Themes of
Work and Love
in Adulthood

Themes of Work and Love in Adulthood

Edited by

Neil J. Smelser
and Erik H. Erikson

HARVARD UNIVERSITY PRESS
Cambridge, Massachusetts

Library of Congress Catalog Card Number 79-26130

ISBN 0-674-87750-0 (cloth)
ISBN 0-674-87751-9 (paper)

*This collection of essays was prepared
under the auspices of the American Academy
of Arts and Sciences, Western Center*

Preface

THIS BOOK CONSISTS of a series of exploratory probes into the
dimensions of human development in the adult years. As such, it
may be assessed as an intellectual product of selected persons who
from a variety of points of view were led to study issues and unanswered queries concerning adulthood.

Yet, we (and this means readers and writers alike) have every
reason to wonder about this curiosity which has rather suddenly
focused on adulthood as a developmental phase, when, in the past,
we all wrote and read about childhood and adolescence and their
cultural and historical variations. Were we thinking of ourselves as
representatives of a stage that crowned all development? Did we see
ourselves as the wielders of such proven methods of observation that
it was unnecessary to consider our own relative position in the cycle of
human life as a whole? This seems, indeed, to have been the case. For
this reason, it is all the more interesting to see how, in our time,
adults from different disciplinary fields and styles go about studying
other adults *as adults*.

Since we editors are represented in this volume by essays of our
own, and by a lengthy introduction by Smelser, our preface need
only explain how it came about that we selected the writers here assembled in a conference in which they clarified and sharpened their
views in discussion — and how this book then emerged.

The editors had known of each other's work for a long time and
had met at occasional conferences, but a sustained interchange of
ideas was first facilitated by our participation in an informal evening

seminar organized jointly with our friend Dr. Robert Wallerstein, Chairman of the Department of Psychiatry at the University of California in San Francisco. This seminar, which included a number of psychoanalysts and social and behavioral scientists from the Bay Area, met almost every month during the years 1974-1976. It was a lively, free-ranging, provocative vehicle, and through it we discovered a preoccupation that led to the conference we editors organized and to its product, this book. That common preoccupation was with the human life cycle as a whole, focusing especially on the developmental vicissitudes of the adult years. Erikson, whose interest was the product of a long career in the psychoanalytic study of developmental processes, was one of the first observers to emphasize the necessity of looking at each stage of life in the context of the whole life cycle — and vice versa. Smelser, in turn, in his early work on the British Industrial Revolution, had analyzed the dynamics of changing age and sex roles in work and in the family; but only recently, and after a long period of attending to other lines of research, had his interest in the sociological and psychological facets of the life cycle been rekindled. Thus, we came to our common preoccupation from different but complementary directions. While Erikson has been primarily the psychoanalyst fascinated with the sociocultural and historical contexts of psychodynamic processes, Smelser has been primarily the sociologist, but with a concern for the deeper dynamics engendered during his own psychoanalytic training.

We began meeting in 1975 on a periodic basis, and gradually a project plan evolved that we felt would best reflect the current state of research and thinking on adult development. As an organizing basis for the conference, we chose the themes of work and love (see Smelser's introduction). When it then came to identifying names to achieve the best mix of participants, we relied not only on our own judgments but also on the valuable advice of two who were themselves later to participate, Marjorie Fiske and Daniel J. Levinson.

We chose an interdisciplinary group which (including ourselves) comprised sociologists and social psychologists, psychoanalysts, psychologists, an anthropologist, and a historian. We wished to acknowledge, as a central theme, the relativity of adult development, subject as it is to systematic variations along a number of lines — among them, cultural, class, racial, ethnic, and sexual. Our goal was to have an exploratory, comparative conference.

In the fall of 1976, having received the necessary financial support, we sent out invitations to potential participants in which we explained our intentions and asked them to indicate briefly the nature of the contribution they felt most qualified and inclined to make. Participants were asked to submit a brief statement, based on their research, identifying what *they* perceived to be central issues in the study of adult development. By way of additional orienting documents, we circulated to them a statement by each of us — Erikson on issues in the study of adult development, with a preliminary assessment of the Freud-Jung correspondence, and Smelser on the vicissitudes of love and work in Western society, some parts of which survive in his essay (Chapter 5).

The conference took place on May 8 and 9, 1977, at the Center for Advanced Study in the Behavioral Sciences in Palo Alto, California. The participants were given an opportunity to elaborate briefly on their written contributions, but most of the time was given over to unstructured exploratory discussion. It is impossible to convey in a few words the essence of the interchanges that occurred during those two days, but both of us — seasoned veterans of such occasions — agreed on the high level of spontaneity, openness, engagement, and intellectual passion. At the end of the conference we decided that it *would* be worthwhile to have participants put their papers in publishable form. To ensure a unified volume, Erikson and Smelser met to decide on the nature of the revisions that would be requested from each participant. Smelser then went through an editorial dialogue with the participants, who submitted revised, expanded versions of their essays. These have now been assembled here. Thus this volume represents an accurate reflection of views developed during and immediately after the conference.

One detail so obvious that it may escape some readers: on the title page of this book, we editors are not listed according to alphabetical convention. This symbolizes the fact that, while in many important respects we regard both the conference and the book as a collaboration between us — in original inspiration as well as in overall editorial decisions — Smelser assumed a much greater responsibility for the actual work involved. He took the leadership in such matters as arranging the details of the conference, chairing it, drafting the suggestions for revising the original statements into chapters, reviewing the chapters, and, finally, dealing with the sponsors of our project and those who supported it throughout.

For an excuse or, shall we say, explanation of his relatively minor role, Erikson can, of course, take refuge in the fact that his position in life transcends adulthood proper: an emeritus rarely has the necessary machinery for editorial activities at his disposal, even if he could, or would, do all this work.

This study was carried out under the auspices of the Western Center of the American Academy of Arts and Sciences. From a very early moment in our deliberations it seemed natural to us that it should be an Academy project, given the intimacy of the affiliation we both have had with the Academy for many years and the role the Academy has long played in sponsoring programs that bring together participants from several disciplines and a wide geographical range to work on developing themes, such as the study of adulthood. During our earliest discussions and planning we were assisted by Beverly Rowen and Pamela Gullard of the Western Center. As the enterprise developed from a vision into a concrete plan for a conference and a volume, we began to work most directly with Corinne Schelling, Assistant Executive Officer of the Academy, who helped us carry out and coordinate each successive phase, from raising necessary funds to arranging for publication. John Voss, Executive Officer of the Academy, was supportive and cooperative throughout. We single out finally the work of Pamela Gullard and Jane Kielsmeier of the staff of the Western Center, who organized and executed the details of the conference, and of Christine Egan, who assisted Smelser at every stage in corresponding with all parties involved in the endeavor.

For the financial support which made this study possible, we express our appreciation to the Rockefeller Foundation and to the Committee on Research and Planning of the American Academy.

September 1979   *N.J.S.*

E.H.E.

Contents

Themes of
Work and Love
in Adulthood

—————— ONE ——————
Issues in the Study of Work and Love in Adulthood
—————— NEIL J. SMELSER ——————

THIS BOOK IS SIMULTANEOUSLY a product of and, we hope, a contribution to a vigorous intellectual movement of recent decades: the study of the postadolescent, preaged years of the life cycle. This movement has excited interest among sociologists, psychologists, social psychologists, psychoanalysts, and, to a somewhat lesser extent, historians and anthropologists. It has also spread into the popular press, so that by now certain kinds of adult behavior (such as drastic career changes, desertion of a spouse, marked alteration of style of dress) once condemned by a previous generation as manifestations of immaturity are now being regarded by laymen as well as scholars as part of a "normal" episode in adult life — the midlife crisis. Yet the expansion of interest in the adult years has developed as a facet of increased attention to the life course as a whole, while at other times specific phases or problems (for example, the "empty nest") have been singled out for study. To eliminate some of this unevenness, we have undertaken to present in this volume an overview of issues that seem to merit further investigation.

In one respect the recent development of the systematic study of adulthood is akin to filling in the remaining white parts on the map, all the others having been settled or colonized. Social and behavioral scientists have for a long time focused on other phases of life — childhood, adolescence (even preadolescence), old age, and, more recently, youth, which follows and is distinguishable from adolescence but somehow falls short of adult maturity. While knowledge about these stages of life is scarcely complete, it is still true that the adult years have been almost the only phase left to investigate.

1

Why the adult years, arguably the most productive and in some ways the most gratifying years in the life course, should have gone unattended for so long is a mystery. Perhaps the story lies in the fact that it is nearly always adults who study things, and in many ways it is less demanding to study *les autres*. And then why, in recent decades, the adult years should have emerged as especially intriguing is also not well understood. One reason for this new interest may be that the study of *other* phases of life cycle virtually guaranteed that sooner or later adulthood would become a focus of attention. If we concentrate on childhood as developmental, eventually the question must arise, developmental toward what? If we regard old age as somehow or other a decline, it excites the question, decline from what? Moreover, the study of certain processes at one stage of life tends to spread to other stages. If scholars locate the essence of childhood in the processes of socialization and learning, critics do not delay in pointing out that socialization and learning occur not only in childhood but throughout life (Brim and Wheeler, 1966). It is not a much larger step to inquire, then, about distinctive differences between childhood and adult socialization. And having asked that, we have begun the systematic study of adulthood.

Another impetus toward the study of adulthood is the fact that the adult years have become socially more problematic in recent times. This is a special instance of the principle that when *any* phase of social life becomes problematic and therefore the focus of attention, a collective struggle to come to terms with it begins. This struggle is an attempt to give definition to — and thus increasing control over — the problematic phase. For example, it is likely that the modern definition of "adolescence" among politicians, jurists, social thinkers, and the general public came into existence when the years between twelve and eighteen became ambiguous — after the family had lost its control over the courtship, marriage, and economic training of the young, after apprenticeship as the typical initiation into adult work roles became weak, after the factory came to be regarded as an unsatisfactory if not evil place for young people, and before age-graded secondary schools arose as the principal vehicle for organizing those years (Musgrove, 1965; Demos and Demos, 1969). As a result of those social developments, what were to become known as the adolescent years demanded new definition and new social attention. Similarly, the increased salience of old age as a social category and the rise of special lines of inquiry such as gerontology reflected the growing problems of the aged — their increase in relative numbers, their systematic exclusion from the workplace through hiring and firing policies of employers and through institutionalized retirement schemes, and their increasing isolation from children and other relatives who might care for them in later years.

What modern social changes have rendered adulthood more problematical in recent generations? Here I must speculate, but would mention several likely developments. Janet Giele in Chapter 7 points out that because of the declining infant-mortality rates and the growing control over epidemics and plagues, experience with the death of loved ones has become more concentrated in the middle years, when one's own parents die, whereas in earlier periods the experience of the death of loved ones — parents, siblings, and children — was continuous and life-long.

A more widely appreciated — and more modern — phenomenon, also mentioned by Giele, is the lowering of the marriage rate, and, more notably, a tendency for women to concentrate the child-bearing years in the decade following the eighteenth birthday rather than to bear children until they are unable physiologically to do so, as did earlier generations of women. These two developments, combined with the increased life expectancy of adults, have lowered the age when couples must face the "empty nest" and have lengthened that period itself, thus marking off a distinct bracket of years wherein involvement in intimate family relations is lessened.

Late industrial development has also witnessed a vast expansion of professional, semiprofessional, and related service roles, distinguished by a long posttraining, preretirement career that is normally expected to peak in what we think of as the middle years, between forty and fifty-five years of age. This sharpening of the boundaries of a period in middle life for an increasing proportion of the population is another factor that makes adulthood more problematic for modern generations.

The final factor that has helped to turn adulthood into a problematic period is the fact that large numbers of scholars trained and placed in the golden era of expansion of American higher education in the 1950s and 1960s and now themselves somewhere in the neighborhood of midlife are experiencing its problems and perhaps coming to terms with personal as well as scholarly agendas as they pose questions about the nature and significance of the adult years.

Whatever the peculiar combination of reasons for the new prominence of the psychology and sociology of adulthood as a special subject, it is undeniably increasing. At the same time, the subject shows the signs of groping, inchoation, and experimentation that characterize a new field of inquiry. In some cases interest in the study of the adult years surpasses the precision of the definition of the subject matter. Much of the work is interdisciplinary, which may also contribute to the lack of analytic focus. And finally, the study of adulthood has been enlivened but also inhibited by a number of deep and abiding controversies over the nature of that phase of life.

For these reasons it seems premature in this volume to attempt either a theoretical synthesis or a general stocktaking of empirical findings. The first would likely be impossible, given the diversity and the noncomparability of many of the intellectual frameworks that inform the study of the adult years, and the second would likely be a failure, since the corpus of definitively established empirical findings is so limited. Our aim, rather, has been to identify the central issues that have emerged to dominate the study of the adult phase of life — issues that both preoccupy its students and divide them from one another.

THE ISSUES OF WORK AND LOVE

In this book we have chosen to focus on the adult years of the life course but also on two of the most important life phenomena that play themselves out during these years, work and love. This interest is partly personal, rooted in that cryptic phrase, reportedly uttered by Freud in his mature years, that the definition of maturity was to be found in the capacity to love and to work. The sphinx-like character of that statement has contributed in part to its fascination and the extended exploration devoted to it since it was voiced. Nothing endures like a profound and incomplete utterance of a master.

Beyond that, we believe the statement to have much psychological and sociological validity because of the centrality of the two phenomena in adult life. On the psychological side, the adult years mark the development and integration of cognitive and instrumental capacities that enable people to reach whatever heights of purposeful, organized mastery of the world they are capable of reaching. Too, the adult years are those in which people are able to reach their maximum of mutually gratifying attachments to other individuals, though this capacity is also often restricted by superego restraints and ego defenses. (Freud spoke of the *capacity* to love and to work, but that did not imply that all individuals realize that capacity in the full.) On the sociological side, society — especially in contemporary times but to a degree in the past as well — has constructed some of its major institutions to specialize in work and love. In particular, the spectacular development of the modern occupational-bureaucratic complex has provided the locus of most of the work activities of society, and the modern family has become the preferred institutional arena for the cultivation and expression of love and related affects (see Chapters 5 and 6). Modern social organization, in short, has taken ample cognizance of—perhaps even overstressed—the centrality of work and love in human affairs.

We are aware of some difficulties in giving a sharp, analytic definition to either work or love. Freud's own discussion of the two was vague and incomplete, and he appeared to take their definition largely for granted (see Chapter 2). Furthermore, we are unable to find any precise set of definitions in the psychological or sociological literature and none has been advanced in this volume. Indeed, there is reason to believe that the two phenomena overlap with each other almost to the point of fusion. It is possible to point out a number of elements common to the two in Freud's writings: both work and love involve libidinal attachments to objects, personal and impersonal, though the mix is different for each; both work and love have an element of sublimation; both kinds of attachments can serve as the basis for the integration of diverse activities, for identification, and for personal identity; both work and love are dependent on interpersonal relationships—love obviously so, but work as well, in interactions and identifications involved in developing skills and capacities, and in cooperative and conflictual work relationships; work and love are in important respects substitutable for one another, in that varying amounts of libido and resources may be devoted to one at the expense of the other. Marjorie Fiske's "hierarchies of commitment" include commitments both to work and to interpersonal relations, and some of her empirical evidence suggests that when someone experiences a deterioration in one of these lines of commitment, that person is likely to adapt in a self-protective way by giving greater importance to another line of commitment (see Chapter 11). Leonard Pearlin makes a similar observation when he speaks of the "rearrangement of priorities" as a means of coping with stressful situations in adult life (see Chapter 8). In the light of these evident similarities between the processes of working and loving, it might be appropriate to regard the two as different names for a very similar process of human adaptation, both involving a fusion of the different psychic forces—impulse, discipline or control, integration, and object attachment.

Despite these difficulties in defining, conceptualizing, and perhaps even distinguishing between work and love, the two phenomena stubbornly refuse to go away as central psychological and social forces. They impose themselves continually upon our attention, and to ignore them is to ignore two of the fundamental things that make the world go round.

THE PREOCCUPATION WITH PATTERN

The study of the adult years is not an entirely new intellectual movement. Students of history and politics have concentrated on the actions of adult actors; economists study the behavior mainly of adults in the market; social psychologists generally survey adults as a means of assessing attitudes toward a given issue or topic; and sociologists' study of role behavior has concentrated on adult behavior. What is novel about the movement is a preoccupation not with adult behavior as such but rather with adult*hood*. By that is implied the study of the processes of adaptation and change in the life situation over the span of the adult years.

The main preoccupation of students of adulthood has been with whether life processes in these years are patterned, and if so, how they are patterned. These issues of patterning not only dictate most of the agendas for theoretical formulation and empirical research but also constitute the bases on which different theorists and empirical research workers take their stands and generate their polemics. Several issues have come to the fore among scholars who have worked recently on patterns of adaptation and change in adulthood:

(1) If we succeed in defining and setting off a period in life that can be identified as adulthood, what are the general characteristics of processes that transpire within that period? Is adulthood best regarded as a noncumulative parade of life situations — events, crises, responses, adaptations, successes, and failures — or is there some kind of cumulative or developmental pattern in the adult years?

(2) If the adult years are patterned, how "strong" are the patterns? Is the journey through the adult years to be regarded as a few loose directional trends, which are forever being deflected by unanticipated events? Or, alternatively, is it possible to identify certain developmental regularities that persist despite divergent life experiences and idiosyncratic personal histories?

(3) If persistent developmental patterns can be identified, is it possible to regard these patterns as a series of distinctive stages?

(4) If stages of adult development are identified and postulated, by what dimensions are they characterized?

(5) Whether conceived as noncumulative change or as patterned development, what are the sources or determinants of change in adulthood? Is the character of those years dictated mainly by physiological processes of maturation and decay? Or is change molded mainly by the sociological agendas implied by a person's changing role relationships through the adult years? Or is there some

kind of autonomous psychological process akin to a life design that plays itself out despite biological and sociocultural constraints?

(6) Can the processes of change in adult life be regarded as involving growth, stagnation, deterioration, directionlessness, or perhaps some combination of all these?

(7) Is it possible to evaluate experiences in adulthood? Is one kind of adult experience to be regarded as more creative, fulfilling, or gratifying than another?

Although these issues are phrased in terms of individual change, they parallel precisely the issues that historically have dominated theories and controversies about the character of social or cultural evolution. All one has to do is to rephrase these questions at those analytic levels to open all the thorny issues of linearity, evolutionary stages, the moving force (for example, technological) of evolution, the role of historical accidents in human evolution, and the possibility or reality of evolutionary progress. Indeed, the degree to which the evolutionary model (as well as the criticisms of that model) dominates the contemporary study of adulthood is most remarkable.

LIFE CONTOURS

Let us begin to discuss these issues of patterning by first examining the notion of ideal life contours. Take a familiar example of a professional role in contemporary American society—a medical doctor, an engineer, or an academic. After a period of prolonged training, the person is certified and assumes the role. According to general expectations, a person's involvement in that role—whether measured by level of power, level of responsibility, or level of rewards—is expected to grow steadily through the adult years, level off in the late fifties or early sixties, perhaps decline a bit, by the same measures, in the years just prior to retirement, and then cease abruptly upon retirement. Represented in crude graphical form, the contour resembles the following:

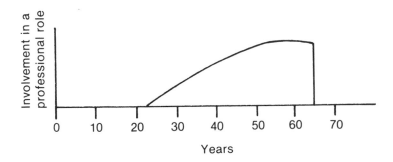

A different contour illustrates the expectations for another occupational role, the semiskilled blue-collar worker. Typically the assumption of role responsibility occurs earlier than for the professional, peaks in terms of responsibility and rewards earlier, has a longer period of leveling off, but has an equally abrupt termination with retirement:

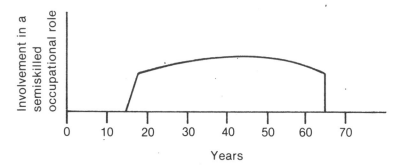

Both types of occupational contours would be modified if we took into account delays and interruptions because of family responsibilities.

Contours can be generated for other facets of social existence as well. In a society with monogamy as its ideal system of marriage, it is expected that people will marry at some point in their young years (say, between sixteen and thirty) and will remain married until their own or their spouse's death, yielding a simple contour, thus:

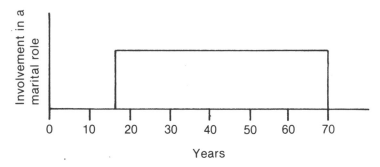

In actuality, of course, the marital contour is often one of serial monogamy, in which case the contour would be subdivided into a number of successive involvements and uninvolvements in marital roles. Many other contours could also be constructed, for example, the contour of the assumption of various legal rights and responsibilities (for example, liability to criminal prosecution, right to vote, right to purchase alcoholic beverages, and so on), or the contour of membership in a church or other organization.

One of the most interesting contours of life is the chronological contour, one that is plotted against time. I regard this as a cultural or normative contour, like those previously illustrated, because the counting of time is a normative matter, and in principle could be — and indeed has been in other times and civilizations — calculated in ways different from that mode we now take for granted. The contour is this: from the moment a person is born until the moment of death, life is counted in units of equal value (minutes, days, months, years, decades) which pass and are never repeated. Time is conventionally regarded as passing steadily, cumulatively, and nonrepetitively. In that sense one's relationship to time is always the same; one is always in time and time passes at the same rate at all times, even though it may not seem to do so. Similarly, everyone stands in an equal relationship to time (in the sense that time is passing everyone by at the same rate), even though we sometimes say that one person's time is more valuable than another's. The graphical representation of this contour would be the simplest possible:

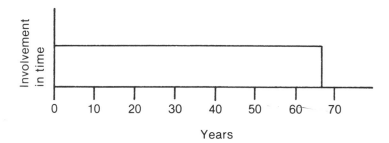

The life contour calculated according to time is of supreme and unique importance in our own cultural tradition because it is the contour against which and in terms of which all other contours — occupational, marital, legal, and so on — are measured; it is the horizontal axis for all contours.

It is also possible to plot a number of ideal-type physiological contours as well. In terms of the development of physiological capacities (muscular strength, reaction time, ability to coordinate body movements), the typical person undergoes a long process of maturation, reaching a peak in the middle to late twenties, then experiencing a gradual and possibly accelerating deterioration from that time until death occurs:

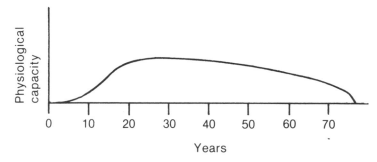

Different contours would result, depending on the kind of physiological variable chosen (for example, sexual drive, keenness of the senses, and so on).

Finally, we should consider the possibility of describing psychological contours as well, such as the one depicted by Roger Gould (Chapter 10; Gould, 1978), in which people are regarded as accumulating during childhood a number of rigid and self-protective myths, all of which serve to inhibit their capacity for gratification and growth. Gould regards the years between adolescence and middle life as the period for the progressive shedding of these myths, and the corresponding growth of freedom, gratification, and self-realization. Daniel Levinson's conceptualization of a life-structure and its vicissitudes could also be regarded as a kind of psychological contour (see Chapter 12). While perhaps still vague in formulation, this notion of a psychological career constitutes the focus of several of the contributions to this volume.

The various sociocultural contours depicted — and others could be added — constitute a series of programs or agendas for a person's life course that determine to some degree his life history or personal career. This determination is only partial, however; a number of variables can affect life contours.

For example, contours may vary in cultural and normative content. Clearly the ideal-type professional career sketched above depends on the institutionalization of the particular occupational roles that are prevalent in modern, developed societies but often absent in others. The economic life contour of the Gusii woman sketched by Robert LeVine (Chapter 4) — which involves an adult life of child care and productive farm work — is very different from that of the contemporary American woman whose work is primarily household management and child care, or paid employment in the labor market, or both. Contours, then, vary historically and cross-culturally as values, norms, and social structures vary.

Contours also vary according to the degree to which the events and transitions which give them shape are inevitable. The chronological contour is a case of the inevitable contour, with the incessant and unchanging passing of time and the inevitability of death. At the other extreme, certain transitions and sequences are not at all inevitable—marriage, divorce, parenthood, church membership, advanced occupational training. In the middle, there are many events and sequences which, though in principle are not inevitable, are nevertheless very likely to occur as part of a contour. The degree of likelihood depends on the normative and opportunity structures. Any society has expectations, exercised both formally and informally, that define the appropriate age for certain events—enrolling in school, beginning work, marrying (Neugarten, Moore, and Lowe, 1968). The fact of being born a man or a woman also "loads the dice" with respect to educational and occupational opportunities (see Chapter 7), as does being born a member of a minority or majority group, or being born in a certain neighborhood or region of the country. These constraints do not make transitions and sequences in the life course inevitable, but they do make them highly probable.

Contours vary according to the degree to which events and sequences are reversible or revocable. Becoming a Ph.D. is not normally a reversible act; neither is becoming a mother. Marrying, however, can be revoked by divorce, and taking a job can be revoked by quitting or being discharged.

Contours may vary according to the definitiveness with which sequences and events are scheduled. Assuming the right to vote is a precisely scheduled event, occurring on every person's eighteenth birthday; completing one's education is only loosely scheduled.

The degree to which contours are socially defined as salient to the individual may vary. In our own society, both the work and family contours are considered to be salient; the history of a person's membership in voluntary associations is not so important.

Contours vary according to the degree that they are publicly noticed by ritual (for example, religious confirmation, college graduation, birthday celebrations) or permitted to pass without such acknowledgement.

Contours vary according to the ways in which they are interrupted by unanticipated events, such as premature death, debilitating illness, unemployment, and so on (see Chapter 8).

The interrelations of contours with one another vary. For example, long professional training—until, say, age thirty—delays a person's entry into the labor force well beyond the age of legal majority, beyond the traditionally expected age of marriage, and even beyond the traditionally expected child-bearing years. For a person in a working-class career, entering the labor force, leaving the parental home, attaining legal majority, and becoming a parent are more likely to be compressed into a few brief years beginning at age seventeen or eighteen (Rubin, 1976).

Finally, culturally defined contours may vary according to the degree to which they are accepted or regarded as legitimate by different groups in the population. At any given time there will be individuals and groups in a society who reject the legitimacy of entering the occupational world and having a career, reject the desirability of getting married and having children, and so on. This variability concerns above all the degree of consensus on the definition and valuation of life contours in a population.

Such are the major lines of variability of the different life contours that constitute the constraining sociocultural agendas for a person's journey through the life course. Taken together they spell out the relative degree of freedom or choice that is left to the individual. Insofar as a person's life has ingredients that are inevitable, irreversible, tightly scheduled, and normatively dictated, to that extent it is predetermined, leaving little room for choice. But as the illustrations indicate, not all contours possess all of these restraining features, and each personal history is not determined entirely by biological and sociocultural agendas. Furthermore, we may expect individual differences in the ways people come to terms with the inevitable, irreversible, and binding features of the life course. For this reason it is important to leave room for the notion of personal career, characterized in its own right, above and beyond the influences which play upon it. The personal career always unfolds in relation to its environmental agendas but not solely according to their dictates.

THEMATIC VARIATIONS IN THE STUDY OF PERSONAL CAREERS

What is the character of the personal career? First, we may ask whether the individual's environment, including the agendas represented by the life contours, is itself orderly or not. Our contributors assume a wide variety of positions on this issue. Three of them — Erikson, Gould, and Levinson — are most explicit in their attention to the psychological processes involved in the passage through adult life. Certain assumptions concerning the social order can be drawn from — or perhaps read into — the contributions of each. While Levinson explicitly insists on the importance of a developmental perspective in the study of the life course, he nevertheless posits an institutional nexus of roles through which a person passes (while at the same time reminding us that they cannot yield a full account of the individual life course). He develops the notion of "major life events," some of which occur as integral parts of and at expected points in the life contour and some of which are interruptions. These constitute, for Levinson, a framework within which an individual fashions his or her life structure (see Chapter 12).

Erikson and Gould can also be read from the standpoint of their assumptions of orderliness of the environment, even though neither is as explicit as Levinson on this score. Most of Erikson's readers and critics have tended to see his stages of adult life as expressions of autonomous psychological development. However, his own characterization of the adult phases includes reference to the fact that going through them is "essential not only for the individual cycle of life but also for the cycle of generational sequence as supported by the basic structure of societies" (Erikson, 1977). This suggests a certain societal orderliness, and indeed could lead to the conclusion that the various stages of adult development are triggered by expectations imposed by one or more of the life contours. For example, the adolescent crisis of intimacy versus role refusal could be triggered by the sociological fact that during these years the adolescent is being asked to assume positions of role responsibility in the "adult" world. Similarly, the conflict between intimacy versus exclusivity is linked most closely with the familial life contour, especially the establishment of love relations as the basis for the marital role. The conflict of generativity versus rejectivity, characteristic of adulthood, can be read as being a psychological manifestation of the involvement in the parental (caring) as well as the work role. In short, Erikson's psychological stages appear to be rooted in the orderliness of the person's social and biological contours and occur roughly in the sequence that these contours impinge on that person.

Similarly, in Roger Gould's account of a person's progressive liberation from childhood myths and the relationship of this liberation to life contours, there is a sequence of new involvements which contradicts fixed childhood assumptions and leads ultimately to liberation from them. Thus, in the late teens and early twenties, leaving home, which becomes a reality as that time approaches and the expectation of the culture is perceived, challenges the assumptions of dependency and parental omnipotence. During the twenties, when we are confronted with decisions about the adult enterprises of work, family, and marriage, a further set of assumptions about parents' virtues and power is challenged. The dismantling of childhood myths during the thirties is triggered by growing marital, parental, and occupational responsibilities, and the further mythical dismantling in midlife appears to be rooted in the experience of the death of others and the sense of finiteness of one's own time. Most of Gould's discussions, like Erikson's, focus on the psychological dynamics involved in these transitions of adult life. But at the same time, Gould's scheme, like Erikson's, makes certain assumptions about an ordered set of social involvements (especially in work and family roles) that parallel and indeed precipitate the different phases of adult development (see Chapter 10).

Another point on the continuum from order to fragmentation of the social milieu is revealed in Leonard Pearlin's contribution (Chapter 8). He sees a person's external circumstances as rooted in the organization of the larger society. With respect to the experienced strains of life, he finds that young people are more likely to be bombarded with the strains of unemployment and marital discord, but these strains are likely to be transitory. Older people's work and intimate affective relations appear to be more stabilized, but they are more burdened with chronic, irreversible stresses. Thus, while Pearlin concentrates on the incidence of disturbing events in the course of adult life, his account emphasizes that those events are likely to occur at specified periods in the adult years, and therefore are more nearly predictable.

A different account of the social milieu of the life course is given by Marjorie Fiske (Chapter 11). While she acknowledges the importance of major institutions — particularly occupational and family institutions — through which her subjects pass in life, she stresses the general chaos of the world that has resulted from rapid social change. She argues that "most people in Western societies would probably agree that the senses and sensibilities of the individual are under greater bombardment than ever before," and that "many people appear to utilize whatever fragment of the self best fits the demands of the immediate situation." She argues that even such general values as generativity have been challenged by the acceleration of generational differences and increased challenges by the young.

Janet Giele (Chapter 7) also notes a certain destructuring or fragmentation of the sociocultural environment, in the sense that norms of behavior appropriate to different ages and for each sex have been challenged and have become more indefinite in recent decades. In that sense she, like Fiske, sees a less predictable social order. Yet her evaluation of the significance of that change differs from Fiske's. Far from regarding the indefiniteness as a source of uncertainty or chaos, she regards it as an opportunity for greater personal self-realization through the transcendence of traditionally limiting age and sex-role norms. One senses a deep dilemma lurking in these contrasting formulations: Are clarity and structure in the environment to be regarded as psychologically comforting or as imprisoning? Are lack of clarity and structure to be regarded as disorienting or liberating? Or are both reactions invariably present? In all likelihood both are present, but we know too little to be able to determine under what conditions each will dominate.

Our contributors, then, develop an array of assumptions concerning the degree of order and stability of those aspects of the sociocultural environment that impinge on the life course. In assessing their formulations, it seems imperative that we acknowledge the variability of the sociocultural environment. This variability takes at least two forms. First, societies and cultures—and within them, groups and subgroups—differ with respect to normative expectations concerning the content, timing, and sequencing of role involvements. Second, within any society or group, we may expect variability with respect to the clarity, organization, and integration of these expectations—which in turn are related to the pattern of social change being experienced by the society or group. This evident variability calls for a certain caution in attempting to define universal or even general stages or phases of adult development in a strict descriptive sense. There are probably universally occurring *issues* of adult life that arise from biological and social exigencies—issues such as organizing the care of the young and helpless or confronting the finiteness of human life—but the socially preferred ways of confronting these issues, as well as the outcomes of those confrontations, should be expected to display great variation.

The assumptions one makes about the nature—including the orderliness—of the sociocultural environment have definite implications for one's view of the patterning of the individual's personal career. At one extreme, if the theorist or researcher regards the sociocultural environment as patterned, he may see this as the source of patterned development for the individual. On the other hand, if the sociocultural environment is regarded as fragmented or chaotic, the patterning of personal careers either is likely to be denied or is considered to be caused by influences other than the sociocultural environment.

A second thematic variation in the study of personal careers depends on the relative importance of the external (mainly social) and the internal (mainly psychologically developmental) determinants of adult life processes. While both sets of factors are generally acknowledged to be involved in complex interplay, scholars—including those represented in this book—vary considerably both in their theoretical posture and in the factors they stress in empirical research. Questions of the relative explanatory force of the different classes of variables, and, perhaps more important, of the ways in which these variables combine to produce behavioral and developmental processes, though important, remain largely unanswered. Rather than review the different social and psychological factors invoked in this volume and then cast some sort of vote for the significance of this or that factor, let me venture a few hints about our thinking on these issues by referring to a couple of selected examples of research reported in this volume.

The first example concerns the interesting research of Melvin Kohn and his colleagues on the relationship between the substantive complexity of work (which could be regarded as a social or external factor in that it involves the characteristics of work) and intellectual flexibility (more nearly a psychological variable). This research— especially the longitudinal studies—suggests that work which involves the complex management of people, things, and ideas tends to generate a more complex and adaptive intellectual style generally, and also infuses other, nonwork aspects of an individual's life. Yet at the same time, their data suggest that the relationship between the two variables is truly reciprocal, and that one can predict subsequent complexity of work on the basis of earlier measures of intellectual flexibility. What, then, is the likely causal direction between the two? The answer is "both," evidently, and that answer suggests a theoretical and research strategy that concentrates not on the impact of one variable on another at a discrete point in time but rather on complex interactive circles, both benign and vicious. Such circles may begin very early in life when children from culturally advantaged families develop skills and other qualities that result in their being placed in classroom situations and tracks that are relatively complex and demanding, which in turn contribute to further development of intellectual flexibility. The opposite circle leading to intellectual brittleness and substantive simplicity is not difficult to envision or illustrate. Regarded causally, however, the variables of intellectual flexibility and substantive complexity, whether in an educational or work setting, are both cause and effect, depending on the point at which one cuts into the circle. Furthermore, by the time individuals reach the age and stage of career development studied by Kohn and his colleagues, they have already inherited a long circle of mutual causation that in some sense determines both their level of intellectual flexibility and the substantive complexity of their occupational assignment (see Chapter 9).

One promising way to further understand these developmental circles is to study situations in which the circle has been broken or deflected by some life event. I have in mind, for example, the prolonged unemployment of persons who have experienced a lifetime of intellectual flexibility and involvement in substantively complex educational and work settings. Will the intellectual flexibility endure, or will it deteriorate through lack of continuous demands for complex functioning? Or consider the case of previously deprived persons who are given some unusual opportunity (a scholarship for study or involvement in a promising occupational training program). Will the inherited circle foredoom the opportunity to failure or limited success, or will exposure to a new, more demanding environment break through that heritage? Or, more generally, what conditions are likely to lead to one or the other outcome? Studies directed by questions such as these promise to lead us further in assessing the relative strength and significance of a person's current social situation and his psychological resources.

Another illustration, reported by Fiske (Chapter 11) but also found more widely in the literature, is that from a certain period in midlife, men tend to lay less stress on mastery, achievement, and independence and to give more expression to passivity and dependence, and that women tend to do just the opposite. Assuming for argument's sake that these findings are generally valid, are they to be explained primarily as a matter of psychodynamics, for example, as a "return of the repressed," the result of a growth process whereby a person at a greater level of maturity and freedom permits gratification of that which has been denied earlier? Or are they to be explained in role or social terms, with adult men responding realistically to anticipated rejection from the world of achievement through retirement, and women responding realistically to the end of involvement with the world of children that calls for a stress on caring and loving? While these possible explanations are inevitably difficult to unscramble, some progress might be made by studying variable situations. Do men who retire at radically different times in life (professional athletes, career military men, professors and clergymen) manifest different personal careers in their struggle with and expression of dependence and passivity? Do women who never marry and bear children—and thus never (or always) experience the empty nest—have a typical career with respect to dependency and mastery? Do women who bear children until very late in the reproductive years and women who continue to be heavily and responsibly involved with children as grandmothers experience the same tendencies toward assertiveness and mastery as women whose children leave them in midlife? Comparative studies could begin to throw additional light on the relative explanatory power of the adaptive and developmental models.

A third thematic variation in the study of personal careers concerns the ultimate shape the investigator believes those careers will take—that belief usually being based on a mixture of empirical evidence and theoretical conviction. The model emerging from Fiske's studies, for example, is one of somewhat pathetic, self-protective, situational adaptation without any particular overall pattern. She speaks of "backward and forward movements which often occur in rapid succession," "the possibility of recurring periods of identity diffusion . . . over far shorter intervals than [she] had reason to expect." The main empirical evidence for this view lies in the frequent fluctuations in commitments to different spheres or hierarchies over relatively short periods of time among her subjects. Trends in shifting commitments make their appearance largely because of the changing occupational and familial involvements of her subjects. Fiske is not explicit about whether this process yields any "growth" in terms of the accumulation of adaptive capacity or richness, but at least one statement suggests she is dubious: "It is probable that more complex and autonomous people can grow old gracefully and comfortably in our time only if they belong to a more privileged class, where life-style options remain more open. It is regrettable indeed that the more self-generating people among the great middle-class majority of our population become, as they reach late middle and old age, deprived of the arenas in which they could serve as role models for the generations behind them, and for whom later life becomes the period of greatest frustration."

Fiske's model is partly explained by what she sees as the rapidity of contemporary social change and the resulting chaos. To notice the discontinuities and chaos in contemporary society, however, does not necessarily lead to these pessimistic conclusions. Researchers who retain a belief in the individual's capacity to tolerate and even resolve social ambiguities and contradictions envision various kinds of creative synthesis and growth emerging from the confusion of a disordered social environment (Lifton, 1976).

A variation of the theme of continuous struggle and adaptation is taken by Pearlin, who regards adulthood as "a time in which change is continuous, interspersed with occasional quiescent inter-ludes." The degree of order adulthood manifests depends in large part on the occurrence of scheduled and nonscheduled events, upon a person's vulnerability to these events, and upon systematic differences in a person's ability to cope with them — differences which stem from social-structural, especially class, differences in society.

Erikson, Gould, and Levinson stress that crisis and adaptation yield some kind of cumulative development. Formal comparison among the three is somewhat difficult, since they have made their contributions in different historical and theoretical contexts. In many respects Erikson's efforts to epitomize the dynamics of adult development precede by at least a generation the new intellectual movement — which he himself inspired in some measure — that fo-cuses on adult development itself and in which both Gould and Lev-inson are important figures. Erikson's interest grew as an integral part of his lifetime efforts, originating in psychoanalysis, to construct a psychosocial theory of development over the entire life cycle, in-deed of the cycle of generations. In this respect Erickson is not and did not aspire to be a theorist of adult development as such but rath-er a theorist of development generally, of which adult development constitutes one part. The work of Gould and Levinson is more focus-ed on distinctive processes and stages characteristic of the adult years. There are significant differences among the two as well, with Gould emphasizing the major shifts in ego adaptations — in the direc-tion of liberation from childhood fantasies — and Levinson concen-trating more on a kind of personal career of transition-crisis-adaptation sequences which are rooted in an individual's changing social situation but which nevertheless unfold with a developmental regularity.

Despite these differences in scope and aspiration, the concep-tions of the three lend themselves to comparison and contrast with respect to their level of determinacy (or indeterminacy). Erikson's model of adult development is a complex mixture of determinacy and indeterminacy (Erikson, 1950). On the side of determinacy, he envisions a definite sequence of stages which follow on and build on one another. In addition, he suggests definite age ranges for the var-ious stages of the life cycle from infancy to old age, though — on the side of indeterminacy — he does not fix exact or unvarying chronolog-ical ages for each stage or the transitions between them. His theory of development is also lent determinacy by its principle of epigenesis —

the principle that for a given developmental process to transpire, others have to have transpired before it, and that the resolution of any given prior crisis is not fixed for all time but must develop further at all subsequent stages. Yet at the same time the principle of epigenesis is not a completely fixed one; each developmental stage has a measure of its own autonomous dynamics. It is not totally determined — only conditioned and shaped — by past crises and resolutions. Finally, while Erikson envisions a definite and limited number of basic psychosocial antitheses (for example, intimacy versus exclusivity in early adulthood) and a definite series of possibilities for growth, disturbance, ritualization, and ritualism as outcomes for each stage, his developmental scheme does not pretend to postulate specific outcomes for any stage for every person.

The developmental processes characterized by both Gould and Levinson are more determinate on some counts. Gould envisions the years from the late teens to the late forties as being a continuous challenge to and freeing from protective assumptions. Furthermore, the challenges are in a definite order, occurring during a specific span of years. The first major challenge, for example, is to the assumption that "I'll always belong to my parents and believe in their world," and the dynamics of freeing oneself from it occur between the ages of sixteen and twenty-two (Gould, 1978). Gould's analysis is, to be sure, qualified from time to time. The major transition to the period beyond midlife is seen to occur around age forty-five with the denial of evil and death being the last major assumption to be dismantled. But there is some variability in this, and Gould sees this variability rooted mainly in people's role involvements: "This major transition in life does not occur sharply at age forty-five. Cycles of work, family and marriage extend in varying degrees into the fifties. For some men the work plateau may not be reached in the early forties but later on, so the disillusionment with the 'magical' pay-off of work is delayed to the late forties or early fifties. For some, having a family of children who are still young or parents who remain healthy and active continues throughout the forties, supporting the illusion of safety in life despite contrary messages. For some women, the excitement of a new career or the luxury of having only a career and not also a home and children to worry about, can lend a temporary new sense of power just as the old power of youthful attractiveness fades" (Gould, 1978, p. 307).

Levinson's theory and findings on the life structure are not so specific as to the precise psychic content as are Gould's, but on the basis of empirical materials gathered from in-depth interviews of forty adult men in several walks of life, he maintains that there are definite phases of structure building and structure changing that appear to concentrate within specific age ranges, never varying more than one or two years in each direction from a critical year and marking a similar kind of transition (for example, the age-thirty transition) for all the subjects (Chapter 12; Levinson et al., 1978). Obviously the content of the periods of stability and transition varied with the major life involvements (occupational and familial, mainly) of the different men, but Levinson's conclusion is that timing of the various crises and resolutions is remarkably invariant, and that the entire sequence of these episodes constitutes a developmental life structure for an individual.

Thus the positions in this book, with respect to the overall pattern of the personal life course — as well as the empirical evidence relating to that structure — appear to run the gamut from chaos to order. Although each has at least a limited base of supporting empirical evidence, it is impossible to imagine how all of these formulations, contrasting as they are, could be correct. Part of the confusion is no doubt conceptual; the notions of order and chaos are relative terms that vary according to the questions asked, the language used to ask them, and the scope of the life course considered. Thus, while in the short run Pearlin's model is one of a person adapting to whatever exigencies — scheduled or nonscheduled — that are experienced, in the long run a pattern emerges because the timing and content of the exigencies are not random. Fiske, while observing the rapidly shifting commitments to different arenas of involvement, nevertheless envisions certain general longer term trends in the aging process. Even in the life structure depicted by Levinson, which appears to be the most definitely patterned of all, certain transitional crises, if described without reference to the longer term pattern of life, certainly appear to be chaotic and directionless. At the very least, then, the study of adulthood calls for a certain amount of conceptual ordering, with greater precision about the levels of generality and scope on which apparently contrasting findings are based.

Part of the confusion is also likely to be methodological. To continue with the same illustrations, Pearlin's data consisted of responses to a number of standardized questions administered to a Chicago sample, focusing specifically on stress and emotional response to stress. Fiske's interview schedule contained a wider range of variables and also incorporated a temporal or longitudinal dimension for individual subjects. And Levinson's approach made an effort to assess the overall life situation of his subjects largely through biographical reconstruction and in-depth exploration through interviews. Variations in sampling and methods of data gathering do not necessarily dictate substantive differences in outcome, but clearly Levinson's — and, to a lesser extent, Fiske's — methods of investigation are more likely to show evidence of patterned, developmental processes over long time spans than are Pearlin's.

A similar caution can be voiced with respect to the issue of whether the life course involves some kind of growth. On this issue, again, the contributors present an array of assessments. The models of Gould and Erikson, for example, clearly imply cumulative processes of growth, but the same cannot be said for the adaptive models ventured by Pearlin and Fiske. But growth, too, is a relative concept. Like pattern, its presence or absence, is dictated in part by the questions posed and by the scope of the life span considered. Whether or not a given process is regarded as growth depends also on the criteria by which that term is defined. Two investigators may agree on the empirical fact that in the later years of adulthood men and women become more resigned and conservative in a variety of ways. But whether this is to be interpreted as growth to some plateau of vision and wisdom or whether it is to be seen as defeat and retreat is unclear, and neither interpretation depends on the facts but rather on the framework for evaluation that the individual investigator uses.

In light of these observations, I suggest that both the formulations about the degree to which the life course is patterned or ordered in some absolute sense and the attendant controversies involve an unfortunate reification of the notion of pattern or structure. What should be sought instead is, first, a careful formulation of the questions to be asked, the analytical levels to be opened, and the time spans to be considered in the inquiry. Then those variables that make for regularities, continuity, and pattern and those variables that make for disruptions or that impose new directions or change in adult lives should be systematically incorporated into models of the life course. The question of chaos versus orderliness as absolutes would disappear and the question would be seen as one of understanding the variability that occurs under different circumstances. Or, in other words, the question of orderliness versus chaos would give way to development of conceptual constructs whose usefulness as explanatory models could be assessed.

Finally, while we are far from having either a formally developed theory or a corpus of definitive empirical findings that explains the development of the life course, we do have strong indications of what such a theory—and its relevant empirical base—cannot do without. I would suggest that any formulation of a theory of the adult life course must contain the following minimum ingredients:

(1) A statement of the continuous and repeated *challenges* to a person over the life course, both anticipated and unanticipated. These challenges are created by changes in the physiology of the organism, psychological orientation, interpersonal relations, pressures from institutionalized norms, and exposure to cultural values and definitions.

(2) A statement of the *resources* available to the individual who faces this array of challenges. These resources can be regarded in a positive sense, as facilitating adaptive responses to the challenges, or in a negative sense, as constituting constraints or obstacles to coping. The resources, like the challenges, operate at different levels—the physiological, psychological, interpersonal, social-structural, and cultural.

(3) A statement of the *adaptive responses* that take place when life-course challenges and individual resources confront one another in concrete situations. Above all attention should be given to the conditions under which different types of adaptive responses dominate.

(4) A statement of the *historical accumulation* of a person's responses and orientations. Evidently, one is not immune from one's own past history; and indeed, the life course can be regarded as an accumulation of historical precipitates which themselves constitute in part the challenges one confronts and the resources one brings to meet those challenges. A description of individual history demands some sort of developmental perspective on the study of the life course, even though it is still an open question as to whether that perspective should be one of growth, growth-and-decline, progressive commitment of personal resources, progressive realization of freedom, or some mixture of these.

ORGANIZATION OF THE VOLUME

These introductory remarks have been designed to provide a conceptual map on which the following contributions can be located in relation to one another and in relation to the dominant issues in the study of work and love in adulthood. What follows is a brief rationale for how the editors have organized those contributions sequentially.

The two essays in Part I are historical in character. Both deal in unusual ways with work and love in adulthood from the perspective of the psychoanalytic tradition, which informs many of the essays in this volume and which remains one of the most important intellectual influences on the study of the life course. Erikson and I felt that a necessary ingredient in this book was an essay on Freud's own treatment of the topics of work and love. We asked Nathan Hale, who has written about the history of psychoanalysis, to undertake this task. In Chapter 2 he reveals the vague and somewhat uncritical character of those ideas in Freud's writings, but at the same time examines a number of personal factors and the cultural forces in his Viennese environment that shaped his views. For his contribution Erikson selected an extremely important series of episodes in Freud's adult life, manifested concretely in his correspondence with Carl Jung. In a sense, Erikson's analysis is a sequel to his earlier study of Freud's correspondence with Wilhelm Fliess. The essay here is remarkable for its demonstration of how very complex and inclusive an intergenerational relationship can be, for in this one both men mobilized their own pasts, their current situations, and their dreads of and hopes for the future. Their relationship encompassed all the ingredients of adult life — generativity, creativity, stagnation, and rejectivity — in complicated sequence. It not only involved the two men themselves, but absorbed, conditioned, and sometimes almost destroyed their relations with many significant others in their lives. And above all, these episodes reveal the enormous potential of both work and love to fluctuate, combine and recombine, break down, and rebuild in the course of a meaningful interpersonal relationship.

The rest of the book is organized according to influences that impinge on the individual life course, in sequence from the macroscopic to the microscopic. Part II is concerned with the most general kinds of cultural and historical variations in the structuring of work and love relationships. Robert LeVine, our lone anthropological voice, argues that even in cultural settings as diverse as contemporary America and contemporary Gusii society in Kenya, the life course displays general commonalities, but the cultural expectations, as well as the social-structural and demographic realities of the two societies, are so different that they serve as a caution against cultural myopia in generalizing from life-course sequences observed in our own society. My essay also deals with variations in the sociocultural structuring of work and love relations, as illustrated by trends in Anglo-American society during the past few centuries. In it I demonstrate how certain dominant cultural trends relating to the segregation of work and love relationships have been modified and deflected by the class, religious, and economic differences between Great Britain and the United States, and how each society has developed its own normative agendas for experiencing work and love in adulthood.

Whereas my essay stresses the structuring of adult work and love relationships, Ann Swidler's underscores their adaptability. As she traces the transformation of the love ideal from medieval times to its more contemporary forms, she illustrates how the love ideal, because of its adaptibility, is a truly extraordinary cultural resource. It serves both to resolve contradictions or conflicts within the culture's ideology (for example, choice versus commitment) and to fulfill either or both sides of the ambivalence inherent in those situations.

The remaining parts of the volume are somewhat narrower in analytic scope, focusing on life-course processes within more limited cultural and historical contexts. Part III concentrates on the social-structural determinants of those processes.. After a review of themes in recent life-course research, Janet Giele explores the implications of the gradual erosion of age and sex-role norms in contemporary society, arguing that this breakdown contains the possibility, at least, that people may now experience fuller, more flexible, and more gratifying lives insofar as previously prohibited lines of experience and expression become available to them. Leonard Pearlin traces variations in people's exposure to distressing events and in their ability to cope with these events, concluding that at least part of the variation is systematically explained by sociological variables such as social class and occupational role. And finally, in an even more focused treatment, Melvin Kohn argues that the structuring of adult work experiences — particularly with respect to the complexity of their demands — has general significance for the quality of experience over a wide range of adult attitudes and activities.

Part IV concentrates on the individual life course, though, as we have seen, each author makes some reference to the influence of sociocultural factors on that life course. The Levinson and Gould contributions make use of explicitly developmental models — though these differ from each another substantively — with definite benchmarks and processes of change. Skeptical of such developmental theories, Marjorie Fiske's formulations resemble more nearly an adaptive kind of model, wherein people fall back on a variety of resources and classes of commitments as they experience different kinds of distress and disappointment.

I would like to call attention finally to several partial but excellent reviews of the literature in several of the essays: Giele on research relating to the life course and adult development; Kohn on the study of work; and both Levinson and Fiske on the adult life course. Together these reviews can be taken as a guide to the central research traditions that inform the contents of this volume.

References

BRIM, ORVILLE, JR., AND STANTON WHEELER. 1966. *Socialization after childhood.* New York: Wiley.

DEMOS, JOHN, AND VIRGINIA DEMOS. 1969. Adolescence in historical perspective. *Journal of Marriage and the Family,* 31:632-638.

ERIKSON, ERIK H. 1977. Adulthood and worldviews. Paper presented at the American Academy Conference on Love and Work in Adulthood, Palo Alto, May 6-7.

————. 1950. *Childhood and society.* New York: Norton.

GOULD, ROGER. 1978. *Transformations: growth and change in adult life.* New York: Simon and Schuster.

LEVINSON, DANIEL J., CHARLOTTE DARROW, EDWARD KLEIN, MARIA LEVINSON, AND BRAXTON McKEE. 1978. *The seasons of a man's life.* New York: Knopf.

LIFTON, ROBERT J. 1976. *The life of the self.* New York: Simon and Schuster.

MUSGROVE, FRANK. 1965. *Youth and the social order.* Bloomington: Indiana University Press.

NEUGARTEN, B. L., AND J. W. MOORE, AND J. C. LOWE, 1968. Age norms, age constraints and adult socialization. In *Middle age and aging,* ed. B. L. Neugarten. Chicago: University of Chicago Press.

RUBIN, LILLIAN B. 1976. *Worlds of pain: life in the working-class family.* New York: Basic Books.

PART ONE
Historical Background

TWO
Freud's Reflections on Work and Love
NATHAN HALE

ALTHOUGH FREUD WROTE very little about work and love in mature, "normal" adults, an examination of his views is a useful and revealing undertaking, first, because his influence on American social thought has been pervasive. A second reason is that his reflections were not complete or systematic, and so it is likely that they were governed by important, unexamined assumptions. Three of these beliefs that dominated Freud's views of love and work have been singled out for particular attention by later commentators: the pervasiveness of scarcity, the domination of the unconscious by the instincts of love and death, and the sharp differentiation of sexual roles. Attitudes toward Freud often have been determined by the quite different assumptions of his critics about these three fundamental issues. After considering the nature of Freud's reflections on work and love and the conditions of late nineteenth-century Europe and its Viennese variant that influenced those views, I will examine the attitudes toward Freud of a few important commentators from Thomas Mann to Robert Heilbroner and Kate Millett, each of whose responses were governed by new or different assumptions about scarcity, instinct, or sexual roles.

Freud's reflections on work and love were those not of a systematic social philosopher but of a physician. They must be culled from the slender corpus of his social thought, from the testimony of his personal life, beginning with his early letters, and from his voluminous clinical and psychological studies. In all three sources, work and love were often intertwined. For example, in the context of his social thought, they combined to make civilization possible. On a personal level, after enduring the ascetic poverty of the student, Freud, as the young Jewish professional male, unendowed by privilege, had to earn a living before he could marry; only effort and postponement could create the conditions for lasting satisfaction.

From the outset, Freud's clinical practice was overwhelmingly devoted to young adults between twenty and forty for whom the problems of work and love were poignantly acute. The earliest neurotic patients about whom he wrote were young women who could not acknowledge love or sexuality that social norms forbade: Miss Lucy R., the governess in love with her brother-in-law; Katharina, the peasant girl, unable to acknowledge the sexual nature of her father's advances; Dora, in love with her father, with her father's friend, and with her father's friend's wife. But it was among Freud's male patients that difficulties in both work and love were conspicuously combined. Chiefly, they were young men, anxious, obsessive, or hysterical, who could not complete their professional education, perhaps a degree in law or philosophy, and who thus indefinitely postponed an adult career and the fulfillment of the adult male role in marriage and family. They chose inappropriate sexual objects which disgusted them; often they fled from both work and love altogether.

From these cautionary clinical cases and from Freud's social thought, bald normative prescriptions can be derived. Reduced to the simplest level, both work and love are governed by the search for the same goal: more lasting, realistic, and socially responsible pleasure. Artistic creation and scientific discovery are the highest and most intensely enjoyable kinds of work because in them, sublimated energies of sexuality and aggression play a major role. Work not only attaches the individual to reality but "gives him a secure place in the human community" (Freud, 1964d, pp. 79-80, 102). Optimal love includes the working through of ambivalence, fantasy, disgust, and narcissism. Optimal love also includes the adult union of sexuality and affection in marriage and caring for the young, the functions Erik Erikson has developed into the concept of generativity. Work and love can function optimally only in the context of civilization, which jointly they make possible.

Yet the harsh realities of nature, the human body, and human society sharply circumscribe the satisfactions of even optimal work and love. Reality, governed by scarcity, dictates inevitable frustration, the toleration by all mature adults of restraint and postponement. Material scarcity makes work a necessity; the scarcities of nature dictate inequalities of talent and energy, and, accordingly, social rewards will differ. Scarcity also gives value to love and to the loved object; the finite limits of the mother's love, for instance, underlie the jealousies of the Oedipus complex. Adult satisfactions within civilized society are of necessity less intense than the direct discharge of impulse among primitives and children (Freud, 1966d, pp. 89, 97, 108).

Even love itself operates like a fixed bank account in each person. Withdrawals from the direct satisfaction of the component sexual instincts augment the amounts of sublimated energies. And only sublimated sexuality and its aim-inhibited ties are capable of curbing aggressive instincts for the sake of social solidarity. Thus the mature adult must recognize responsibilities to society and to culture by accepting the limited satisfactions afforded by sexually inhibited aims. At the same time mature adults should attempt to reduce the number of those who oppose civilization to a minority by mitigating economic and cultural burdens (Freud, 1966b, p. 50; 1966d, pp. 79-83, 104-105, 112-113, 143-144; 1966f, pp. 8-9).

The acceptance of frustration dictated by scarcity and of responsibility to others and to culture in general constitute an almost banal stoical ethic: work and love are ancient prescriptions. What gives Freud's notions their unique quality is the weight he assigned to the unconscious and to the instincts of sexuality and aggression as the two forces within it. Both drives are illimitable and uncircumscribed in fantasy, yet they must operate in a reality dominated by scarcity and by fixed quantities of energy.

Before turning to the cultural determinants of Freud's system, it is important to place it in developmental perspective, perhaps the best-known aspect of his thought. What allows the mature adult to accept reality, including scarcity and postponement, and to concur in sublimation? First, the child must relinquish a sense of omnipotence, fed by the womb and by early nurture; he must renounce partial sexual drives, then Oedipal objects, and later, excessive family attachments, thus acquiring his first modes of judgment and independence. His curiosity must be cultivated, and education must tactfully reinforce biological instinctual curbs by setting limits which are firm but not overdrawn. The mature adult must learn to know the nature of his own drives so that they can be accepted or rejected, according to a moral standard which Freud left unexamined as "self-evident." Reclaimed from the unconscious and from an unrealistic sense of guilt, the strengthened and mature adult can most effectively maximize real satisfactions, discharge social responsibilities, and achieve reasonable pleasure in work and in love.

Freud sharpened his views on work and love by cultural comparisons and by unusual sensitivity to the interrelations of culture and personality. He contrasted modern civilization with classical antiquity and with primitive man, the modern elite with the modern masses, and, very briefly, the Soviet Union with western Europe. None of these comparisons is systematically pursued, but each illuminates an aspect of work or instinctual life. For instance, Freud argued that in classical civilization, sex was so readily available that the value of love became debased. The asceticism of Christianity was required to restore love to a position of decent scarcity. In his own contemporary civilization a woman's value depended on her chastity and her exclusive possession by one man — in other words, on her scarcity. Moreover, the expression of sexuality differed among the educated elite and the masses. The latter, with their easy-going ways, were franker, more sexually expressive. The restraints of civilized sexuality had become so restrictive among the former that there were few who did not suffer from neuroses, impotence, or frigidity (Freud, 1966j; pp. 165-208). Freud also contrasted the restraints of modern civilization with the behavior of man's primitive ancestors, curbed only by force and necessity. Among moderns, the Russian Communists furnished one example, among many, of the persistence of human aggression. Promising equality and the satisfaction of material needs, they hoped to curb hostility. But nonetheless they are armed with the "most scrupulous care," and "keep their supporters together" by hatred of "everyone beyond their frontiers" (Freud, 1966k, pp. 211-212; 1966d, pp. 112-113).

Freud's views of work changed little from his first letters to his fiancée in the 1880s to *Civilization and Its Discontents,* almost forty-five years later. Scarcity dictated the necessity of work, which Freud often equated with effort. He distinguished between the toil of the masses, imposed and harsh, and the pleasurable discoveries and artistic achievements of the gifted few. Yet the pleasures of art and discovery often required hard preliminary effort. His creation of psychoanalysis, he insisted, remained the result of painstaking, constant, cumulative labor. Although he treated patients on a precise schedule, he wrote only when the spirit moved him, as an artist might, and insisted that no other method functioned for him. Thus his enduring work in its final form flowed easily, perhaps pleasurably, once the painful ground had been securely laid (Jones, 1957, vol. 2, p. 395).

Although his attitude toward work remained constant, Freud's view of love changed, from stereotyped romantic passion to criticism of excessive civilized repression. First came dissatisfaction with the prudery of physicians and of society in denying the sexuality of women. In 1908 Freud made his concerted attack on "modern civilization's" code of sexual morality. By unduly restricting sexuality, civilization warped the personality, creating neuroses and the double standard and, on the part of the strong, defiance of convention. Marriage itself was unsatisfactory, postponed too long when sexual desires were strongest, complicated by ineffective methods of birth control and unwanted pregnancies (Freud, 1966e, pp. 181-205). By 1910, in the essays on the vicissitudes of the sexual instinct, it became apparent that not merely culture but something in the sexual instincts themselves thwarted satisfaction. Culture and instinct together made the fusion of sexuality and affection difficult, a complex achievement for modern civilized man, not the simple result of growth (Freud, 1966j, pp. 165-208).

Freud's ambivalence toward civilization abated somewhat after World War I had revealed the fragility of civilized life. Analysis of neuroses suggested that aggression and the death instinct were as important as sexuality. By 1920 it had become clear to him that only aim-inhibited sexual feelings could effectively counter man's innate aggression; only thus could sociality be preserved. Freud's experience with the psychoanalytic movement had demonstrated that work in common did not suffice to mute narcissism and hostility. That role was reserved for aim-inhibited eros. Yet, aggression, deployed in limited, socially restricted doses, was essential for both work and love: in each it was important not to "give way" to others but energetically to pursue love objects and working goals (Freud, 1966a, p. 159n1).

HISTORICAL INFLUENCES ON FREUD

The serious attempt to trace the influence of Freud's historical milieu on aspects of his thought began in the 1920s. At that time Karen Horney (1927) first attempted to discern the social determinants of Freud's conception of woman, an effort that led her to an increasing emphasis on cultural as against biological determinism. By 1970 Henri Ellenberger had placed Freud clearly within the context of nineteenth-century medical psychology, and the historian Carl Schorske (1973) has used Freud's dreams as evidence to unravel his attitude toward the politics and culture of Habsburg Vienna (Janik and Toulmin, 1973; McGrath, 1974).

Some of Freud's insights seem timeless, in the sense that he captured what appear to many of us to be enduring and universal aspects of the human condition. But there are also unexamined contradictions and assumptions in Freud's views that reflect singularities of time and place. To understand these it is helpful to look for determinants in the intellectual tradition and culture to which he was exposed. What is significant are the choices Freud made within the intellectual and cultural milieux he knew. Views similar to Freud's can be found among his contemporaries and immediate predecessors. English Darwinists emphasized struggle and scarcity; Wagner paired love and death; Schopenhauer emphasized the unconscious and irrational will; Gustav Le Bon distrusted the masses and assumed an inequality of talents; William James defined the human condition by the capacity for postponement. But at the same time alternative views existed. For example, most psychologists assumed a wide variety of innate drives and the supremacy of consciousness; Marx posited a final utopia of equality, abundance, and harmony; John Stuart Mill, whose work Freud translated, proclaimed the equality of the sexes.

It can be argued that the social conditions of Habsburg Vienna and Freud's own position as an upwardly mobile Jew created a special identity that at least in part dictated Freud's choice among the intellectual traditions to which he was exposed. This identity sometimes reflected and sometimes deliberately countered the prevailing Viennese environment. That same social environment had molded many of the young adults whom he treated, except that often they were more financially secure than he and of higher social status. But Freud's interpretation of their experience and of his own was also determined by the particular medical, intellectual, political, and cultural contexts, in which he worked.

The importance Freud ascribed to the unconscious reflected a combination of influences. Beginning with Liebault's investigation of hypnotism, the last three decades of the nineteenth century saw a growing interest among European physicians and psychologists in mental operations and personality traits outside ordinary awareness. This medical and psychological interest was paralleled by a philosophical tradition going back to Schopenhauer which Freud hardly could have escaped and which placed the determinants of action not in conscious reason but in often unacknowledged will and passion. These medical and philosophical traditions were given particular plausibility by political circumstances. In Habsburg Vienna the organs of liberal government — constitution, cabinet, and judiciary — were impotent compared with the real power exercised by aristocratic patronage. The reality of political power lay not with the surface institutions but in the personal influence behind their facade (Ellenberger, 1970; Johnston, 1972).

Not only the importance Freud ascribed to the unconscious but his selection of the drives within it reflected a general intellectual tradition and particular aspects of Viennese life. Strongly influenced by Darwinism and its emphasis on animal instincts, Freud ultimately reduced them to love and death (Sulloway, 1979). Where Freud's contemporaries were pleased to discover a multitude, his choice of this pair suggests the influence of particular theoretical needs and cultural conditions. Already prepared by intellectual currents in which unconscious will and passion had been equated and by a medical tradition that emphasized the unconscious, Freud discovered erotic drives in his adult women patients, in the form of repressed sexual wishes. They were the wishes of young women who had been raised in what may have been a stringent Jewish version of Victorian middle-class reticence; his own wife, for instance, had come from a strict, rabbinical home (Zweig, 1943, pp. 67-91). The particular degree of repression made sexuality of special importance to these patients. But it was in his male patients that the vicissitudes of the sexual instinct became most apparent, and these, it seems clear, also reflected a particular cultural outlook. The Viennese middle and upper classes accepted a standard by which their women were presumed to be chaste until marriage, while men were libertine, that is, they accepted precisely that split between sexuality and affection that Freud emphasized as a major impediment to adult sexuality. His discussion of this split, as the Vienna Society Minutes indicate, assumed exactly this behavioral pattern, which was based in part on the Viennese acceptance of sensuality among males and lower-class women (Nunberg and Federn, 1967; Esslin, 1972). Toward the close of the nineteenth century, beginning with Krafft-Ebing, Viennese intellectuals and their public were preoccupied with the problems of sexuality. This preoccupation may well have made Freud's emphasis on the role of sexuality easier, and the evidence seems clear that the degree of shock it aroused among the Viennese has been grossly exaggerated. Interest in the problem of sexuality as well as the double standard were European, not merely Viennese, phenomena, but it was in their Viennese manifestations that Freud knew them most intimately.

Although the pairing of sexuality with death was common to a number of European thinkers, the Viennese emphasis on eroticism and destruction was unusually strong, as was the identification of death with Nirvana. In fact, it is precisely the Nirvana-like aspect of death, the special hallmark of late nineteenth-century Vienna, that has always posed problems for Freud's interpreters. Freud's obsession with his own death may have been not only personally idiosyncratic but also reflective of the culture in which he lived. After falling to the floor "in a dead faint" during an argument with Jung in Munich in 1912, he revived and his first words were, "How sweet it must be to die" (Johnston, 1972, p. 243; vol. 1, p. 317). Freud resisted giving aggression and death a place in his system until the discovery of the compulsion to repeat traumatic experience in the shell-shocked soldiers of World War I. Yet, unlike Anglo-American physicians who decided that the war neuroses proved that the instinct of "self-preservation" was supremely important, Freud insisted that death, the drive to return to the inorganic, was as powerful as eros.

If the pairing of eros and death reflected Viennese preoccupations, Freud opposed the culture around him in important respects. He developed a particularly rigorous version of a common nineteenth-century identity—the ascetic, virtuous, hard-working professional scientist, exemplified in his teachers, Meynert and Brucke (Ellenberger, 1970; Sachs, 1944).

Freud's identity reflected, perhaps, his position as an upwardly mobile Jewish male, a generation away from the ghetto. His professional ambition was fostered early by parents who sacrificed for their firstborn son and granted him special status within the family as a scholar. His career required the utmost austerity, and his financial circumstances remained tenuous and difficult during the early years of his marriage and the birth of his children. Indeed, his genteel poverty, the lot of the young professional on the make, persisted into the late 1890s. The mobility, sacrifice, and poverty cannot be exaggerated as an explanation for Freud's insistence on scarcity, frustration, and postponement (M. Freud, 1957; Jones, 1957, pp. 154-156; Rieff, 1959; Bakan, 1958; Cuddihy, 1974; Gay, 1978). It was as if the harshest aspects of the Darwinian struggle were made plausible by the conditions of Freud's personal life. The austerities of World War I and the immediate postwar years only could have confirmed their plausibility.

Freud's upward mobility and his vision of the masses below and of professional competitors on all sides reinforced his lifelong acceptance of the inequality of talents. Freud viewed the sublimated pleasures of art and science as reserved for a gifted elite, which in particular ways he saw as Jewish. On September 4, 1883, in a letter to his fiancée, Martha Bernays, Freud distinguished between the deep discoveries in science that Jews pursued, sometimes at peril of exhausting their nervous systems, and the ordinary, less daring routine work that gentiles tended to perform (Freud, 1960, p. 54; Pulzer, 1964, pp. 4-14). Among Vienna's Jews, ambition for the truly great achievements in art and science burned bright. Perhaps in the example of his Jewish contemporaries, whose astonishing rise he witnessed, he saw that aggressive competition, "not giving way" spinelessly to others, standing one's ground, was a prerequisite to achievement. Acceptance of competition and the suitable deployment of aggression appeared to be necessary for adult work and love, while absence of aggression often marked his neurotic patients. It also was for the elite — in this instance, Sigmund and Martha — that the pleasures of eternal, romantic, and disciplined affection were reserved. For the masses — and Freud could have added for aristocrats — sex and love were more frequent, more casual, and therefore less worthwhile. The persistent anti-intellectualism of the Viennese masses, and in the 1880s their growing antisemitism, may have confirmed Freud's sense of estrangement from them, despite his undertone of envy at their easy pleasures.

The simultaneous pursuit of art and science also was a particular Viennese preoccupation, a local intensification of a nineteenth-century professional pattern, exemplified again in Freud's teachers and especially in his admired contemporary Arthur Schnitzler. It is logical to suppose that Freud's view of art as pleasurable but useless, a substitute for action in the real world, admirable but in its way impotent, reflected the aestheticism that the Jewish Austrian bourgeoisie adopted after the defeat of its political ambitions in the 1870s. Similarly, Freud's use of science, notably the "young science" of psychoanalysis, as a scalpel to cut away the falsities of official, paternal authority, both temporal and spiritual, may also have reflected the renunciation of Freud's first political ambitions in the Viennese context (Schorske, 1973; 1961). In Switzerland, on the other hand, where authority was more democratic and where God could be approached by individual Protestant confrontation — indeed where major psychologists such as Theodore Flournoy were avidly investigating mediums for hints of the subliminal — psychological science, in Jung's hands, would bolster, not undermine, religious authority.

There is a final respect in which Freud's views of adult work and love seem particularly time- and culture-bound, namely in his assumption of fixed sexual roles. Ignoring the implications of his own argument that culture, not biology, associated passivity with the female and activity with the male, Freud insisted that the woman's true sphere was primarily domestic, "the family and sexual life," while the "work of civilization has become increasingly the business of men" (Freud, 1966d, pp. 103-104; 1966i, p. 116). Only in a culture in which women do not pursue professional careers and are above all housewives and mothers is such role differentiation possible, and only there could women's professional ambitions be seen as the derivative of penis envy.

The historical fate of Freud's reflections in important instances has been governed by changing attitudes toward scarcity, unconscious drives, and sexual roles. It also has been affected by changes in the status of the psychoanalytic movement. While psychoanalysis still was fighting for recognition, Freud easily could be seen as an iconoclast. After the enshrinement of the psychoanalyst as a psychiatric authority, especially in America, critics could regard Freud as an upholder of the existing order.

It is in Europe, in cultures where psychoanalysis has been less closely identified with a psychiatric establishment, that Freud has been seen most clearly as a liberator. For Thomas Mann, Freud's message called for a humane, modest freeing of the playful, artistic aspects of the unconscious. Writing in exile, aware of the Nazi worship of the primitive and irrational, Mann could view Freud as a liberator from illusions in the tradition of Schopenhauer. Freud was the proponent of a profound realism about the nature of man, the domination of the conscious by the unconscious. The "physicianly psychologist" pointed the way to a "blither humanism," a "bolder, freer relation to the Id . . . productive of a riper art than any possible in our neurotic, fear-ridden, hate-ridden world" (Mann, 1937, pp. 40, 42). Freud had clearly revealed the role of regression to playful childhood, and of identification with the father, and of the union of both these functions, regression and identification, in the work of the artist. What is distinctive in Mann is his insistence that Freud's insights, though cautionary, are nonetheless joyful, giving wider scope and understanding to creative regression. It is also among Europeans that efforts to reconcile Freud with Marxist hopes for the future have been most conspicuous and persistent. Yet, those, such as Wilhelm Reich and Eric Fromm, who have attempted this reconciliation usually have altered Freud's theory of instincts, rejecting particularly the death instinct (Jay, 1973; Habermas, 1971).

The Americans are responsible for turning Freud into a proponent of unremitting toil. David Riesman, writing in 1950 from the easy American assumption that the problem of scarcity had been solved and that the world's food could be grown in flowerpots, saw Freud as a crabbed nineteenth-century bourgeois, a puritanical

Malthusian, imposing on a generation for whom the possibilities of leisure and play were newly important the mortgage of "reactionary and constricting ideas" (Riesman, 1954, pp. 176-178). To Freud, work was real, art and play unreal. Yet this interpretation underplayed the sublimated pleasure Freud associated with artistic creation and scientific discovery. It ignored as well that continuance of the child in the adult which he associated with greatness. Freud wrote that it was Leonardo's instinct for play that later "found its way into the activity of research" (Freud, 1966h, pp. 127-128). the transplanted European, Herbert Marcuse (1955), also assumed the possibility of abundance in the mid 1950s, while acknowledging the pervasiveness of scarcity in Freud's social thought. But he argued that Freud's theories envisioned, in a benign environment, the transformation of sexuality into a playful, utopian eros, automatically taming the death instinct.

Recently, as some futurologists predict that scarcity once more could become the lot of mankind, Freud has been used to suggest the usefulness of an authoritarian society. The transition to a postindustrial order, Robert Heilbroner (1974) has argued, requires consideration of the interests of the future and of mankind as a whole. Yet, the power of identification, the basis of loyalty and morality, he construes Freud as suggesting, is limited in all probability to the national state, an immediate substitute for the family. Mankind and the future are too remote to generate libidinal ties or identifications. Hence in the perilous transition, the human need for authority must be acknowledged, an authority based on the early helplessness of the child and his nurture by parent figures. This vision symbolizes Freud's transformation from a figure of liberation to a symbol of authority.

A somewhat similar change has occurred in American perceptions of Freud's theories about women. In 1910, the anarchist Emma Goldman, who heard Freud's lectures at Clark University, argued that Freud had demonstrated that the "inhibitions of thought imposed upon woman for the purpose of sexual repression," accounted for her "intellectual inferiority." Goldman wrote before Freud and later psychoanalysts had fully developed the theory of penis envy to which they attributed woman's ambition to fulfill roles traditionally reserved for males. By the 1960s for Betty Friedan and particularly for Kate Millett, Freud had become the major counterrevolutionary ideologist who destroyed the movement for woman's freedom begun by John Stuart Mill. Betty Friedan based her case partly on the vulgar popularizations of Freud's traditionalist view of woman's role by some American psychoanalysts and writers

(Friedan, 1963). Millett (1970, pp. 178, 187-189) argued that a "philosophy which assumes that the 'demand for justice is a modification of envy' and informs the dispossessed that the circumstances of their deprivation is organic, therefore unalterable, is capable of condoning a great deal of injustice . . . it is not difficult to see why Freud finally became so popular a thinker in conservative societies . . . Apart from ridicule, the counterrevolutionary period never employed a more withering or destructive weapon against feminist insurgence than the Freudian accusation of penis envy." Again, it is the European Marxist Juliet Mitchell (1974) writing in a nation where psychoanalysis is not identified with established medicine, who sees Freud's conception of penis envy as a brilliant portrayal of woman's oppression in a patriarchal, bourgeois society.

And finally, in America, Freud's view of instincts has been drastically shorn of its biological and mythical aspects. American psychoanalysts have been strongly influenced by environmentalist sociology and psychology. Within these disciplines the concept of instinct became increasingly attenuated and divorced from constitutional or biological factors. This began in the 1920s when the exuberant lists of late nineteenth and early twentieth century psychologists finally led a Chinese colleague, Z. Y. Kuo (1921), to catalogue more than one thousand separate instincts and then to argue that it was time the concept be reexamined or dismissed. Instincts have been redefined as needs, drives, or vectors that are organized by the social environment. Within psychoanalysis, human drives have been increasingly interpreted as modified by object relations. Whatever justification may be found in Freud's later writings for this development, it nevertheless represents a major shift in emphasis. Most recently, with Roy Schafer (1976), Freud's entire metapsychological structure has been jettisoned in an attempt to make psychoanalysis conform to a major tradition in modern American philosophy, the analytic school represented by Gilbert Ryle. In the process, psychoanalysis is being shorn of much of its mythical and literary resonance.

Thus, in those cases where local cultural or intellectual tradition impinged drastically on Freud's vision, he has been harshly dealt with by subsequent generations. And these generations, in turn, inadvertently create parochialisms of their own.

References

BAKAN, DAVID. 1958. *Freud and the Jewish mystical tradition.* New York: Van Nostrand.

BRODY, BENJAMIN. 1970. Freud's case load. *Psychotherapy: Theory, Research, Practice,* 7:8-12.

CUDDIHY, JOHN MURRAY. 1974. *The ordeal of civility: Freud, Marx, Levi-Strauss and the Jewish struggle with modernity.* New York: Delta.

ELLENBERGER, HENRI. 1970. *The discovery of the unconscious.* New York: Basic Books.

ESSLIN, MARTIN. 1972. Freud's Vienna. In *Freud: the man, his world, his influence,* ed. Jonathan Miller. London: Weidenfeld and Nicolson.

FREUD, MARTIN. 1957. *Glory reflected.* London: Angus and Robertson.

FREUD, SIGMUND. 1966a. A case of homosexuality in a woman. In *Complete psychological works of Sigmund Freud,* ed. James Strachey, vol. 18. London: Hogarth Press.

———. 1966b. A case of hysteria. In *Complete psychological works of Sigmund Freud,* ed. James Strachey, vol. 7. London: Hogarth Press.

———. 1966c. A case of obsessional neurosis. In *Complete psychological works of Sigmund Freud,* ed. James Strachey, vol. 10. London: Hogarth Press.

———. 1966d. Civilization and its discontents. In *Complete psychological works of Sigmund Freud,* ed. James Strachey, vol. 21. London: Hogarth Press.

———. 1966e. 'Civilized' sexual morality and modern nervousness. In *Complete psychological works of Sigmund Freud,* ed. James Strachey, vol. 9. London: Hogarth Press.

———. 1966f. Future of an illusion. In *Complete psychological works of Sigmund Freud,* ed. James Strachey, vol. 21. London: Hogarth Press.

———. 1966g. Inhibitions, symptoms and anxiety. In *Complete psychological works of Sigmund Freud,* ed. James Strachey, vol. 20. London: Hogarth Press.

———. 1966h. Leonardo da Vinci and a memory of his childhood. In *Complete psychological works of Sigmund Freud,* ed. James Strachey, vol. 11. London: Hogarth Press.

———. 1966i. New introductory lectures on psychoanalysis. In *Complete psychological works of Sigmund Freud,* ed. James Strachey, vol. 22. London: Hogarth Press.

———. 1966j. Contributions to the psychology of love. In *Complete psychological works of Sigmund Freud,* ed. James Strachey, vol. 11. London: Hogarth Press.

———. 1966k. Why war? In *Complete psychological works of Sigmund Freud,* ed. James Strachey, vol. 22. London: Hogarth Press.

———. 1960. *The letters of Sigmund Freud,* ed. Ernst Freud. New York: McGraw Hill.

FRIEDAN, BETTY. 1963. *The feminine mystique.* New York: Norton.

GAY, PETER. 1978. *Freud, Jews and other Germans.* New York: Oxford University Press.

GOLDMAN, EMMA. 1910. *Anarchism and other essays.* New York: Mother Earth.

HABERMAS, JURGEN. 1971. *Knowledge and human interest,* trans. Jeremy J. Shapiro. Boston: Beacon Press.

HEILBRONER, ROBERT. 1974. *An inquiry into the human prospect.* New York: Norton.

HORNEY, KAREN. 1927. The flight from womanhood: the masculinity complex in women as viewed by men and women. *International Journal of Psychoanalysis,* 7:324-339.

JANIK, ALLAN, and STEPHEN TOULMIN. 1973. *Wittgenstein's Vienna.* New York: Simon and Schuster.

JAY, MARTIN. 1973. *The dialectical imagination: a history of the Frankfurt School and the Institute of Social Research, 1923-1950.* Boston: Little, Brown.

JOHNSTON, WILLIAM. 1972. *The Austrian mind.* Berkeley: University of California Press.

JONES, ERNEST. 1957. *The life and work of Sigmund Freud.* 3 vols. New York: Basic Books.

KUO, Z. Y. 1921. Giving up instincts in psychology. *Journal of Philosophy,* 18:645-663.

MANN, THOMAS. 1937. Freud and the future. In *Freud, Goethe, Wagner.* New York: Alfred A. Knopf.

MARCUSE, HERBERT. 1955. *Eros and civilization: a philosophical inquiry into Freud.* Boston: Beacon Press.

MCGRATH, WILLIAM J. 1974. Freud as Hannibal: the politics of the brother band. *Central European History,* 7:31-83.

MILLETT, KATE. 1970. *Sexual politics.* New York: Doubleday.

MITCHELL, JULIET. 1974. *Psychoanalysis and feminism: Freud, Reich, Laing, and women.* New York: Pantheon Press.

NUNBERG, HERMAN, and ERNST FEDERN, eds. 1967. *Minutes of the Vienna psychoanalytic society.* New York: International Universities Press.

PULZER, P: G. J. 1964. *The rise of political anti-semitism in Germany and Austria.* New York: John Wiley.

RIEFF, PHILIP. 1959. *Freud: the mind of the moralist.* New York: Viking Press.

RIESMAN, DAVID. 1954. Themes of work and play in the structure of Freud's thought. In *Individualism reconsidered.* New York: Doubleday Anchor.

SACHS, HANNS. 1944. *Freud: master and friend.* Cambridge: Harvard University Press.

SCHAFER, ROY. 1976. *A new language for psychoanalysis.* New Haven: Yale University Press.

SCHORSKE, CARL E. 1973. Politics and patricide in Freud's interpretation of dreams. *American Historical Review,* 72:328-347.

———. 1961. Politics and the psyche in fin de siècle Vienna. *American Historical Review,* 66:930-946.

DE SOUSA, RONALD. 1974. Norms and the normal. In *Freud: a collection of critical essays,* ed. Richard Wollheim. New York: Doubleday Anchor.

SULLOWAY, FRANK. 1979. *Freud, biologist of the mind: beyond the psychoanalytic legend.* New York: Basic Books.

ZWEIG, STEFAN. 1943. *The world of yesterday.* New York: Viking Press.

--------- THREE ---------
Themes of Adulthood
in the Freud-Jung
Correspondence
--------- ERIK H. ERIKSON ---------

THE CORRESPONDENCE BETWEEN Sigmund Freud and Carl Gustav Jung began in 1906 and ended in 1914. Its publication contains about 350 letters each from Freud and Jung, and six from Frau Emma Jung to Freud. William McGuire, the editor of the exceptionally well-annotated publication, rightly states that these letters bear "acute witness to the complex interplay of these two unique personalities." At the same time, he shares with Ernst Freud and Franz Jung—the two men's sons who together decided that this correspondence should be published—a justified apprehension that readers may pay more attention to the inadvertent self-revelations of these sages than to the historical complexity of their encounter. He concludes: "The dialogue inevitably tempts analytical and psychoanalytical interpretation, philosophical rumination over its beginnings and its effects and its 'meaning,' and the weighing up of its aggressions, projections, magnanimities, shafts of wisdom, seminal particles, and whatever else could be put into the balance" (Freud and Jung, 1974a, p. xii).[1] (In passing, I must point out that the word "seminal" which is here used to characterize the forcefulness of the correspondents' insights, in the German edition (Freud and Jung, 1974b) is *zukunftstraechtig*, that is, "*pregnant* with future": which must give us a warning of how the best translation can aggravate the complexity of such "interplay.")

McGuire further states that the sons of the two correspondents, in concluding an agreement to publish the letters, prudently stipulated that they were to be treated "like historical documents . . . in order to guarantee impartiality" (p. xiii). I think that we must concur with this definition and, in fact, make the very most of it: for only when seen in all their historical relativity can such data even begin to serve psychoanalytic interpretation. I, therefore, intend to offer in these pages a "life-historical" as well as historical introduction to these letters, hoping thereby to demonstrate a certain thematic order in this assemblage of very uneven communications. From the historical point of view we must consider relative to each other the following phenomena:

(1) Correspondence is a form of communication which varies in intensity and meaning with personality and culture. The correspondence under consideration here is, in some way, typical of an exchange which had to serve as a medium of intimate affiliation under conditions when for many months no direct encounters such as visits or even telephone talks were possible. During the long intervals between meetings, a mixture of affiliative and antagonistic expectations are apt to be cultivated which, at the time of reunion, can lead to remarkable breakthroughs not only of shared imagination but also of personal affects. As to the general role of their letters in the life histories of the correspondents, I may claim, or admit, to being rather one-sidedly prepared to elucidate Freud's investment in this correspondence because it fell to me to write a review of his correspondence to another doctor, Wilhelm Fliess, when it was first published in 1950 (Freud, 1954) — then every bit as much of a surprise as the Freud-Jung letters are now. I will, in fact, enlarge, by way of introduction, on the history of that other "historical document."

(2) Freud and Jung were, of course, two creative doctors in the position of founding a new clinical art-and-science which was to have a tremendous impact on human self-enlightenment. Moreover, this new field made it incumbent on them, as Jung put it, to "make a profession out of analyzing man's resistance to the Unconscious," which, most importantly, included the (for doctors, then most revolutionary) obligation to study and to understand their own resistance to their own unconscious, even when they would prove to harbor, say, truly unheard of infantile dependencies. And these innovators could not possibly know to what extent they were endangering their own and each other's sanity by paying an as yet unsystematized and unritualized attention to insights which had been hidden in symbols and rituals throughout human evolution.

(3) When engaging in such interplay the two correspondents lived through their respective stages of adulthood — an aspect of the matter to which I will pay particular attention. In fact, I will select themes of adulthood on the joint frontier of work and love. Freud

was fifty when the correspondence started, a turning point in anyone's life, and one peculiarly significant for him. Some of his most important works had been written and the outline of his new science well-circumscribed. But he had for years worried over the completion and, above all, the survival of that work—and over his "successor." His children, by then, were all in their teens and during the correspondence, with one exception, entered their twenties. Jung, in turn, was just over thirty, married only a few years, and in the early bloom of his work, while his children, with one exception, were all born during the time of this correspondence. Since I have committed myself to ascribing to middle adulthood a crisis of generativity which includes procreativity as well as productivity and creativity (Erikson, 1950), we must explore how the correspondents' relative positions on the scale of stages are reflected in these letters. But because of Jung's age we will also have to consider the prior crisis of intimacy which I have ascribed to young adulthood and which includes marital and parental intimacy as well as the creative intimacy of work affiliation and friendship. This will prove all the more relevant since it so happens that at the beginning of the Fliess correspondence (1887 to 1902) both Freud and Fliess had been near thirty, recently married, and about to become fathers.

(4) Finally, there is a pervasive historical aspect in all correspondence, and here I mean history itself. The correspondence between Freud and Jung came to a bitter end in the very year, 1914, when empires and monarchic systems tottered. Some surprising themes in the correspondence can, I believe, only be understood as a reflection of a contemporary imagery then reaching a crisis: I mean Freud's preoccupation with the question of a successor (even if, in calling Jung his "crown prince," he seems to mock such imagery) and their remarkable references to power spheres as they began to wonder what, in the capitals of the world (Berlin, London, New York), would become of the psychoanalytic movement. Actually, when World War I broke out they had indeed effected a kind of international psychoanalytic underground which after the war quickly organized and gradually became dominant in the psychiatry of the Western world.

As I, then, select from the many fascinating strands in this body of correspondence some specifically adult and historically acute themes, I hope to be in accord with a statement of Freud's in another correspondence, namely, with Sandor Ferenczi (Jones, 1953). Especially in view of the search of some reviewers of this correspondence for leftover infantile complexes which might explain some of the

writers' more irrational images and affects, I quote here an ex-
quisitely adult remark: "One should not strive to eliminate one's
complexes but to come to terms with them: they are the legitimate
guiding forces of one's behavior in the world (November 11, 1917, II,
452).

The editor summarizes the letters' contents as follows:

> The account of the relationship of Freud and Jung from 1906 forward is,
> of course, contained in the letters in this volume—the gradual warming
> of mutual regard, confidence, and the affection, the continual
> interchange of professional information and opinions, the rapidly
> elaborating business of the psychoanalytical movement, the intimate
> give-and-take of family news, the often acerb and witty observations on
> colleagues and adversaries, and at length the emergence of differences,
> disagreements, misunderstandings, injured feelings, and finally
> disruption and separation. (p. xix)

Certainly, all these are eminently adult issues, mostly dominated by
rational inquiry and pervasive common sense. Yet, I must trace
through them matters of maturational conflict which characterize
adulthood both as a stage within the individual life cycle and as a
stage within the cycle of generations. It is hoped that such phenomenological groundwork will permit readers to recognize corresponding
configurations in the lines of other persons in other personal, cultural, and historical contexts—including, perhaps, their own lives.

SHADES OF FLIESS

A brief review of the Fliess correspondence takes us back to
Freud's thirty-first year. Ernest Jones (1953, I, 387) calls this friendship "the only really extraordinary experience in Freud's life," which
is an extraordinary remark: but one can well see where this friendship may have provided for Freud the one truly playful and intimate
intercommunication of ideas at a time when psychoanalysis had not
yet become a field beset with "political" issues. True, Freud, with his
early works, had reached out to the scientific and literary public. But
even after the appearance of "The Interpretation of Dreams" he
could only report: "Not a leaf has stirred." So he called Fliess his "one
and only public" (*Mein einziges Publikum*). And, indeed, Fliess, a
well-trained otolaryngologist in Berlin, was quite apt to indulge in a
flight of theories (Freud once entered him in a hotel register as a
'Universalspezialist) so when the two men met for what Freud called
their *congresses à deux*, they no doubt could count on resounding
and playful echoes in each other. It was to Fliess that Freud first en-

trusted the manuscript of his early ambitious "Project for a Scientific Psychology" (Freud, 1954). He was, however, undoubtedly too trusting when he let themes of his self-analysis—the first in history—enter the correspondence and thus (as yet unknowingly) made Fliess the recipient of that special confidential appeal which we now call transference. Thus, when the correspondence became more intimate, Freud did not hesitate to admit (in those days of bearded manhood) that "there can be no substitute for the close friendship which a particular, almost feminine side of me calls for" (Freud, 1954, letter no. 318). He sought in Fliess, Freud mused in a letter, "The Other" (*den Anderen*, unfortunately translated as "the others"), a simple term which, as we shall see, can cover one's "double" or counterpart in a variety of categories: in the Jung correspondence we will encounter it in Freud's almost illusional demand for a true (a non-Oedipal) successor. I say it with some hesitation, but both these correspondences convey the impression that Freud, supremely aware as he was of human ambivalence and deception, was in his younger years a true and sometimes tragic believer in a kind of spiritual friendship. I will discuss this later. At any rate, in his self-analysis during the Fliess period Freud recovered and understood many early childhood memories, all the way back to his mother and the vivid memory of his peasant Nanny who had taken him to the Roman church and had made him witness the ceremonial approach to the Ultimate Other.

But as to Freud's passionate need for a friendship in his early adulthood—a stage to which I ascribe the antithesis of intimacy versus isolation—I repeat that this was for both Fliess and him the period of a somewhat late marriage, the beginning of their (then relentless) parenthood, and, of course, a time of special economic pressure. That this, in Freud's life, coincided both with his most creative period and with his self-analysis (that is, his encounter with a number of inner Others) called all the more for that creative intimacy with a responsive man which a correspondence can provide. But such male intimacy may well also harbor a generative (and jealous?) competition with the young wife, who, after a prolonged betrothal, was embarked on her procreative mission: the very year after the correspondence began, Mrs. Freud gave birth to her first daughter, followed by three sons and two more daughters. Generativity, of course, demands that, having decided what we care *about*, and what and whom we care *for*, we stake out what and whom we must and can take care *of*. And if a sense of stagnation is the antithesis of generativity, we can well see where especially creative and productive men may, at such a time in their own lives, be afraid of becoming (relatively) stagnant because of their new professional and marital obligations.

But here I must add another component of generativity which is strategic for such correspondences: I mean self-generation, the care given more or less consciously and more or less verbosely (for only creative people have their own words for such things) to one's own continued identity renewal, tied as it now is to a net of commitments. The mutual support of such further development is the main psychosocial function of friendship. It permits a reciprocal narcissistic mirroring which allocates to each partner the self-love necessary for creative activity and yet also, by intimate critique, keeps it within necessary limits. How the attending mutual indulgence—here in a gradually professionalized form—is apt to threaten friendship itself, we will observe in both correspondences.

If care in its many meanings is the dominant strength and concern of the middle years, the fear of stagnation was, in Freud, aggravated by another major theme which strongly emerges in the first correspondence and reaches into the second. Freud, so it seems, expected to die early; and he was, at times, wracked by ideas of not "making it," whether this concerned the night train that would take him on a vacation, or that great future when his ideas would be sure to survive: his destination, then, and his idea's destiny. Related to this was a Rome complex: ever again, he wonders whether he and Fliess might arrange to meet in Rome, a wish which found its ritual expression in the words "Next Year in Rome!"—obviously, a Roman version of the Jewish prayer, "Next Year in Jerusalem!" That all of this, indeed, harbored a Jewish world image, according to which the diaspora ever again renews the traditional exile just as one is "getting there," can be seen from Freud's identification both with Moses, the supreme lawgiver who was never to see the Promised Land, and the Semitic warrior Hannibal, who never conquered Rome. We will come back to some of these themes at the very end of the Jung correspondence. In the meantime, they remain illustrative of the fact that even the most rational and scientifically minded adult lives in a more or less conscious world view formed by ancestral images evoked in childhood or by those of an emerging new ideology—or both.

Freud's strange images of fate, furthermore, remind us that in viewing the life of a genius (even more so than the lives of others) we must avoid assigning all too circumscribed chronological ages to the stages of life. In creative persons the adolescent crisis (in our terms, that of identity versus role confusion) is apt to be both aggravated and prolonged: and we can and will see a continuing struggle in

Freud between the early role models of the leader and the scientist, the healer and the thinker. In such a person, the intimacy crisis, too, can be delayed. And while generativity will be in the center of our attention, we also note in Freud's experience of time a premature old age crisis. For if that crisis is characterized by the antithesis of integrity versus despair, an early despair over a possibly unfulfilled life is strangely obvious in these letters as his sense of personal integrity begins to include that of his ideas, and as in utter isolation he takes possibly catastrophic chances by insisting on instinctual theories abhorrent to many of his colleagues and sometimes acceptable only to men whom he himself does not much respect.

In the meantime, we will not be surprised that Dr. Fliess, the otolaryngologist, was able to take neither the evolving ideas nor the affiliative needs of his strange friend. In 1902 they broke with each other, not without some paranoid reactions on Fliess's part and some mournfully traumatic ones on Freud's.

This very end, however, provides us with another adult theme: I mean rejectivity, which I would call the antipathic trend corresponding to the sympathetic one of generativity. For he who cares must also learn to know what or whom he simply does not care to care for – or, indeed, to *have* cared for. And Freud and Fliess not only broke with each other but also agreed to destroy their correspondence. And here we come to a special fate of both the Fliess and the Jung correspondences, namely, their chance survival. While Freud had destroyed Fliess's letters and assumed his own to have been destroyed, Fliess's widow sold Freud's letters, together with other papers, to a Berlin book dealer who happened to show them, in the eary thirties, to Marie Bonaparte. One of Freud's most trusted friends, and his analysand at the time, she of course acquired them. Moreover, she refused to hand them over to Freud, who wanted them destroyed even then. And so they were published in 1950 — forty-eight years after the last letter was written.

What must interest us here is that the Jung correspondence, too, lay rejected by both their correspondents in some files and bundles, and Jung's letters were, in fact, considered lost until Anna Freud found them stacked away in a closet in Maresfield Gardens in London – in 1954, forty years after the conclusion of the correspondence. In the meantime, Jung, when asked, had called the correspondence alternately "unimportant" or "accursed" (*verflucht*) and in utter ambivalence had agreed to have them published thirty, twenty, fifty, or one hundred years after his death. Freud and Jung both had sons who were architects, and these artistic men knew and agreed that the letters, after the correspondents' death, had to see the light of day. No doubt, however, the writers had, at the end of their friendship, not only rejected each other but also part of their own past selves: and we may conclude that they had to reject each other all the more in order to escape too much self-disdain.

THE MANDATE

During the Fliess period Freud has formulated his basic clinical and theoretical orientation and had found his style. We need only to remember some of the major works of that time to know that psychoanalysis already existed: "The Interpretation of Dreams" (Freud, 1964, IV, V), "The Psychology of Every Day Life" (Freud, 1964, VI) and "Jokes and Their Relation to the Unconscious" (Freud, 1964, VIII) had been published. In the Jung years and with Jung's initial help Freud would establish the psychoanalytic movement.

When Jung first wrote to him in 1906, however, Freud still felt markedly isolated. He had gone on, almost grimly, with his mission: his basic "Three Essays on the Theory of Sexuality" (Freud, 1964, VII) did little to endear him to the medical world. True, he now was a "titular professor" in the Medical School of the University of Vienna, but as a Jew and as himself he had forfeited the academic chances he craved: he was doomed to private practice. The "Psychological Wednesday Evenings" in his waiting room in Berggasse 19 had started, and was to expand from a membership of three to twenty. But while in acute need of understanding and discussion, Freud never thought much of the style of Viennese intellectual life: and not long thereafter he was to write to Dr. Karl Abraham that he hoped that future leadership would prevent psychoanalysis from becoming a "Jewish national affair."

It was under these conditions that Jung's first public references to Freud rang like clarion calls. In his foreword to "The Psychology of Dementia Praecox" he wrote: "But, I told myself, Freud could be refuted only by one who has made repeated use of the psychoanalytic method and who really investigates as Freud does; that is, by one who has made a long and patient study of everyday life, hysteria, and dreams from Freud's point of view. He who does not or cannot do this should not pronounce judgment on Freud, else he acts like those notorious men of science who disdained to look through Galileo's telescope" (Freud and Jung, 1974a, p. xvi).

Significantly, he then added: "Fairness to Freud, however, does not imply, as many fear, unqualified submission to a dogma." Freud responded: "I am confident that you will often be in a position to back me up [*bestaetigen*, to confirm me], but I shall also gladly accept correction" (1F).[2]

Jung was relatively young, but he was firmly advancing in the world-renowned psychiatric establishment of the Swiss "Burghölzli" presided over by the truly powerful Manfred Bleuler, who, so Jung informed Freud, was on the verge of "conversion." And it was through Jung's mediation — and even before Jung's first visit — that Freud received in 1907 (he was then over fifty) the first visit from a foreign believer, and later one of his most inner circle: Max Eitingon. And soon the "congresses" of the Fliess period would become real conferences — and yearly ones. If Freud, however, sought in Jung a true and un-Viennese academic connection who could provide access to the psychiatric centers abroad, Jung, in fact, admired in Freud the genius free of academic encumbrances. Together, they produced in those first letters some of the most ingenious diagnostic discussions extant — discussions which, to my regret, have (literally) no place in this essay. Yet, I must quote two small examples of Jung's analytic clarity: "The paranoiac always seeks inner solutions, the hysteric outer ones, probably, and often quite obviously, because in paranoia that complex becomes an absolutely sovereign and incontrovertible fact, whereas in hysteria it is always a bit of a comedy, with one part of the personality playing the role of a mere spectator" (72J). And again: "The notion that obsessional ideas are, by their very nature, regressive substitutes for action sounds very convincing to me. The formula for D.pr. [Dementia Praecox] ideas would be: regressive substitutes for reality" (168J). However, only a study of the clinical sketches presented in these letters and of the great case histories published during this period can convey some of the mutual enrichment of observational acumen. Here I must add, however, that these very attempts to differentiate between neurotic and psychotic states not only phenomenologically, but also in their dynamics and genesis, involved the correspondents in reconstructions leading back into ever earlier periods and down into ever more primitive layers of the human mind. Nevertheless, Jung's style as a proponent and junior statesman of a new psychiatric way of thinking was firmly rooted in observation and broad experience. While he was secure in his new conviction, however, he also felt the need to remain adaptive: "If I appear to underestimate the therapeutic results of psychoanalysis, I do so only out of diplomatic considerations" (7J). But he soon found that diplomacy would not help: the psychiatric world at large was ready to "give him up," too. And so before long Jung confessed that "it is no small thing to defend *such* a position before *such* a public," and this all the more as he knew that "my upbringing, my milieu, and my scientific premises are in any case utterly different from your own" (9J). Yet, Freud insisted:

> I should like to repeat in writing various things that I confided to you by word of mouth, in particular, that you have inspired me with confidence for the future, that I now realize that I am as replaceable as everyone else and that I could hope for no one better than yourself, as I have come to know you, to continue and complete my work. I am sure you will not abandon the work, you have gone into it too deeply and seen for yourself how exciting, how far-reaching, and how beautiful our subject is. (18F)

In such statements a certain rhetoric is sometimes lost in translation; thus, Freud at the end of the first sentence really appoints Jung *Fortsetzer* and *Vollender*, literally: "continuer" and "completer." At the same time he attempted to demarcate almost phobically Jung's territory of action as well as the domain of his thought. After Jung had visited the famous Janet in Paris Freud wrote: "I was very glad to hear that you are back at work at Burghölzli . . . I should have been very sorry if your Vienna complex had been obliged to share the available cathexis with a Paris complex. Luckily, as you tell me, nothing of the sort happened, you gained the impression that the days of the great Charcot are past and that the new life of psychiatry is with us, between Zurich and Vienna. So we have emerged safe and sound from a first danger" (34F). And soon his new mandate seems to have forced on Jung a certain militant commitment which he could make convincing to himself only by turning more militantly rejective against the nonbelievers, as well as against his competitors at home. Thus, Jung reports from the Premier Congrès International de Psychiatrie, in Amsterdam:

> I spoke this morning but unfortunately couldn't quite finish my lecture as I would have exceeded the time limit of half an hour, which wasn't allowed. What a gang of cut-throats we have here! Their resistance really is rooted in affect . . . A ghastly crowd, reeking of vanity, Janet the worst of the lot. I am glad you have never been caught in the bedlam of such a mutual admiration society. I constantly feel the urgent need of a bath. What a morass of nonsense and stupidity! But in spite of everything I have the impression that the ferment is working. (43J)

No wonder that under such conditions the sudden appearance of an ideological brother seems like a shaft of light announcing a new kind of man: "Now for a great surprise: among the English contingent there was a young man from London, Dr. Jones (a Celt from Wales!), who knows your writings very well and does psychoanalytical work himself. He will probably visit you later. He is very intelligent and could do a lot of good" (44J). But this means that Jones is not yet a potential competitor, as *may be* one Jung's own younger staff members:

> In one of your earlier letters you asked for my views about Dr. [Karl] Abraham. I admit at once that I am "jealous" of him because he corresponds with you. (Forgive me this candour, however tasteless it may seem!) There are no objections to A. Only, he isn't quite my type. For instance, I once suggested that he collaborate on my writings, but he declined. Now he pricks up his ears whenever Bleuler and I talk about what we are investigating, etc. He then comes up with a publication . . . He is intelligent but not original, highly adaptable, but totally lacking in psychological empathy, for which reason he is usually very unpopular with the patients. I would ask you to subtract a personal touch of venom from this judgment. (39J)

Freud's sense of cautious recruitment makes him, in return, ask a "racist" question: "By the way, is he a descendant of his eponym?" (40F). Jung, still cautiously, claims not to know, but slurs Mrs. Abraham with a kind of clinical and national jargon which will at times become rampant in the letters: "I fear I have painted Abraham (who is what his name implies) in too dark colours. Of his antecedents I know nothing whatever—which is characteristic. The emotional rapport is missing but I don't feel it's my fault. A. often has mild ideas of persecution about me. His wife comes from Berlin, and suffers from Berlinese autoerotism with all its psychological consequences. That rubs off on A." (41J). *Autoerotic*, I hasten to clarify, then meant something like *narcissistic*.

Later, Jones (twenty-eight, whom Jung, thirty-two, calls a "young man") visits Jung in Zurich and proposes a first psychoanalytic congress in Salzburg which will, he thinks, be attended by at least two Englishmen. Freud is delighted: "Your Englishman appeals to me because of his nationality; I believe that once the English have become acquainted with our ideas they will never let them go. I have less confidence in the French, but the Geneva people must be thought of as Swiss" (55F). He adds that Abraham is going to visit him. These few selections from the first year and a half of correspondence set, I think, a pattern for scenarios that will rapidly include other persons and countries. By 1909, both Jung and Freud were to speak and receive honorary degrees in the New World: at Clark University in Worcester.

As to Freud, it had, by then, become only too clear that he was going to fight for Jung's soul as that of his true successor who would vouch both for the founder's and the new field's integrity — and immortality.

Here a particular form of father complex began to manifest itself which is, no doubt, part of male generativity, although it is noteworthy that then — as it is today — a father complex was usually considered something a *son* had. Freud did not hesitate to address Jung as "son" and "heir." Touchingly, and in line with his own Moses complex, he would also call him his "Joshua" who *was* going to see the Promised Land. Here one cannot overlook that Jung's very name is related to *Juenger*, the German word for Christ's disciples. As for the "empire" to be inherited, Jung found himself addressed as "Alexander" even as he was asked to occupy the new field's top chairmanships and editorships as soon as they materialized.

While all such designations often had, of course, a humorously poetic ring, the imagery employed was part of a patriarchic world image which also entered the dream life of the times, as will be seen from Jung's report of a dream of his "convert" Bleuler:

> After I had broken down his cover-resistance through the last dream-analysis, the following dreams came out at the party, accompanied by venomous asides (he told them to me in front of the company, all unsuspecting — as if to prove how little he understands dream-analysis!): He was the guest of the German Kaiser, who looked like a fat grocer, sodden with drink. In a second dream he was summoned to Berlin in order to analyse the Kaiser. But he didn't get round to that, for the Kaiser locked him in the cellar. (222J)

There gradually emerges in these patriarchal relationships a theme which — in view of Freud's and Jung's increasing emphasis on son Oedipus as the model of the core complex of all complexes — can only be called the Laius complex. For the reader of today cannot overlook the fact that Freud's persistent warnings regarding the temporal limits of his own life and the sure betrayals threatening the immortality of his ideas take on an oracular ring reminiscent of Laius' received message: Oedipus *was* going to betray him. And, indeed, Freud, besides expressing his general moody disbelief in the next generation, threatened Jung directly: "My one-time friend Fliess developed a dreadful case of paranoia after throwing off his affection for me, which was undoubtedly considerable" (70F). Jung responded, as yet naively: "The reference to Fliess — surely not accidental — and your relationship with him impels me to ask you to let me enjoy your friendship not as one between equals but as that of father and son.

This distance appears to me fitting and natural" (72J). He did not sense yet the presence of both Oedipus and Laius, waiting in the wings of the enfolding scenario of fathership and sonship.

THE CORE COMPLEX: FATHERS AND SONS

As I now relate some of the most tragic personal encounters between the correspondents, I must remind the reader once more of the special dynamics governing this particular combination of regular correspondence (for Freud demanded, because he needed, near weekly letters) and very rare personal meetings. Some of our themes appear in these letters, and especially also in personal meetings in between letters, in such dramatic form just because these men were embarked on an inner voyage of discovery engulfing them in unknown turbulences. For after all, the very ethos of their search— almost a new kind of Caritas—demanded that these members of a patriarchal and authoritative medical world face in themselves exactly those borderlines of normality beyond which their patients were lost—that is, the borderlines between normal and neurotic conflict, between neurosis and psychosis, and between fantasy and mythology: all the way down and back to earliest ontogeny and to prehistoric phylogeny.

The first encounter between the two men occurred when the Jungs visited the Freuds in Vienna. The two men did not seclude themselves in Freud's study until after a family dinner with, no doubt, excellent wine. The two wives waved to them through the closing study door as to a couple of newlyweds: "Enfin seuls!" Jung could confess to Freud only half a year later that "my veneration for you has something of the character of a 'religious' crush. Though it does not really bother me, I still feel it is disgusting and ridiculous because of its undeniable erotic undertone. This abominable feeling comes from the fact that as a boy I was the victim of a sexual assault by a man I once·worshipped. Even in Vienna the remarks of the ladies ('enfin seuls,' etc.) sickened me, although the reason for it was not clear to me at the time" (49J). And underscored: "*I therefore fear your confidence.*" Jung makes further remarkable confessions induced, no doubt, by the vortex of associations aroused by the new, the psychoanalytic, kind of confessional. At any rate, the German words for "I was the victim" are *Ich bin unterlegen*—literally, "layed under," that is, I submitted. It is probable that a true transference played into the panicky reaction to being privated with the great man. Furthermore, it is said that Jung as a boy for many years shared his father's bedroom.

On a second visit there arose between the two men, during a discussion of parapsychology at the dinner table (that is, in the presence of the young Freuds) an acute, if somewhat ridiculous, authoritative conflict: they suddenly heard a loud noise in a bookcase, and Jung predicted firmly and correctly, in spite of Freud's strenuous disbelief, that another one would follow in a matter of minutes. "That last evening with you," Jung wrote later, "has, most happily, freed me inwardly from the oppressive sense of your paternal authority" — while Freud wrote: "It is strange that on the very same evening when I formally adopted you as eldest son and anointed you — in *partibus infidelium* — as my successor and crown prince, you should have divested me of my paternal dignity, which divesting seems to have given you as much pleasure as I, on the contrary, derived from the investiture of your person" (139F). Here, the words "divested" and "investiture" are in German *entkleidet* and *Einkleidung*, that is, "disrobed" and "clothing" and thus imply a more primitive mode of exposing a kind of nakedness.

And then there was, on the boat to America, a decisive moment marking, as Jung claimed later, his definitive disappointment in Freud's ethical superiority. The two men and Sandor Ferenczi apparently made a daily ritual out of analyzing one another's dreams. Jung years later reminded Freud that one day "our analysis, you may remember, came to a stop with your remark that you 'could not submit to analysis *without losing your authority*.' These words are engraved on my memory as a symbol of everything to come. I haven't eaten *my* words, however" (330J). Here, the German expression for "submit to analysis" is *sich analytisch preisgeben* — that is, to "give oneself away psychoanalytically," while Jung's supposed "I haven't eaten *my* words" is in German *Ich bin nicht zu Kreuz gekrochen*, literally, "I did not crawl to the cross," a most significant phrase, coming from a Lutheran pastor's son.

Finally, in reference to Freud's fainting spells, first in Bremen before the embarkation for America, and toward the end of the friendship, at a conference in Munich following Jung's apology after a last emotional attempt to clear up a misunderstanding, there are extended accounts both in Jung's writings (1963, pp. 157, 153) and in Jones' biography (1953, I, pp. 347f, 316f; II, pp. 164ff, 145ff). In our context I would simply point out that the German word for fainting is *Ohnmacht* — literally, "without power," a meaning dramatically underlined by the fact that Jung, the powerful mountaineer, carried Freud to a sofa.

My corrections of small details in the English translation is meant only to demonstrate that whoever uses a translated historical document as illustration of a conceptual approach will have to investigate whether the original words support it. My approach here is a configurational one which is one necessary step toward any encompassing psychoanalytic investigation. The configurations noted are all related to highly emotional situations in which one partner in a relationship must "submit," is "exposed," "gives himself away," "crawls to the cross," or "is without power". All this corresponds to a set of space-time configurations which seem to emerge from the evolutionary fact pervading our language as well as our affects, namely, that we humans, as members of a species called *Homo erectus*, must be "brought up" from an especially helpless state and "grow up" through an especially prolonged childhood, in order to take our stand. For these and other reasons, men who appoint one another the "Other" in any of its existential connotations will experience their relationship, more or less consciously, in one of the many terms connoting spatial superiority or inferiority. Seeing the pervasiveness of such themes in some of the letters (remember Bleuler's dream), one can well see why Freud for quite some time considered Adler's ideological determination to make superiority as such *the* central instinctual motive more dangerous to the emerging psychoanalytic metapsychology than Jung's mythological inclinations.

In this connection, there is a most interesting letter in which Freud discusses the age-old mythological theme of "the unequal pair of brothers," one of whom appears higher in breeding, taller in stature, stronger in constitution, or, as it were, more immortal than the other. He ascribes to a mythologist, Paul Ehrenreich (of whom he says that he "for once forgot his science and consequently had a good idea"; 274F), the interpretation that the weaker double, in primitive imagination, is symbolized by the afterbirth, which in some tribes is ritually treated as the twin who died. Here, then, is the fraternal and sororal aspect of the existential problem of I-consciousness and self-love: Narcissus, we remember, fell in love with and drowned in his dead twin sister's image. In his letter about such "double" brotherhood, incidentally, Freud mentions the possible existence of a *phylogenetic memory*, to which Jung (the future proponent of a collective unconscious) responds enthusiastically.

But then there is, of course, the firstborn, not only ahead of his own afterbirth but of all his brothers and sisters. Freud, in his protest over Jung's "spookery," complained that this happened just after he had anointed him his *oldest* son, thus marking him, according to the best monarchic and patriarchal principle, as the one who came first and thus is his natural heir. Here fathers and oldest sons collude against all latecomers; but this also forces the oldest into the role of Oedipus, if only in the sense that the time of his succession depends on the father's death: and, indeed, for the sake of a secure, a true succession, Freud almost promises to die early. As far as I know, Freud has not acknowledged that oracle-ridden Laius is as necessary to the Oedipus complex as is Oedipus—who in Kolonos will fall victim to *his* sons—for the whole complex is, of course, a generational matter. At any rate, the tragic outcome of Freud's and Jung's friendship assumes a somewhat comic connotation (in the antique sense) if one remembers that one main criterion for Jung's fidelity in theoretical matters was his credal acknowledgment of the Oedipus complex as the core complex of emotional development and as being even "at the root of religious feeling" (270F). But this never made sense to Jung in ontogenetic terms: he looked for its phylogenetic and mythological significance. In order eventually to come into his own, Jung, at the very end, had no choice but to do away with the whole father-son business and—as we shall see—treat Freud with untranslatable "helvetic" cussedness as a brother—and a child.

In the meantime, however, Freud and Jung indulged in what in terms of that day can only be called a collusion of their Laius complexes in the way in which they wrote to each other about the generation of followers in Vienna and in Burghölzli who became ready to take over the future of psychoanalysis—some in Vienna by "betraying" Freud's original ideas and some in Burghölzli by "betraying" Jung and becoming lifelong Freudians. In 1909 Freud wrote: "I believe on the contrary that the younger men will demolish everything in my heritage that is not absolutely solid as fast as they can. Developments in psychoanalysis are often the exact opposite of what you would expect to find in other fields. Since you are likely to play a prominent part in this work of liquidation, I shall try to place certain of my endangered ideas in your safekeeping" (169F).

At this point, let me present a brief "family tree" of the generational structure of this emerging professional hierarchy. The list is topped by a truly great great grandfather—no other than Johann Wolfgang von Goethe, whom Jung claimed as an (illegitimate) ancestor. There follows a very concrete grandfather of a pervasively reliable and yet critical stature, from the new world: James Putnam, M.D., of Harvard, born in the 1840s. In the father category are Freud and Bleuler—1850s. In the 1870s was born the generation of men who somehow had to become clusters of brothers in a psychoanalytic movement: beside Jung, Alfred Adler (really the oldest) and then Ferenczi (Budapest), Abraham (Berlin), and Jones (London). And then there was "little Rank," as Freud referred to him, born in 1886, who was secretary of the Wednesday evenings throughout the Jung period and beyond. Rank was only four years older than Freud's oldest son. A dropout, he was still studying Greek and Latin so as to finally graduate.

This factual list must be followed by some references to the way in which some of these people are first mentioned in the letters, and this mostly in a (totally impartial) scurrilous manner. In reporting this I am glad to have introduced for this whole matter a dignified conceptual term, namely, adult "rejectivity" — in this correspondence a kind of playful denunciation which, besides Freud's fate-bound mistrust and Jung's acute jealousy, signified the test which all these persons had to pass in order to qualify for the new special species of psychoanalyst. And, unnecessary to say, I consider this an "adult theme" of pervasive importance, for such — here often playful — rejectivity, besides enlivening professional gossip and book review sections, *can* be employed in all manner of national, religious, and racial discrimination. Consider, then, what Jones came to read when he was the first to peruse these old letters in preparation for his Freud biography: "Jones is undoubtedly a very interesting and worthy man, but he gives me a feeling of, I was almost going to say racial strangeness. He is a fanatic and doesn't eat enough. 'Let me have men about me that are fat,' says Caesar, etc. . . . He almost reminds me of the lean and hungry Cassius" (87F). And a few months later: "I find the racial mixture in our group most interesting; he is a Celt and consequently not quite accessible to us, the Teuton and the Mediterranean man" (103F).

Ferenczi was and remained for years Freud's sole companion on many vacation trips, when his receptivity and imagination undoubtedly provided Freud with something he had missed since the best days with Fliess. But receptivity can go to too far. As Freud reported to Jung: "My travelling companion is a dear fellow, but dreamy in a disturbing kind of way, and his attitude towards me is infantile. He never stops admiring me, which I don't like, and is probably sharply critical of me in his unconscious when I am taking it easy. He has been too passive and receptive, letting everything be done for him like a woman, and I really haven't got enough homosexuality in me to accept him as one. These trips arouse a great longing for a real woman" (212F).

But to quote Jung, too, and in regard to the man who was to come closest to Freud's scientific style: "I have an undisguised con-

tempt for some of colleague A's [Abraham's] idiosyncrasies. In spite
of his estimable qualities and sundry virtues, he is simply not a
gentleman. In my eyes just about the worst thing that can happen to
anyone" (91J).

Finally, Freud's characterization of two more Viennese and his
general conclusion regarding any "school":

> Sadger [Isidor Sadger] that congenital fanatic of orthodoxy, who
> happens by mere accident to believe in psychoanalysis rather than in the
> law given by God on Sinai-Horeb. (77F)

> Unfortunately, [Wilhelm Stekel] has the best nose of any of us for the
> secrets of the unconscious. Because he is a perfect swine, whereas we are
> really decent people who submit only reluctantly to the evidence. (160F)

> To tell the truth, I would rather you did not identify any particular school
> with me, because if you do I shall soon be obliged to confess that my
> pseudo-students or non-students are closer to me than my students *sensu
> strictiori*. Also, I should not like to be held more directly responsible for
> the work of Stekel, Adler, Sadger, etc. than for my influence on you,
> Binswanger, Abraham, Maeder, etc. (127F)

It should be added, however, that Freud in his letters to Ferenczi
was apt to confront him directly with some of the difficulties he had
with him; and that in the analysis of his own dreams he recognized
some of Ferenczi's "womanly" attitudes as comparable to his own
behavior in relation to Fliess. Nor can I omit the remark that Freud's
derisive utterances, as has been seen, often reflect a certain humorous and respectful rejection, while Jung's can be characterized by
what he himself calls his "Helvetic" crudeness.

But there are in these letters also most searching and compassionate references to the tragedies caused by the confrontation of
sensitive co-workers with the data of the unconscious — in those early
days when neither a "training analysis" nor a theoretical training was
as yet formalized. Among the professional patients who became colleagues and the colleagues who became patients there was one young
Dr. Johann Jacob Honegger, an age-mate of Rank, who, so it seems,
could not "take" his analysis with Jung. Here, Freud intervened.

> Grandfathers are seldom harsh and I doubt if I have even been so as a
> father. It is unreasonable of you, I think, to expect his working methods
> to be as independent of the human libido as yours: we agree that he
> belongs to a later generation, that he has had little experience of love thus

far, and is in general of softer stuff than you. We would not want him to be a copy of yourself. He will be far more useful to you as he is. He possesses a fine receptivity, psychological flair, and a good sense of the "basic language." He seems to be exceedingly devoted to you, and his personal value is further enhanced by the present situation, in which you must stand up to our opponents in the Zurich camp. Why then don't you take him as he is and train him on the basis of his own nature, rather than try to mould him to an ideal that is alien to him? (197F)

And after some suicides, including Honegger's, Freud wrote sadly: "It occurs to me that we wear out quite a few men" or, more liberally translated, "that we are using up quite a number of persons" (248F).

TERRITORIES

There are many sober and factual passages in the letters about the founding of journals and the spread of societies abroad. The reader of today is struck by occasional poignant phrases connoting "conquest" which somehow provide the territorial background for such national and racial remarks as we have already noted. Jung can excel in them enthusiastically, but Freud seems to enjoy them, too. To Jung's suggestion that "now it is Germany's turn" (164J), Freud still responded with an appeal to modesty, "while our ultimate conquest of the world still lies so far ahead" (166F). Jung, in turn, likes to refer to psychoanalysis in writing as S Ψ, an equivalent to SJ (Society of Jesus), and to use phrases of credal conquest such as "to send an apostle into the Diaspora" (175J). But Freud, always more political, could speak of "raising the flag of psychoanalysis" and this, of all places, "over the territory of normal love life" (174F); while he could also ask "what to do about Australia?" (244F). That such themes, besides personal inclinations, reflect the world-historic situation can be seen from the fact that something like a Vienna-Zurich axis was clearly envisaged by these men as useful in the establishment of the Vienna-New York and Vienna-London axes.

Nor did the two men after their trip to the New World hesitate to diagnose the American people—Jung, by suggesting a national "Negro complex" which made it necessary for the majority, in the seductive presence of such a sensual minority, to repress its own instinctuality. Freud mused: "In our studies of America, have we ever looked into the source of the energies they develop in practical life? I believe it is the early dissolution of family ties, which prevents all the erotic components from coming to life and banishes the Graces from the land" (223F). Freud was all the more impressed with James Jackson Putnam: "The old Puritan's understanding and conduct are really amazing" (225F).

But then, in all these sometimes raucous, humorous, or thoughtful references to nations and races, there appears an adult theme of both general and very personal significance: I mean territoriality, which pervades procreativity and productivity as well as creativity as an essential adult aspiration endowed with strong instinctual drive. The adult, committed to affiliative intimacy, must accept or stake out a certain territory to be taken care of by him and his own "kind." Depending on personality, social system, and historical situation, this may include such territory as must be conquered for the sake of such care: and in this sense our correspondents most decisively represent the conquering types. As for Freud, we know from the Fliess letters and especially also from "The Interpretation of Dreams" that in his younger years he had entertained dreams of political leadership. In fact, if for this, his greatest book, he chose the Vergilian motto "Flectere si nequeo superos, Acheronta movebo" ("If I cannot bend the powers above, I will move the river of the underworld"), this motto can be seen to signify the powerful wish to conquer the unconscious. But it can also mean the hope that the human mind, once it has, indeed, gained insight into its own unconscious, may learn to influence the traditionally insensitive motivation of those in power. How this may be related to Freud's personal fate as a Jew in the then increasingly anti-Semitic Austrian Empire has been, from a historical point of view, comprehensively treated by Schorske (1973). At any rate, both Jung and Freud were passionately motivated in conquering, beyond international psychiatry, the awareness of the humanistic world.

In regard to the concrete logistics of guiding such conquest, this may be the point to note that Freud soon began to doubt Jung's capacity for organizational leadership, and he honestly confronted him with these doubts. Blaming his own "impatience to see you in the right place and my chafing under the pressure of my own responsibility," he concluded: "As it is, the first months of your reign, my dear son and successor, have not turned out brilliantly. Sometimes I have the impression that you yourself have not taken your functions seriously enough and have not yet begun to act in a manner appropriate to your new dignity" (205F). But then Jung gradually had become irreversibly engrossed in the wider humanistic promises of psychoanalysis. And, indeed, there emerged in both men and between them a certain ideological chill: for it became clear that psychoanalysis was more than a psychiatric "technique" or a research "method" or both. But what was psychoanalysis, in terms of old universal beliefs or of new and ascending ones? What new type of man was the "psychoanalyzed" species to be, and in the context of what human future? And what kind of imagery was to provide psychoanalysis with a universally relevant and yet safe and teachable communicative pattern? Jung, no doubt, early sensed an affinity to something Christian; and, indeed, Freud's statement, made early in the correspondence, that the energy effective in the "transference" (that is, the patient's transfer to the psychoanalyst of infantile affects) was the energy of love, can well remind one of the Gospel story where Jesus, in the middle of a crowd pressing upon him from all sides, felt touched by somebody in such a way that "some energy had gone out of Him." Upon identifying a woman kneeling behind him, and now cured of her dysmenorrhia, he said, "Your faith has healed you." At any rate, it is not surprising that Jung, who could count among his basic identifications that of a hereditary parson, felt that there was a credal as well as scientific aspect to the love-energy assumed to be active in healing. Freud, in turn, although he recognized something specifically Judaic in the nature of his own mystic inclinations, nevertheless decided that the then budding Ethical Movement was as far as he would go in terms of a larger group association, for as he confessed: "the ultimate basis of man's need for religion is *infantile helplessness*, which is so much greater in man than in animals. After infancy he cannot conceive of a world without parents and makes for himself a just God and a kindly nature, the two worst anthropomorphic falsifications he could have imagined. But all that is very banal. Derived, incidentally, from the instinct of self-preservation, not the sexual instinct, which adds its spice later on" (171F). So Freud suggested that Jung inquire at a coming meeting whether, perchance, some psychoanalysts could see a place for psychoanalysis in the Ethical Movement.

Jung, however, felt inspired otherwise, and this, as he admits, in a "stormy" fashion. "A genuine and proper ethical development cannot abandon Christianity but must grow up within it, must bring to fruition its hymn of love, the agony and the ecstasy over the dying and resurgent god, the mystic power of the wine, the awesome anthropophagy of the Last Supper—only *this* ethical development can serve the vital forces of religion" (178J). In German, the last sentence of this inspired paragraph reads quite differently (and I italicize) "only *this* ethical development can bend (*macht* . . . *dienstbar*) the vital forces of religion to *its* service." And he rejects Freud's proposal:

The ethical problem of sexual freedom really is enormous and worth the sweat of all noble souls. But 2000 years of Christianity can only be replaced by something equivalent. An ethical fraternity, with its mythical Nothing, not infused by any archaic-infantile driving force, is a pure vacuum and can never evoke in man the slightest trace of that age-old animal power which drives the migrating bird across the sea and without which no irresistible.mass movement can come into being. (178J)

Freud turns sarcastic: "An ethical society does not need religion any more than a voluntary fire brigade does" (179F); while Jung, for the moment, gives in — "My last letter was naturally another of those rampages of fantasy I indulge in from time to time" (180J) — and promises to submit the ethical association matter to the Nuremberg Congress. But Freud loses interest.

A few letters later Jung strongly confronts Freud with the paradoxical fact that the *opponents* of psychoanalysis had started to see in it a movement which has "all the trappings of a religion" and to which they, in turn, react with a kind of religious horror. And he adds, referring to Swiss pastors: "The keen interest of our theologians is suspicious" (206J). But it is vacation time, and Jung announces his intention to bicycle to Northern Italy: "Rome in particular," he adds, "is not yet permitted to me" (206J). (He was never to set foot on Roman soil.)

The abortive idea of an actual tie with some bigger organization representative of the philosophical horizon of the new field was followed by the highly personal attempt of each correspondent to clarify his own interpretive relation to the world views of the past — a search which led Jung to the investigation of "creative fantasy" and to the concept of the collective unconscious. To Freud's remarks on the symbolism of the afterbirth he had responded:

I am most grateful for this contribution since it fits in very well with certain other observations which have forced me to conclude that the so-called "early memories of childhood" are not individual memories at all but phylogenetic ones. I mean of course the *very early* memories like birth, sucking, etc. There are things whose only explanation is *intrauterine:* much of the water symbolism, then the enwrappings and encoilings which seem to be accompanied by strange skin sensations (umbilical cord and amnion). Just now my Agathli is having dreams like this; they are closely related to certain Negro birth-myths, where these envelopments in slimy stuff also occur. I think we shall find that infinitely many more things than we now suppose are phylogenetic memories. (275J)

Before this, he had again announced his continued interest in occultism, astrology, and mythology and almost begged: "There are strange and wondrous things in these lands of darkness. Please don't worry about my wanderings in these infinitudes. I shall return laden with rich booty for our knowledge of the human psyche" (254J).

Freud, who was about to shed the company of Adler and the Adlerians ("the whole Adler gang"), had begun to pursue in open secrecy his own inquiry into the origin of religion which was to lead him to totem and taboo: "Since my mental powers revived, I have been working in a field where you will be surprised to meet me. I have unearthed strange and uncanny things and will almost feel obliged *not* to discuss them with you. But you are too shrewd not to guess what I am up to when I add that I am dying to read your 'Transformations and Symb. of the Lib'" (268F). Jung would continue to plead:

> I don't think you need have any apprehensions about my protracted and invisible sojourn in the "religious-libidinal cloud." I would willingly tell you what is going on up there if only I knew how to set it down in a letter. Essentially, it is an elaboration of all the problems that arise out of the mother-incest libido, or rather, the libido-cathected mother-imago. This time I have ventured to tackle the mother. So what is keeping me hidden is the *katabasis* to the realm of the Mothers, where, as we know, Theseus and Peirithous remained stuck, grown fast to the rocks. But in time I shall come up again. (300J)

In the meantime, however, the mother theme had made itself heard on homeground and in other than mythological ways.

A WOMAN'S VOICE

Freud and Jung, over the years, report about their family life, and the procreative and the creative father-son themes are often intertwined. The Freuds' sons and daughters, of course, were in their late teens and twenties, getting ready to go their own ways, while the Jung family was just coming into its own. Freud reported on such events as joint vacations, the oldest daughter's betrothal and repeated medical problems, the sons' graduations, and one son's dramatic accident. The foreboding of his own old age attaches itself to such reports, too: "My second son has his final examination behind him and has gone off on his first trip alone. The eldest has got his face chopped up in a student duel and been very brave about the whole thing. Little by little the young people are becoming independent and all of a sudden I have become *the old man*" (150F). The last three words are in English. A more fateful mood characterizes the reaction to the oldest daughter's protracted problems: "I have returned rather depressed from our lovely Diet of Nuremberg. Analysis [of my depression] leads far afield to the distress which the state of my daughter's health causes me—I have been trying in vain to replace her" (185F). And again: "My daughter's health is definitely a little better; I don't dare expect any more. One becomes so anxious and resigned in old age!" (190F).

Freud was fifty-four years old then. There was, of course, much sympathy on the Jungs' part. An incident in son Martin Freud's life, however, was drawn into the intra- and interfamily analysis cultivated by the Jungs. Martin had broken a foot while skiing and Freud's report vividly depicts the dangerous circumstances, such as the young man's lying "motionless in the snow for five hours before help came," and this at an altitude of some 7,800 feet, while it was another two and a half days before he could be brought down to a hospital. "Well," Freud added, "I suppose such accidents are determined by the same causes as those of non[psycho]analysts' sons" (231F). But Jung challenges him: "From a very discreet source a little of your son's 'complex' story has come to my ears. Is Martin his mother's favourite? I am sure you know the rest as well as I do" (235J). Freud, surprisingly, responds by hinting at his son's "secret motives" and claims that he himself had

> definitely expected the accident. He had told me nothing about this projected skiing trip. I knew that a few days before he had been in a fight in the barracks yard and was expecting to be called before the court of honor . . . But something seems to be wrong with your combinations. He is not his mother's favourite son; on the contrary, she treats him almost unjustly, compensating at his expense for her over-indulgence·towards her brother, whom he resembles a good deal, whereas, strangely enough, I compensate in my treatment of him for my unfriendliness towards the same person (now in New York). (236F)

Finally, there are references to a worrisome duodenal ulcer suffered by Ernst Freud. Reading all this, one cannot help thinking of the picture (reproduced in Jones, 1953, II, 192-193) of proud Freud, in his sixtieth year, with his uniformed and be-medaled sons Ernst and Martin. But the younger the Freud "children," the more are they apt in this correspondence to be included in fond references to "my people" or simply *Kleinzeug* ("small fry"). Thus, the youngest, Anna, does not seem to be mentioned by name at all—she whom fate and giftedness later selected to fill the very role of a caretaker and successor more simply and more naturally than did Jung, or anybody else.

As for the Jung family, one daughter was two, a second just born when the correspondence started. Freud was frankly apprehensive as to what it would do to Jung's spiritual son-ship, if Jung became the father of a "real" son:

In the meantime, I venture to hope, fate has made you a father again, and perhaps the star you spoke of on our long walk has risen for you. The transfer of one's hopes to one's children is certainly an excellent way of appeasing one's unresolved complexes, though for you it is too soon. Let me hear from you; until then I assume that the valiant mother is well; to her husband she must indeed be more precious than all her children, just as the method must be valued more highly than the results obtained by it. (116F)

The German text, more humorously, speaks of the "single results." And, indeed, son Franz came next, and one more daughter two years later.

It was only then that Emma Jung, abruptly and without her husband's knowledge, entered the correspondence in a historical fashion: as a woman, she apparently could not tolerate any longer what to her appeared to be a spurious interplay of creative and pro-creative themes in the communications of these men. I think Emma Jung deserves to be quoted extensively as she reacts, in October 1911, to Freud's visit in September. She first wonders whether, maybe, he felt in disagreement with her husband's latest book, *Transformations of the Libido*: "You didn't speak of it at all and yet I think it would do you both so much good if you got down to a thorough discussion of it. Or is it something else? If so, please tell me what, dear Herr Professor." She then refers to a certain overly resigned mood which she claims Freud had displayed, and concludes "that your resignation relates not only to your real children (it made a quite special impression on me when you spoke of it) but also to your spiritual sons; otherwise you would have so little need to be resigned . . . Please do not take my action as officiousness and do not count me among the women who, you once told me, always spoil your friendships" (following 277J). Whatever Freud answered (his letters to her are not preserved), Emma Jung reminded him a month later of other resigned remarks concerning his family:

This made such an impression on me and seemed to me so significant that I had to think of it again and again, and I fancied it was intended just for me because it was meant symbolically at the same time and referred to my husband. . . .I wanted to ask then if you are sure that your children would not be helped by analysis. One certainly cannot be the child of a great man with impunity, considering the trouble one has in getting away from ordinary fathers. And when this distinguished father also has a streak of paternalism in him, as you yourself said! . . . You may imagine how overjoyed and honoured I am by the confidence you have in Carl, but it almost seems to me as though you were sometimes giving too much—do you not see in him the follower and fulfiller more than you need? Doesn't one often give much because one wants to keep much? (following 279J)

She then protests that nobody need to fear premature age who has discovered what she innocently calls the *Jungbrunnen* of psychoanalysis—in translation, the "well of youth" but, of course, also literally the "Jung-well"—and concludes: "And do not think of Carl with a father's feeling: 'He will grow, but I must dwindle,' but rather as one human being thinks of another, who like you has his own law to fulfill."

In two further letters Emma Jung seems eager to correct the impression her letters had made on Freud:

I . . . just wanted to raise the question whether [his children's] physical symptoms might not be somehow psychically conditioned, so that there might for instance be a reduced power of resistance. Since I have made some very astonishing discoveries in myself in this respect and do not consider myself excessively degenerate or markedly hysterical, I thought similar phenomena possible with other people too. I shall be grateful for enlightenment . . . Please write nothing of this to Carl; things are going badly enough with me as it is. (following 282J)

As pointed out, it is interesting to behold that Emma Jung, too, initiated her brief correspondence when she was approaching thirty—the age of Freud, Fliess, and Jung when they started their correspondences. But while the men pursued their creative interests in competition with their wives' procreative preoccupation, Emma Jung apparently wanted to save Freud's children as well as Freud himself and, above all, her husband from what she perceived as a morbid attempt on Freud's part to appropriate Jung. At any rate, her valiant female reaction expresses a generativity more dedicated to the developmental needs of living mortals than to immortal ideas. Her letters, however, seem to have ended Freud's references to the young Freuds in further correspondence.

SEPARATE WAYS

By this time, as already reported, a certain secretiveness begins to shroud the work of both men, as they searched back into primary origins. Freud, significantly, had warned Jung against straying too far into mythical territory, urging him "to return to our medical motherland" (232F)—a designation which may give us an inkling that our main fields may symbolize maternal sources of creative fertility, as well as a territory with guarded boundaries. Freud was on his way to totem and taboo. Jung became concerned:

Your letter has got me on tenterhooks because, for all my "shrewdness," I can't quite make out what is going on so enigmatically behind the scenes. Together with my wife I have tried to unriddle your words, and we have reached surmises which, for the time being at any rate, I would rather keep to myself. I can only hope that your embargo on discussion will be lifted during your stay here. I, too, have the feeling that this is a time full of marvels, and, if the auguries do not deceive us, it may very well be that, thanks to your discoveries, we are on the threshold of something really sensational, which I scarcely know how to describe except with the Gnostic concept of "Sophia," an Alexandrian term particularly suited to the reincarnation of ancient wisdom in the shape of Ψ A. I daren't say too much, but would only counsel you (very immodestly) to let my "Transf. and Symb. of the Lib." unleash your associations and/or fantasies: I am sure you will hit upon strange things if you do. (269J)

Freud answers:

I am glad to release you as well as your dear wife, well known to me as a solver of riddles, from the darkness by informing you that my work in these last few weeks has dealt with the same theme as yours, to wit, the origin of religion. I wasn't going to speak of it for fear of confusing you. But . . . I find, much to my relief, that there is no need for secrecy. So you too are aware that the Oedipus complex is at the root of religious feeling. Bravo! What evidence I have to contribute can be told in five minutes. (270F)

At this time both men find it necessary to reiterate how different they feel they are from one another — an emphasis which, no doubt, contributed a mighty motive to Jung's work on such polarities as introversion and extroversion and the animus and the anima, not to speak of the psychological types. Freud, too, was thinking along these lines: "I can see from the difficulties I encounter in this work that I was not cut out for inductive investigation, that my whole make-up is intuitive, and that in setting out to establish the purely empirical science of Ψ A I subjected myself to an extraordinary discipline" (288F). But then, Freud also more sharply characterized differences in therapeutic approach. Referring to Oskar Pfister as well as Jung, he gathers

that neither of you has yet acquired the necessary objectivity in your practice, that you still get involved, giving a good deal of yourselves and expecting the patient to give something in return. Permit me, speaking as the venerable old master, to say that this technique is invariably ill-advised and that it is best to remain reserved and purely receptive. We must never let our poor neurotics drive us crazy. I believe an article on "counter-transference" is sorely needed; of course we could not publish it, we should have to circulate copies among ourselves. (290F)

As the critical year of 1912 commenced, more sinister implications begin to announce themselves. Strangely, it was an issue that touched Freud's "tenderness"—a word he used freely—which first really alarmed him. He had heard from Pfister that Jung had been bitten by a dog. That he had not written to Freud about it directly and, in fact, did not even respond to Freud's subsequent inquiry seems to have touched the sensitive nerve of unrequited maternal concern. Jung, in turn, felt left out when Freud briefly visited Ludwig Binswanger in nearby Kreuzlingen without informing him—an incident which Jung was to call the "gesture of Kreuzlingen" and which led to that confrontation in Munich where Freud fainted after Jung had apologized for the "misunderstanding." All this only deepened and yet also forced to the surface Jung's lasting sense of characterological differences. "I am glad we were able to meet in Munich, as this was the first time I have really understood you. I realized how different I am from you. This realization will be enough to effect a radical change in my whole attitude . . . I am most distressed that I did not gain this insight much earlier. It could have spared you so many disappointments" (328J). Relying on his hope that such insight will make it unnecessary to "give up our personal relationship," Jung now becomes more intransigent in theoretical and ideological matters: "I am ready at any time to adapt my opinions to the judgment of someone who knows better, and always have been. I would never have sided with you in the first place had not heresy run in my blood. Since I have no professorial ambitions I can afford to admit mistakes" (303J). And he quotes Zarathustra, speaking to his followers:

> You had not yet sought yourselves when you found me.
> Thus do all believers—.
> Now I bid you lose me and find yourselves;
> and only when you have all denied me will I return to you.

Finally, the lines were clearly drawn between Freud's sexual-biological theories and Jung's cultural and mythological ones:

> Like you, I am absorbed in the incest problem and have come to conclusions which show incest primarily as a fantasy problem. Originally,

morality was simply a ceremony of atonement, a substitutive prohibition, so that the ethnic prohibition of incest may not mean biological incest at all, but merely the utilization of infantile incest material for the construction of the first prohibitions. (I don't know whether I am expressing myself clearly!) If biological incest were meant, then father-daughter incest would have fallen under the prohibition much more readily than that between son-in-law and mother-in-law. The tremendous role of the mother in mythology has a significance far outweighing the biological incest problem — a significance that amounts to pure fantasy. (312J)

Evidently the object of the prohibition is not to prevent incest but to consolidate the family (or piety, or the social structure). (313J)

When Jung, finally, announced that in his invited lectures at Fordham University "his version of ψ A" won over many people who had been "put off by Freud's sexual approach to the neuroses" (323J), Freud knew that he had acquired a rival and potential demeanor rather than a "successor."

I will spare myself and my readers quotations from those letters which typically marked the moment when the generative goals of these two men proved definitely split and when vindictive rejectivity took over. According to the differences in age and temperament, Jung had the greater need to pull his senior down, while Freud withdrew, as it were, upward. Jung, at first, only threatened that he would "turn his lyre a few tones lower" (333J). But soon, he demotes Freud himself in a way which I quote only because it marks the total breakdown of the father-son dimension. Freud is, he claims,

reducing everyone to the level of sons and daughters who blushingly admit the existence of their faults. Meanwhile you remain on top as the father, sitting pretty [bleiben schoen oben als Vater].

You see, my dear Professor, so long as you hand out this stuff I don't give a damn [sind mir ganz wurscht] for my symptomatic actions: they shrink to nothing in comparison with the formidable beam in my brother Freud's eye. (338J)

Finally, he addresses Freud as a child: "If I offer you the unvarnished truth," he writes, as 1913 commences, "it is meant for your good, even though it may hurt" (343J).

Freud "proposes that we abandon our personal relations" (342F). By then the monarchic problem of succession had been quietly resolved by Jones's suggestion that the "old guard" which had formed around Freud become an unofficial committee which would oversee the further fate of psychoanalysis — and was to do so through the years of World War I. Ferenczi joined in, and so did Rank, Sachs, and Abraham (and much later, Eitingon). The transformation of an "old guard," attending a monarchic succession, into a "central committee" guiding a new international movement obviously corresponded to major political and ideological changes soon to take over history itself.

If I were presenting these pages to a seminar, I would now suggest a moment of silence. We could then begin to discuss the various dimensions of this historical document. A further pursuit of my own approach would make it mandatory to emphasize the *epigenetic character* of the psychosocial stages here utilized for a clarification of some adult themes. To put it briefly: in principle, each of these adult stages has rudimentary roots in all previous stages of childhood and youth and thus in the previous generations; and each will contribute both vulnerabilities and strengths to the subsequent stages — and the next generation. But I would also enlarge on the relationship of all these psychosocial developments to the basic psychosexual theory postulated by Freud in those early days (see Erikson, in press).

There are two documents which throw some final light on the ex-correspondents' struggle with their deepest historical identifications. In 1914 *Imago* published an anonymous article on "The Moses of Michelangelo," which Freud later acknowledged — and legitimized — as a "non-analytic love child" of his (Freud, 1965, XIII). Freud had seen Michelangelo's statue often since his first visit to Rome in 1901. In September of 1912 he reported to his wife from Rome that he was visiting Moses every day (Jones, 1953, p. 365). Not until the following year, however, and during "three lonely September weeks" when he "studied it, measured it, and sketched it" was he reasonably certain that his thoughts on Michelangelo's statue should be published. And so it appears that Freud's "Moses" was written in the same month in which he also reported on his divergencies with Jung in his "On the History of the Psycho-Analytic Movement" (Freud, 1964, XIV), where he comes to the conclusion: "The truth is that these [Jungian] people have picked out a few cultural overtones from the symphony of life and have once more failed to hear the mighty and primordial melody of the instincts" (Ibid., p. 62).

His new interpretation of the Moses statue asserted that Moses was by no means depicted as a "man filled with wrath about to throw down the Holy Table," but that he, almost oppressively solemn and calm, "would remain sitting like this in his wrath forever" (p. 269) with a sense of "pain mingled with contempt" (p. 279). A nonviolent Moses, then, and one who (in our terms) continues to generate a sense of lawfulness, as he keeps his own rejectivity in bounds.

Jung, in turn, who in 1913 had had some dreams of large catastrophes such as a sea of blood that was inundating Europe, had a repetitive dream in April, May, and June 1914, according to which "in the middle of summer an Arctic cold wave descended and froze the land to ice . . . All living green things were killed by frost." The ·third dream, however, had an unexpected ending: "There stood a leaf-bearing tree, but without fruit (my tree of life, I thought), whose leaves had been transformed by the effects of the frost into sweet grapes full of healing juices. I plucked the grapes and gave them to a large, waiting crowd" (Jung, 1962, pp. 176, 170). Thus both Freud's identification with Michelangelo's vision and Jung's dream-vision of himself as a gospel figure describe gestures of such magnitude and significance that the wrath in the first and the threatening devastation in the second are wholly transformed.

Freud then was nearly sixty, Jung forty. However we may have learned to judge the later course of their respective lives, we must agree that in much of this correspondence both men cared greatly.

Notes

My work on this essay was much facilitated by a grant from the Maurice Falk Foundation to the Department of Psychiatry of the Mt. Zion Hospital in San Francisco.

1. All page references, unless otherwise noted, are to this work.

2. Letter no. 1, written by Freud. In referring to the letters, I will use the designations given to them in both the German and the English editions.

References

Erikson, Erik H. In press. Components of a psychoanalytic theory of psychosocial development. In *The course of life: psychoanalytic contributions toward understanding personality development,* ed. Stanley Greenspan and George Pollock. Washington, D.C.: U. S. Printing Office.

———. 1950. *Childhood and society.* New York: Norton, rev. 1963.

Freud, Sigmund. 1964. *The complete psychological works of Sigmund Freud.* Ed. James Strachey. London: Hogarth Press.

———. 1954. *The origins of psychoanalysis: letters to Wilhelm Fliess, drafts and notes, 1887-1902.* Ed. Marie Bonaparte, Anna Freud, and Ernst Kris. London: Imago; New York: Basic Books.

FREUD, SIGMUND, and C. G. JUNG. 1974a. *The Freud-Jung letters: the correspondence between Sigmund Freud and C. G. Jung.* Ed. William McGuire; tr. Ralph Manheim and R. F. C. Hull. Princeton: Princeton University Press.

———. 1974b. *Briefwechsel.* Ed. William McGuire and W. Sauerlander. Franfurt am Main: S. Fischer Verlag.

JONES, ERNEST. 1962. *Memories, dreams, reflections.* Ed. Aniela Jaffe. New York: Pantheon.

SCHORSKE, CARL E. 1973. Politics and patricide in Freud's *Interpretation of Dreams. American Historical Review* 78.

PART TWO

Cultural Variations and Historical Changes

FOUR

Adulthood among the Gusii of Kenya

ROBERT A. LEVINE

OUR UNDERSTANDING of adulthood in other cultures is fragmentary. Ethnography deals with the institutional and ideological environments of adults and their activities, beliefs, and values; but social anthropologists have rarely examined this material from the perspective of the individual life course. In this chapter, I shall do so for one African society, to illustrate how this perspective can provide ethnographic data on the conscious experience of adulthood and establish a basis for comparative psychosocial investigation. The shared vocabulary, beliefs, and values described here through person-centered ethnography include those collective representations of the self which form the context of personal introspection. In moving through the life course, each person examines himself concurrently, retrospectively, and prospectively in terms of standards derived from his cultural environment. These self-evaluations play a central role in the regulation of self-esteem and are thus salient aspects of personal experience. By taking the viewpoint provided the individual by his culture, we can explicate the conscious meanings that activities and processes related to work and love have for adults of that culture, and come closer to an understanding of their unconscious meanings. Thus, an ethnography of the life course — a descriptive account of indigenous conceptions of ontogeny — is a first step toward the cross-cultural psychology of adulthood that is currently missing.

It is a long way from the life course in one African society to a general conception of human adulthood. Even a single instance of cultural variation, however, can indicate how well our homegrown ideas travel to people of differing circumstances. The Gusii, for example, have a simple society in socioeconomic terms, with a domestically based economic production and no specialized occupational roles. This situation can provide a testing ground for concepts of adulthood that presume entry and exit to an occupational role for each person (or each male) and an occupational identity for each role incumbent. Similarly, for the Gusii as for our own ancestors, childbearing is not confined to young adulthood; women continue giving birth until they are no longer able to do so, usually in the fifth decade of life. With a median of ten live births, they have children as much as thirty years apart in age. Gusii men, because of polygyny, can have even more extended parental lives. By taking a younger wife (or several) after his first reaches menopause, a man fathers infants into his sixties or seventies, long after his eldest sons and daughters have begun doing so. These demographic realities create life structures differing from those familiar to us and provide a different context for self-evaluation along the course of adult life. Our psychosocial conceptions of human adulthood must be constructed or modified to encompass the experience of persons living under such conditions. Thus are we drawn to the ethnographic facts.

The facts of a culture do not speak for themselves; they are given voice by the ethnographer, who selectively organizes the data he records and translates. My reconstruction of the life course as the Gusii view it is necessarily interpretive in this sense, but I have kept theoretical interpretation to a minimum so that the Gusii organization of subjective experience in adulthood could emerge as much as possible from the ethnographic material rather than being imposed on it. A brief introduction to the historical and cultural context of the contemporary Gusii provides a background to their "life plan," that is, their shared conception of the desirable life course.

CULTURAL BACKGROUND

The Gusii, who currently number close to a million, live in western Kenya, surrounded by Nilotic-speaking peoples (Luo, Kipsigis, Maasai), but are part of the great Bantu-speaking majority of Africa south of the equator; their culture has both Bantu and Nilotic affinities. Western Kenya has long been a region where diverse peoples met, merged, fought, and migrated. The Gusii moved to their present highland position (about fifty miles south of the equator and twenty miles east of Lake Victoria) toward the end of the eighteenth century, thereby gaining elevation on their Luo neighbors and putting distance between themselves and the Maasai. In addition to relative security from attack, however, migration gained the Gusii a fertile, well-watered, healthy, and abundant land, most of it over 5,000 feet above sea level. They have lived in these green hills ever since, in a busy isolation, expanding their settlements, crops, and (until recently) herds.

Gusii institutions were not differentiated into political, economic, and religious spheres; patrilineal descent groups of varying scope provided the organizational framework for all social behavior, and all functions were vested in kinship roles. The Gusii polity before the British conquest of 1907 consisted of seven named territorial divisions, each of which was a cluster of intermarrying, localized patrilineal clans without permanent leadership positions or centralization. The clans, and the divisions in which they were located, occasionally fought with one another and only united in the face of external threat. Even lineage segments of a clan conducted blood feuds against each other, though these could be settled by informal councils of clan elders according to an established set of rules. In this insecure environment, the homestead of a single patriarch, that is, a man, his wives, and their sons living in a cluster of houses on their own land, constituted in many respects an autonomous unit of defense and internal governance. They also constituted a largely autonomous unit of economic production, with the women doing most of the cultivation, the young men and children herding the cattle, sheep, and goats, and older men supervising and making decisions in all spheres. The division of labor was entirely by age and sex; each man could build a house and thatch a roof, each woman make baskets—in addition to their roles in primary subsistence activities. They depended on (part-time) specialists only for iron tools, hide preparation, medical treatment, and some ritual services. Neighbors cooperated in house building, agricultural work teams, and herding, with young men of a local lineage segment jointly tending and defending the herds in cattle villages (until their abolition by the British in 1912). Each homestead, however, supplied its own food and met many of its other needs as well. There were no temples or shrines; most rituals were performed at home in the same setting where all other activities took place, often with the patriarch as chief officiant. Thus, there was no sharp boundary between the domestic and other spheres of life, and domestic organization assumed functional primacy in day-to-day activities.

This situation was reflected in Gusii ethnosociology, their vocabulary of social relationships. Gusii concepts of social order drew heavily on domestic imagery. Terms for doorway, house, and hearthstone were used metaphorically to denote corporate group (at any level, including nation), subgroup, and localized lineage (at a level approximating the local community), respectively. Gusii proverbs and rituals relied on domestic metaphors, representing social and religious experience in a language of familiar physical objects, routine actions, and everyday encounters. It would not be an exaggeration to say that Gusii domestic arrangements constituted their model of the world, a dense reservoir of valued prototypes for interpreting the flux and ambiguity of extradomestic relationships.

The Gusii domestic group or homestead as a multifunctional unit and a model for social experience presents a large topic for ethnographic description. The present account is limited to its basic structural features, those economic and social functions that set the background for understanding the Gusii life course. The Gusii term *omochie* denotes a settlement based on primary kin relationships (parent-child and husband-wife), governed by its elder or patriarch (*omogaaka bw'omochie*) — who is sometimes referred to as its owner (*omonyene*) — under whose direction the family members cooperate in a variety of economic, military, and ritual tasks. The males of the homestead, normally the patriarch and his sons, constitute a minimal corporate lineage, an *egesaku* at the lowest level in the genealogical pyramid of patrilineal descent groups sharing that vernacular designation. Until the last decade, polygyny was a cardinal feature of the homestead. The patriarch had several wives — at least two, ideally four, occasionally eight or more. Each wife had her own house with its own yard, surrounded by the fields allocated to her by the patriarch, which she was responsible for cultivating, the produce from which was stored in her own granary. When each of her sons married, he built another house, nearer the mother's than to those of her co-wives, for himself and his wife. There were also children's or bachelor's huts (*chisaiga*, sing. *esaiga*) for older boys to live in before marriage, and the patriarch himself — who ideally rotated among his wives, but often stayed longer with the youngest — sometimes slept in *esaiga* as a retreat from domestic strife.

Another cardinal feature of the domestic group — one that remains — is virilocal residence — the men are permanent residents from birth to death, but the women come from other (*exogamous*) clans as reluctant brides. Since the intermarrying clans occupy distinct territories and in the past carried out military actions against each other, the transfer of women at marriage has always been heavily formalized and highly coercive (from the bride's point of view). At home, this marital residence pattern means that men are related by blood to their neighbors, but women are related by blood only to their own children—something they never lose sight of. Despite their initial position as clan strangers, however, women have a good deal of economic and social autonomy (their own fields, granaries, houses) in the circumscribed world of the homestead.

The world of the Gusii homestead as experienced by its inhabitants is a unit of economic expansion and social control. In precolonial times land was abundant and a homestead head had access to as much land as his family could cultivate and use for grazing. The more wives he married, the more land he could bring under cultivation, the more daughters he could marry off to bring in cattle as bridewealth, the more sons he could have to herd and defend the cattle and keep the homestead safe from outside attack. The ideal was proliferation—of wives, children, herds, and crops—and economic conditions permitted these to be mutually reinforcing. For many Gusii men, now as then, cattle husbandry is the prototype for expansion in general—a man invests in initial nurturance and supervision, the cattle grow and multiply, he divides the herds and replicates the cycle, they enrich him by indefinite expansion. The patriarch is the investor and supervisor of domestic growth in all its forms.

Before 1907, those men whose investment skills, combined with initial good fortune, enabled them to acquire numerous wives and sons gained not only in productive labor but in many other ways. The adult sons, obedient to the patriarch, operated as his private army, defending the herds and constituting a military presence in the locality that intimidated potential interlopers on the land. A man with six or more wives and grown sons would inhabit an entire hill and become known far and wide as the patriarch of that area. His poorer lineage mates from the surrounding homesteads would frequent his visitors' hut (*etureti*), be provided food and drink by his wives, and give support to his prestige, authority, and influence in the settling of disputes. Such a man, an *omotureti* (so called because of the hut), would play a major leadership role in the mobilization of his clan to meet external military threat; this meant in effect an alliance of the various homestead armies together with the warriors living in lineage-based cattle villages (*ebisoraati*). Since there were no permanent superordinate structures of leadership, the foremost Gusii leaders were wealthy polygynists whose wealth and power were based primarily on the proliferation of domestic husband-wife and father-son bonds. With many sons, they became the founders of lineage segments named after them and thus achieved the only kind of personal immortality recognized in Gusii belief.

The Gusii homestead is also a prototypical moral order. It involves a highly prescriptive organization of activities in space, an organization viewed as the embodiment of the highest moral ideals by which Gusii are supposed to live. Moral planning and normative prescription pervade the design and arrangement of houses, rooms, ornaments, footpaths. Each married woman has her own house, and the patriarch is forbidden to enter the house of his son's wife under any circumstances. The adult son is forbidden to go beyond the entrance foyer in his mother's house — the house he had lived in as a child. The husband is forbidden to climb to the loft in his wife's house. These homestead restrictions, together with others concerning sexual modesty and respect, represent a code of propriety effective throughout the clan, regulating the elder and younger alike and enforcing incest rules, marital rights, respect for paternal authority, and checks on that authority. This system of control has more ramifications than can be explored here. Our present emphasis is on its location in the homestead, where many other activities take place, similarly prescribed by custom: for example, birth, male and female initiation ceremonies, weddings, burials (just outside the house), sacrifice. The homestead is a stage on which most of life is played according to a traditional script with specific directions for the design of sets and the locations and movements of the actors. This script, as a normative structure, represents one functional role of domestic group life, another equally important function being its role as a vehicle of economic expansion. With both of these aspects in mind, we can turn to the Gusii life plan.

STAGES AND TRANSITIONS

By "life plan," I mean a people's collective representation of the life course viewed as an organized system of shared ideals about how life should be lived and shared expectancies about how lives are lived. My assumption is that every people has a life plan in this sense — it is the normative aspect of their culture viewed from the perspective of the individual — though it is elaborated as explicit ideology in some cultures and not in others. For the Gusii, as for many peoples of nonliterate tradition, there is no written doctrine or formal ideological statement concerning the life course, but there are beliefs and values of varying degrees of explicitness about how life is and should be lived.

To understand the Gusii life plan, the first step is to know the terms of Gusii discourse about their lives: divisions of the life course, the labels that apply to them, and the meanings of the labels. The labels appear below in Ekegusii and English translation.

Infant: *ekeŋwerere*   Infant: *ekeŋwerere*
Uncircumcised girl: *egesagaane*   Uncircumcised boy: *omoisia*
Circumcised girl: Circumcised boy warrior:
    omoiseke, enyaroka   *omomura, omosae*
Married woman: *omosubaati*
Female elder: *omoŋina*   Male elder: *omogaaka*

Except for infancy, the labels are different for men and women, reflecting their drastically different statuses and social roles in a patrilineal society. The specific term for infant is not used frequently unless special emphasis is being put on the young age of the child; otherwise *omwaana* (pl. *abaana*), the general term for "child," tends to be used for infants and older children alike. The single term for infants regardless of sex is consistent with the claim of Gusii mothers that they do not behave differently to boy and girl babies. When a baby is born, however, its sex is a matter of primary interest, and inquiries are answered with the terms *omoiseke* or *omomura* because the terms for uncircumcised girl or boy, though more accurate, have a derogatory connotation that is out of keeping with the joy and pride of the occasion.

Females have four recognized and labeled life stages after infancy, while males have only three, since there is no special term for a circumcised male who is married but not yet an elder. The difference seems to reflect the fact that women make a fundamental change in their social status and residence at marriage, whereas men do not.

Tracing through the labeled life stages, we begin with *omoisia,* the uncircumcised boy. The word itself is related to *okorisia,* "to herd," and therefore can be literally translated "herd-boy," reflecting the traditional role of young boys in herding goats, sheep, and (after abolition of the cattle villages) cattle. At this literal level it conveys a general fact about the lives of young boys: that they are expected to perform useful tasks (of which herding is one) in response to the commands of their elders. Among those who have been circumcised, however, *omoisia* is used as an insult (acceptable as a jest only among those circumcised in the same year), meaning "uncircumcised," with connotations of childishness and association with women; hence the word carries with it a derogatory connotation.

A boy becomes *omomura* only upon being circumcised and passing through the period of seclusion, hazing, and ceremony that follows. Boys nowadays are circumcised at nine to eleven years of age; it was at age ten to twelve in 1956 and perhaps sixteen to eighteen in precolonial days. The word *omomura* may be derived from the

Maasai word *murran,* "warrior," since the Maasai are considered prototypical fierce warriors by the Gusii and the circumcised Gusii male was a warrior in the precolonial times. The initiation ceremonies that constitute the transition to this stage are considered the most important rites of passage a male Gusii undergoes. This is a passage from childhood, characterized by dependency and intimacy with the mother, to manhood, ideally characterized by not only military bravery but greater personal responsibility within the homestead and preparation for marriage. The altered status of the young man in the homestead is recognized ritually in two events when he emerges from seclusion: his father takes an oath not to punish him physically any more, and he is informed that he must not enter his mother's house until he presents her with a goat, and then only in the entrance foyer. Initiation thus completes the youth's extrusion from the house in which he was born and reared, and it removes him from paternal supervision and discipline — on the publicly stated assumption that he has the sense to behave correctly (which includes obedience to the father). As *omomura,* he lives in his own house in the homestead, and brings his bride to that house.

The term *omomura,* as designating a stage of life, covers an extraordinarily long period — terminating only with the marriage of a man's first child. Thus, a male who is circumcised at age ten, marries at twenty, and whose eldest child is a daughter marrying at fifteen, will be *omomura* for at least twenty-five years. If he married later (as many Gusii do) or had a son first, he could be *omomura* until age fifty — a total of forty years in the status of a "young man." During that time, he will be married and become a father, and it is likely that his own father will die, giving him the opportunity to establish his own homestead. But, though a married man is no longer referred to as *omosae,* "a young lad," his status as *omomura* is unchanged. Thus, though boys are all circumcised and enter the status of *omomura* at roughly the same age, they graduate to the next stage at various ages, depending on when they marry, have children, and so on. The age of a man's marriage, in turn, depends on the availability of cattle for him to use as bridewealth and the availability of cattle depends on his sisters' marriages and the claims on their bridewealth cattle by his older brothers and father. Obtaining the cattle for marriage may involve a man in a bitter quarrel within the homestead or in a long period of work and saving — and hence a long delay in his marriage. For the *omomura,* then, getting married is the most salient personal goal and desired accomplishment, determining the pace at which his future status will be enhanced.

From the viewpoint of the elders, the *abamura* (plural) collectively are potential troublemakers and not entirely mature in their moral judgment. Their high-spirited aggressiveness is associated with their precolonial function as warriors eager for a chance to use their spears on behalf of the community. On the other hand, the elders recognized that this aggressiveness could result in domestic disruptions, which increased after the colonial abolition of the cattle villages brought the *abamura* home. A number of the sayings about them and rules restricting them suggest that the greatest fear was that they might attack their elders, their fathers actual and classificatory. For example, they were (at least until the 1950s) prohibited from drinking beer with their elders; if there was a large beer party, they would have to drink in a different house. Elders justified this explicitly by reference to the bellicosity of the youth when drunk. They were also prohibited from growing beards; if an *omomura* let his beard grow, his father might say, "Do you want to kill me?" (that is, are you pretending to be an old man, which presupposes that I am dead?). The elders expected that *abamura* were not capable of controlling themselves and needed to be checked by their seniors. This expectation operated to excuse misbehavior by the young men, so long as they were not openly disrespectful of patriarchal authority. Even a man in his thirties who committed a crime or mistreated his wife might be excused after reprimand on the grounds that he was *omomura*. Only the elders were presumed to be fully responsible in a moral sense.

The term *omogaaka* has three meanings. In its unmarked form and in contexts defined by customary kinship norms, it is an age-status designation that can be glossed "male elder." This is the most honorable status in Gusii society; the *abagaaka* (plural) represent constituted authority in the community and can invoke sacred sanctions in defense of their authority. An *omomura* becomes *omogaaka* in this sense when one of his children (of either sex) marries, "because there is now someone *outside* who calls you 'father.' " The rationale is that having a son-in-law or daughter-in-law from another clan who must call you "father" qualifies you for a higher status category. In fact, the term of address indicates some genuine social power a man has over his child's spouse, and his status is elevated by its addition, but it is also expected that the marriage will soon make the father-in-law a grandfather—in the long run, a more important consideration. (Since cattle were a relatively scarce resource and were necessary for marriage, the child's marriage is seen as having overcome the major hurdle on the way to grandparenthood.)

In contemporary contexts defined by forms of authority and prestige introduced during or after the colonial period, *omogaaka* is now used as a term of respect, regardless of age, marital status, or the marital status of one's children. In other words, men of importance are called *omogaaka*, in apparent imitation of the identical usage for the Swahili equivalent, *mzee*. Finally, in the context of the homestead, *omogaaka* is understood as an abbreviation for *omogaaka bw'omochie,* "the elder of the homestead," and is best glossed as "patriarch" or "paterfamilias." This is a unique title within the homestead; at any one time, there is only one person who may be addressed *omogaaka*. Thus, a man may have grandchildren, but if his father is still alive, the older man is *omogaaka* of the homestead. If he hears that his sons are using this term of address for their older brother, he might say, "Do you want to kill me?" If someone from the homestead is addressing the grandson of such a patriarch, one may refer to his father as *omogaaka iso*, "your own patriarch," but may not use the term for him without the qualification. It is possible, then, for a man to be *omogaaka* in the community at large, by virtue of his child's marriage, as an automatic elevation in age grade, long before he succeeds to the patriarchal position in the homestead.

The *abagaaka* were, according to Gusii tradition, repositories of moral wisdom and legal judgment as well as authority; they were feared, respected, obeyed, and in many ways depended upon in the making of decisions affecting the welfare of the homestead and the community. The actual power of an elder was a function of his wealth in cattle, wives, and sons, but every patriarch was solely responsible for the governance and spiritual welfare of the entire homestead. In the world of the homestead, a patriarch had the final word, and he could curse those who defied it. He could control the allocation of cattle and land and postpone the inheritance division until his deathbed, thereby keeping his sons dependent on his favor. He could also indulge himself by acquiring young wives in his later years — sometimes with cattle that should have gone to an unmarried son — and by playing favorites among wives and sons.

The status of *omogaaka* as elder and patriarch was terminal, and it was the highest status in Gusii society, but that does not mean that a man's status continued to increase with age. Though there was no recognition in Gusii age terminology of an elder who outlived the authority and wisdom attributed to an *omogaaka*, it appears (on the basis of contemporaneous evidence) that elderly patriarchs — those over seventy, especially if infirm — lost influence and power. Their will was feared, particularly if they had not yet divided the property, but their greater isolation prevented their regulating the affairs of others.

For women, some of the details are similar, but many are different. The *egesagaane,* "uncircumcised girl," was, like her male counterpart, a hard-working toiler at the bottom of the hierarchy in the domestic labor force, but the tasks she performed were different: carrying water from the stream (in pots balanced on her head), caring for babies, and (later) helping her mother in cooking, grinding, cultivating the fields. (If parents lacked children of the appropriate sex, however, boys could be pressed into infant care, and girls could be assigned herding, at least temporarily.) As with boys, initiation ceremonies involving circumcision were the rite of passage to the next age grade, but girls underwent these at a younger age (nowadays seven to eight; precolonial times, early to middle teens) and with a ceremonial content that emphasized themes of sex, marriage, and procreation rather than military valor and social autonomy. Of the two terms for a circumcised but unmarried girl, *enyaroka* literally means "a circumcised thing," and emphasizes the ordeal she has gone through; *omoiseke* is the more general term for a marriageable girl. Nowadays, girls are circumcised so young that there are many years (about seven) between initiation and marriage (at about fifteen years old), but preparation for marriage is a salient theme of life throughout these years. Parents view the unmarried girl with some ambivalence: the mother knows that however attached she is to her daughter, the girl must leave forever; both parents feel they have a right to be compensated for having nurtured her, but are rightly fearful that she will deprive them of the bridewealth compensation by eloping—thus leaving them with no source of bridewealth for one of her brothers.

The timing of marriage in the Gusii life plan is sharply differentiated by sex, reflecting the fact that wives are in greater demand than husbands in this polygynous society. For a typical young man, the timing of his marriage is uncertain; it depends on his family's wealth, his patriarch's willingness to permit him the use of cattle, or his having a sister whose bridewealth can be used in his marriage. Wealthy or fortunate young men may be married by age twenty, whereas unfortunates must postpone it until they are able to raise the bridewealth inside the family or through their own efforts—often until thirty or later. For young women, the timing of marriage is not problematic; like circumcision, it is an event that occurs at approximately the same age for all (fifteen to sixteen) and is another predictable marker of graduation to more elevated status, that of *omosubaati*. The problem is not whether or when they will get married but to whom. A young woman is expected to face marriage with reluctance about leaving home and to resist being taken away when the time comes—even though she has agreed to the match. Some are married to men they like in acceptable circumstances; others are forced by their fathers for reasons of bridewealth into undesirable matches with older men, frequently as secondary wives. There is a period of trial marriage in which the bride is theoretically entitled to call it off if she discovers something terribly wrong with her new home: stereotypically, if her husband is impotent or her mother-in-law a witch. Her father, however, may find it inconvenient to permit return of cattle he has already committed for another purpose and may refuse to honor her complaint with action. Even if she is permitted to come home, she is soon married again to another probable stranger in a strange place where she is expected to live and work with strange people.

The young woman as *omosubaati* faces a period of adjustment that is considered in Gusii belief to be difficult. She is expected to be exceedingly respectful, quiet, and cautious about violating kin avoidance norms. The "home people" are ideally expected to treat her kindly and hospitably and to make her feel welcome, but they may be jealous of her in one way or another and thus embroil her in controversies before she has developed much support in her new home. Furthermore, her domestic and agricultural skills are scrutinized, and she is criticized often with mockery if she is considered lazy, irresponsible, incompetent, or insubordinate. Her progress in gaining respect and social support among women of the homestead and neighborhood depends on many things, including their idiosyncrasies and hers, but in the long run her adjustment requires bearing children early and regularly. As her children grow older, her status increases. The circumcision of her first child of either sex is a joyous event for the mother, a kind of public confirmation of her successful motherhood. When one of her children is married, she graduates to *omoŋina*, "female elder," the highest age grade to which she can aspire. As with the male term for elder, *omogaaka*, however, its use within and outside the homestead is distinguished: a woman who is *omoŋina* through the marriage of her children and becoming a grandparent (as with men, the confirmation of elder status) is not *omoŋina* in the sense of the most senior woman in the homestead if her father-in-law has living wives, even though these wives may be younger than she in chronological age. Being the oldest chronologically but of the younger generation does count for something though:

people in the homestead may begin calling her *omoŋina*, saying they are imitating a grandchild who uses the term for the woman who is visibly older.

As *omoŋina*, a woman has many prerogatives formerly denied her. She can talk more publicly, even to the point of being raucous and openly aggressive; she is permitted to drink beer at beer parties, though not to sit with the men; she can expect a certain amount of help when she needs it from her daughters-in-law and grandchildren. A woman who gives birth at seventeen or eighteen can become *omoŋina* in her early thirties and be a grandmother as young as thirty-five, when she has another decade of childbearing herself. After menopause, in her later forties, she should have circumcised grandchildren, and her primary interests are focused on her sons' and daughters' children, who will visit and joke with her and perhaps live with her. At her husband's death, her sons' claims to land will be based on what she cultivated when he was alive, so she is in effect the trustee of that part of his estate belonging to his sons.

This brief sketch of life stages for Gusii men and women provides no more than an overview of a complex topic, but it does bring some general points to the fore. First, transitions among the life stages of the Gusii are not based simply on chronological age, particularly after marriage. There is a status hierarchy among married adults of each sex; in this hierarchy, those with no married children are at the bottom, those with married children higher, those with grandchildren higher yet, and grandparents with no living seniors of the same sex in the same homestead are at the top. Within the homestead, seniority is based on generational age and, within a generation, on birth order. One moves up by the births and growth of those below and by the deaths of those above.

Getting older is inherently positive if the reproductive cycle is working as it should, that is, if marriage, birth, and death are occurring at expected times and with expected results. If they do not, there is concern, anxiety, potential conflict.

The Gusii life plan as a cultural schema takes account of certain deviations from its normative timetable, particularly ones that threaten the continuity of the minimal lineage based in the homestead. If a patriarch dies without living sons, for example, leaving a postmenopausal widow who has no one with her (since daughters move away at marriage), she can use the cattle from a daughter's marriage to "marry" a woman. The woman comes to live as a wife and has sexual relations with a local man, attempting to bear "sons" for the deceased who will inherit his land and take care of the widow in her old age. Similarly, if a married couple has numerous daughters but no son until the end of the woman's childbearing years, when she is perhaps forty-five and her husband fifty-five (or more), they may reach the ages of sixty and seventy, respectively, without grandchildren living at home and may authorize their son to be married at fifteen (to a woman older than himself) so that they might "see" grandchildren before they die; this young marriage is called *okoboererwa* and is also possible when the mother of sons dies and the bride is brought in to keep house for them in the short run as well as to produce grandchildren as early as possible. Thus, there are extraordinary formal arrangements to call upon when the reproductive cycle does not produce results in accordance with Gusii ideals.

Despite arrangements of this sort to fit exceptional circumstances that deviate from expectations, the Gusii life plan is often experienced as a constraining set of age norms or timetables that stigmatize those who are "off-time." If a man marries late, he will be later than his age-mates in becoming a grandfather and in taking a second wife (if he is dependent on bridewealth from a daughter's marriage) — thus having to suffer the stigma of monogamy in his middle years. If a young woman marries much later than her age-mates — a rare occurrence — everyone knows it must be that her mother is strongly reputed to be a witch. To be on-time in terms of the Gusii life plan means the realization of goals that every Gusii man and woman is supposed to cherish; to be off-time brings mild mockery, severe derision, or — in the case of childlessness — sadness, isolation, and fear.

CAREERS, GOALS, AND STRATEGIES

By examining the Gusii life plan as a series of life stages and transitions, we have seen how the status ideals of Gusii society are culturally scheduled in the life course for both men and women. The life plan, however, can be seen as a trajectory as well as a timetable, and the better one knows Gusii individuals and families, the more one understands the long-term continuities along which they measure their own lives.

First, there are a number of lifelong constraints imposed on men as permanent members of the kin group into which they were born. They inherit, for example, the consequences of ritual neglect by their immediate forefathers. Thus, if a man's father failed to perform one of the funerary sacrifices for his own father, the grandson is believed to be susceptible to affliction until he sacrifices the animal himself. Then there are the effects of birth order, marking a male as *omotaŋani* (the "first," that is, the eldest), *omokogooti* (the last), or

one of the others. A man who is the first son of his father is considered to be "like a father" to his brothers and is expected by the
family to assume leadership and responsibility and exercise authority
throughout his life. If his parents are old, he is expected to marry at a
young age. Lastborns, by contrast, are believed to be spoiled by their
mothers, self-centered, immature in character, and more attached to
home. Gusii consider it appropriate for the lastborn son to stay home
even when others must go away, for he is presumed to remain closer
to the mother and is guardian of the protective medicine (*rirongo*)
for the home. In addition to these fixed effects of birth order, each
man's access to homestead resources is heavily constrained by birth
order. For example, if he is the first son after several daughters, there
will be abundant bridewealth to permit his marriage at a relatively
young age; if there are older brothers competing with him for the
bridewealth of an equal or smaller number of sisters, then he may
have to wait a long time to marry. Similar distributional contingencies apply to such other valued goods (land, magical medicines)
as the homestead might have: a man's access is determined by the
number of competing brothers and his rank in the birth order of
siblings.

A final constraint derived from kinship applies to women as well
as men: it is the obligation of serial reciprocity in relationships over
the lifespan as the Gusii view it. Parents care for their chldren and
consider their nurturance to represent a substantial allocation of resources for which they deserve to be repaid. (Indeed, the word that
parents-in-law use to refer to each other — *chikorera* — literally means
"nurturers" and emphasizes their contribution to the care and
growth of their child.) A young woman compensates her parents with
the bridewealth she brings in; this is their quid pro quo for the female reproductive capacities they have brought to maturity, and the
transaction is largely completed when her bridewealth is paid. The
young man's reciprocation for early nurturance is spread out through
years of filial obligation, but there is a special emphasis on his caring
for his mother in her old age. Serial reciprocity extends to other kin
relationships. When a woman is married, for example, the bridewealth paid for her is used by her brother to get married and creates
an obligatory relationship between sisters-in-law such that the one
whose marriage provided the bridewealth can always take grain
from the granary of the other without asking. Without reviewing all
the relationships of this kind, we can state in general that the Gusii
kinship system creates lifelong obligations of serial reciprocity.

The reference group for the Gusii man consists of the local age-mates with whom he grew up, was circumcised, and remains in some degree of contact; they are members of the same clan and frequently cousins as well, though their relationship is based on being peers and neighbors rather than kinsmen. Women have a reference group of age-mates too, but it shifts during the early years of marriage from the girls with whom they grew up and were circumcised to women at the place they have married into: their co-wives (if their husbands are polygynous), sisters-in-law (husband's brothers' wives), and other wives in the neighborhood. The reference group is the focus of the individual's social comparisons; rather than chart his or her progress or stagnation against an abstract concept of the ideal life stages, the individual measures it invidiously against that of a visible group of peers. In the past (before World War II in the area studied), each year was named after a major event taking place at that time, and people could identify their birth and circumcision by reference to these years; those who shared particular named years of birth and/or circumcision in a given locality recognized each other as age-mates (*abakiare* or *abagesangio*) and observed each other's lives. Nowadays, this recognition comes largely from given names (for men): many of the male children born during the year or two following the death of someone important in that locality will be named after him; they will grow up knowing they are age-mates, and those born in the locality at the same time who were not given the name will nevertheless be included in the reference group. (The same practice holds for girls, but the age-mates disperse at marriage.)

Within this reference group, individuals are constantly (though privately) making comparisons, particularly with respect to movement through the life stages and transitions. The most common motive one can be certain of for Gusii men and women is wanting to move with one's age-mates; the most common anxiety one can attribute to them is that of being left behind. The fear of being left behind plays an important part in the determination of children to be circumcised even when their parents say they are too young, and some join the group in defiance of the expressed wishes of the parents (who are often testing their determination, rather than seriously keeping them back). The same fear, however, may motivate a contemporary fifty-year-old man to take a second wife when his age-mates have, even though economic considerations weigh against it: left behind, he is subject to the mockery of his peers; at a beer party, they tell him to sit near the door so he can get away fast if his one and only becomes sick and threatens to die. Many other points of invidious comparison among age-mates may not be joked about, but age-mates share the concern about being left behind as the others move on along a path of prestige and relative status. With women, the points of comparison are usually fertility, child mortality, and (in polygynous homes) the distribution of the husband's favors; with men, economic resources of all kinds. The reference group of age peers sets the standards by which individuals evaluate themselves and react with a sense of satisfaction or jealousy.

There is more to the Gusii life plan than the permanent kin relationships and keeping up with one's age-mates in the sequence of age statuses. There are long-range goals Gusii pursue, but do not openly discuss most of the time. These pursuits are initially detectable from the measures taken when they are blocked; eventually it becomes possible to understand what these goals are, what strategies are being used to attain them, and what meanings are assigned to success and failure.

One notices, for example, a poor family spending large amounts on diviners and sacrifices intended to restore the fertility of a wife who already has several living children, or relatively old parents taking their firstborn son out of school at a young age so he can marry and have children before they die. Evidence of this type suggests the implicit cultural concept of a reproductive career which, though not represented as such in Gusii terminology, functions as a salient guide for self-evaluation and individual decision making. Similarly, one notices a great concern on the part of adults of various ages with having a proper house; this is perhaps most striking nowadays among young men who live in town but invest in building houses at their rural homes. This finally made sense at the funeral of an old woman who died without a house of her own: a small grass hut (*egesa*) had to be built before she could be buried, and the situation was regarded as a disgrace that would have become a spiritual calamity had not the hut been built. Fragments of evidence, viewed cumulatively over individual lives and concurrently for age-mates, suggest the concept of a spiritual career as a salient cultural construct for the examination of adulthood.

Considerations of this kind have led me to formulate career pathways for the Gusii that are recognizable to them but more explicit than they would ever make them. These formulations are based on evidence that there is a high degree of consensus concerning long-range goals, and that individuals pursue them with perseverance, urgency, personal sacrifice — all symptoms that their personal salience matches their cultural significance.

Each Gusii man or woman, then, pursues three related subjective careers: a reproductive career, an economic career, and a spiritual career. (Although there are some ritual specialists, everyone has a spiritual career.) The reproductive career seems to be the most salient for both sexes. Its goal is to become the ancestor of a maximally expanding genealogy. For women, this means to have children as frequently between marriage and menopause as is consistent with child health, which the Gusii believe to be every two years. A man who fails to impregnate his wife that often will be publicly accused by her of neglect. The woman must have at least one son to take care of her in her old age and whose wives work with her; to have nothing but daughters (who move away at marriage) is second only to barrenness as a disaster. If her husband dies, it is her right as well as her obligation to have a leviratic husband to impregnate her regularly so she will continue to bear children "for the dead man." For men, the goal means not only maximizing his wife's offspring but taking additional wives as he can afford them and so appending their reproductive careers to his. If a man has been a monogamist, he might take a younger second wife when his first wife reaches menopause, for that would extend his reproductive career by a decade or more. The reproductive career as I see it, however, is not limited to the individual's own procreation but includes that of his or her offspring. Grandchildren are as fervently desired as one's own children and, not incidentally, play an essential role in the burial of grandparents.

The economic career is more differentiated by sex because men own land, while women do not, and men now participate in modern employment and business ownership while women do only to a marginal degree. The Gusii man's most cherished economic goal in the past was an ever-expanding herd of cattle to be reared when young and to provide milk and meat when mature. Land was then abundant, and the raising of crops was considered essential but less important than animal husbandry. The ever-expanding herd is conceptually linked in Gusii thought with human reproduction, but in the past it was economically linked as well. Bridewealth was paid in cattle; thus, every daughter born represented potential cattle income. Each son, of course, represented a future demand for cattle, but the sons were permanent family members who served the father by tending his herds and protecting them from raids. Since the expanding lineages of humans and cattle were intimately connected, reproductive and economic goals were not entirely distinct. Furthermore, each additional wife of father or son brought in by bridewealth cattle was assigned new fields to cultivate and made possible cultivation of more available land, while also increasing the reproductive capacity of the family. Successful men had eight or more wives, large herds, and a private army of adult sons from their countless children, representing ideal outcomes of the desired cycle of ever-expanding exchange.

The man's actual role in pursuing these combined economic and reproductive goals was that of an investor and supervisor. If he had sons to do the herding and wives to do the cultivation, then his job was mainly supervisory; if he lacked the field hands, then he did their work himself until the domestic production unit had expanded. But the independent mature man not living under the authority of his father always made all the investment decisions concerning the use of cattle for bridewealth and the allocation of fields among wives. The concept of an economically independent individual acting as supervisor and investor rather than worker has not died out among the Gusii; it is being applied in the modern sector. A man with some capital sets up a shop and then puts one wife in charge of it while another wife runs the family farm; if a surplus is produced, he starts another small business or buys some imported cattle for the farm. A man with some employment income invests in the education of his eldest sons, hoping they will be able to qualify for lucrative jobs and will in turn invest in the education of their younger siblings. The goal of a self-sustaining or self-generating family firm, with the patriarch as entrepreneur, has not disappeared but has found new fields for application. The strategy followed in this economic career also remains the same — that is, exploiting the bonds of obedience that tie wife to husband, and sons to father, for economic gain. But patriarchs nowadays complain that cows are more dependable than humans: you rear them and they give you milk in return, but with your own children, you can never be sure.

In this description of the Gusii reproductive and economic careers, one aspect of change has already emerged: In the past the economic and reproductive careers were inseparable because their goals, though distinct, both required the birth of as many children of both sexes in the family as could be successfully reared to maturity. In the present economy, however, children are an economic liability because they are not needed on the small land holdings, they require school fees to become economically self-sufficient, and the bridewealth system is in disarray. We found otherwise intelligent Gusii parents in 1974 to 1976 pursuing what seemed blatantly contradictory goals in their economic and reproductive careers; they continued to pursue traditional reproductive goals although these have lost their economic rationale so completely that the benefits have all turned to costs, some of them quite severe. How can this behavior be understood?

Part of this answer lies in the subjective aspect of the life course I have not yet described, the spiritual career, which must be understood from the perspective of the middle or later years of a person's life and has its culmination in the posthumous evaluation of the funeral ritual. The spiritual career has its origins in past generations, for the father's failures to perform certain sacrifices decades ago may result in afflictions being visited upon the son and his homestead. Ritual failures during the early part of a person's life, particularly during the initiation ceremonies, may be the cause of afflictions: Should a boy flinch or a girl run away at the moment of circumcision or clitoridectomy, or should the fire go out during the period of seclusion following the genital operation, afflictions through the rest of life will be attributed to this spiritual disaster. After marriage, there are many other possibilities for spiritual vulnerability, for example, failing to perform the proper rituals after the birth of twins or the death of an elder, committing a moral offense like adultery (for a woman), flagrantly violating the rules of kin avoidance that is considered an abomination (*chimuma*), or offending a neighbor who is a witch (*omorogi*). It is necessary to understand the spiritual career in terms of the individual's relationships to the ancestral elders (*ebirecha*) on the one hand and to contemporary kinsmen and neighbors on the other, as diagnosed by the diviners (*abaragoori*). But our focus here is on how these relationships are experienced in the life course of the Gusii individual.

In the subjective context of the spiritual career as defined by Gusii belief, the reproductive and economic careers provide a set of indicators that permit a person to monitor his spiritual condition. In comparison with age-mates, each person looks for indications of relative retardation in moving toward reproductive and economic goals. Incidents of infertility, crop failure, mental disorder, financial reverses, or educational failures are taken as symptoms of destructive intent by ancestors or witches, an intent that can destroy the entire homestead if remedial action is not taken. Such incidents are afflictions (*emechando*), but they are also omens (*ebirage*), signals of a disruption in one's spiritual relationships that must be deciphered by a diviner. The diviner diagnoses the specific spiritual agent to which the destructive intent can be attributed, invoking nonafflictive omens (such as seeing a bird with a white chest, a rat with his tail excised, or snakes wrapped around one another) to establish a coherent account of how the spiritual relationship was ruptured and what must be done to restore it in order to prevent death and destruction. In this context, reproductive delays and economic reverses are signs of impending disaster. The Gusii response to them can be compared to the reactions any of us would have to the spread of an epidemic disease that threatened to kill not only ourselves but our family: panic and the emergency mobilization of resources, without calculating the economic expense.

The goals of the spiritual career, then, are not other-worldly but include the physical well-being of oneself, members of one's homestead, and one's descendants. The ultimate goal is continuity of the lineage, but the most frequently experienced aim is invulnerability to the spiritual dangers that threaten health, fertility, sanity, and economic welfare. Thus progress along the spiritual pathway is monitored through disruptions in the reproductive and economic careers as well as through illness and omens. This monitoring constitutes a form of life review during the adult years, particularly at critical junctures, as when a woman approaches menopause, or when a man finds that his age-mates have become polygynists, or when a mother of any age is afflicted by the crippling of her child. In the process of self-assessment, individuals (and the diviners consulted) use diverse afflictions, including relative poverty and infertility, as equivalent indicators of powerlessness in the face of danger. Thus there seems to be a subjective level of personal experience at which relative positions along the reproductive, economic, and spiritual career pathways are interchangeable tokens of personal power or vulnerability. The three careers, then, are abstractions I have imposed on the goal-seeking behavior of Gusii adults. Their personal experience of self, like their institutionalized roles, is not partitioned into three separate domains but is unified around a sense of potency.

This analysis helps explain the apparent contradiction mentioned above in the economic and reproductive behavior of contemporary Gusii. Even though children today represent an economic cost rather than a benefit, they are experienced as adding to the parents' inner strength, as additional income would. Thus poor parents are likely to feel even more intensely the need to have more children and grandchildren, particularly as they grow older. An ailing man in his late sixties, once a prosperous local leader in agricultural innovation, now an impoverished polygynist whose extensive landholding is crowded with the houses of his quarreling sons, grandsons, and their children, illustrated this tendency when he said that his main pleasure in life was counting the number of people residing in his homestead. Multiply afflicted by illness, poverty, domestic dissension, and the insanity of one son, he experienced the sheer number of his descendants as his remaining source of strength.

Some Gusii men and women, usually in their middle and later years, embark on a quest for personal power by becoming ritual practitioners: diviners, herbalists (*abanyamoriogo*), sorcerers (*abanyamosira*), and performers of particular life-crisis rituals (*abakorerani*). At least ten percent of those over forty in the area studied possessed some kind of spiritual or medicinal power, from virtually fulltime practitioners treating a wide variety of afflictions to those who occasionally treated a particular disease or removed a particular curse. They invariably portrayed themselves as formerly afflicted sufferers who sought relief from powerful healers, often outside of Gusii country, and, having obtained it, decided — sometimes after explicit self-assessment — to take instruction from the same healers and gain the power for themselves. Having become ritual practitioners, they see themselves not only as having the specific powers to remedy certain conditions but as being less vulnerable in general to the dangers that afflict others. Thus one older woman, a senior diviner, said she had been a Christian for many years when the insanity of her firstborn son, uncured by Western medicine, led her to seek indigenous treatment, which cured him and convinced her to give up Christianity and become a diviner. She was the most self-confident Gusii woman I have ever met, secure in the belief that her powers were equal to any dangers that might now befall her. Her male counterpart was a well-known herbalist and sorcerer who said his wife had lost six children in a row when he decided to seek a cure followed by apprenticeship to the practitioner who provided it. He boasted of powers so strong that witches like the ones who had killed his children would not dare now to attack him or his family.

Women, particularly those old enough to be grandmothers, are overrepresented among Gusii ritual practitioners. I believe that their quest for power in the spiritual and medical domain reflects their lack of access to power through an independent economic career and provides compensation for the afflictions in their individual life histories. They are even more heavily represented among the witches (*abarogi*), the secret plotters who magically kill and cannibalize their local enemies. The life histories of witches show them also to be severely afflicted by reproductive disorders, infant mortality, or chronic illness; they are motivated to join the evil band by the offer of invulnerability as well as vengeance against those better off than themselves. They gain the power to harm rather than help others, but, like the healers, they move from being victims of destructive intent to virtual invulnerability from it by the adoption of a ritual identity.

The pursuit of spiritual and medical power by *older* women and men makes sense in the context of Gusii culture for several reasons. Aging is explicitly conceptualized in Gusii proverbs in terms of decline in physical strength and is a source of genuine concern in a culture where each adult performs strenuous tasks for subsistence. It is reasonable to assume that the sense of diminishing physical stamina might motivate some to seek other forms of potency. Second, by the time women and men have reached the age at which their peers are grandparents, they are able to review their lives and make an assessment that is definitive enough to call for drastic action. Like their counterparts in our own society, middle-aged Gusii experience their lives and future performance as limited, and this can occasion a mid-life crisis from which they emerge as ritual practitioners. Finally, parents are in a position of spiritual responsibility for their children and resident grandchildren, even when the offspring are adults, so that death or chronic physical or mental illness affecting the progeny are interpreted as afflictions of their elders; it is the latter who seek cures and the protection of a ritual identity. Thus persons at later phases of the life course are more likely to pursue power in the spiritual realm.

It must be added, however, that when severe afflictions are visited on young persons who must take spiritual responsibility for themselves, they can become ritual practitioners. For example, a young married woman whose child was mentally retarded and crippled by polio became an herbalist in the ensuing years, and a young man who contracted venereal disease eventually acquired the power to cure it in others. But such cases are less frequent than older practitioners.

The final evaluation of a Gusii life is publicly expressed in action at the funeral. Attendance is the most important indicator: the general rule is that the number of people attending is directly related to the number of descendants the deceased had. The funerals of young children, unless murder is suspected, are domestic affairs with few outside mourners. Large funerals, with hundreds attending, are usually reserved for men or women who had many children or grandchildren, all of whom are obligated to come with their spouses and other kinsmen. Some large funerals nowadays, however, are for men who did not have many children but held high positions in the government — indicating an equivalence between economic and reproductive performance — and for members of certain Protestant churches whose congregations recognize the obligation to attend one another's funerals.

The Gusii funeral is a ritual event of great spiritual significance but its manifest evaluative content is centered on the reproductive career. Mourners seem to find deeply satisfying their attendance at the large funeral of an old man or woman whose offspring were numerous. They return full of admiration for the deceased, and this public celebration of fecundity undoubtedly helps maintain the birth rate at a high level. At one such funeral I attended, a sheet of paper was handed around on which were written the numbers of children, grandchildren, and great-grandchildren of the deceased, with a total at the bottom. This quantitative epitaph, symptomatic of spiritual success, was presented with pride to outside visitors. By contrast, the funeral of a thirty-year-old man who had never married or fathered children, indicating spiritual affliction, was not only poorly attended but pervaded by an atmosphere of shame as well as grief. Such public evaluations of the individual life are unique to the funeral rite and are so powerful as definitive statements about the meaning of life that I believe they give shape and purpose to the Gusii experience of adulthood. Having attended many funerals as a child and young adult, every Gusii knows how lives are evaluated at death, when their reproductive, economic, and spiritual continuities ought not end but become appended to those of their descendants. This represents the meaning of life for Gusii adults and sets the goals they pursue until they become ancestors.

WORK AND LOVE IN THE GUSII CONTEXT

The English words "work" and "love" can be unambiguously translated into the Gusii language (as *emeremo* and *obwanchani*, respectively), but their meanings are not equivalent to ours in the contexts of adult life. The precolonial Gusii did not share our presumption that individuals necessarily choose their own occupations and spouses, thereby integrating personal desires with social obligations. For them, a person's assumption of work appropriate to age and sex was conceptualized as automatic conformity to cultural prescription; deviations from the standard pattern were attributed to variations in the domestic labor supply, not voluntary choice. Even in marriage, where choice among alternatives was always explicit, the involvement of patriarchs, intermediaries, and bridewealth negotiations in the traditional selection process took precedence over the preferences of the marriage partners themselves. Socioeconomic conditions have changed, but Gusii discourse about work and love in adulthood continues to reflect indigenous priorities. Normal lives are represented as outcomes of the Gusii life plan modified by differences in economic resources, homestead composition, afflictions, and other externally imposed conditions; individual volitions and hedonistic preference are rarely mentioned spontaneously except in terms of deviance and disorder.

The Gusii life plan discussed above provides the cultural contexts in which work and love in adulthood can be understood from the Gusii point of view. The most salient context for cultural translation is the domestic group, the primary model for Gusii social experience. It is in the domestic scene that reproductive, economic, and spiritual goals are pursued throughout adulthood, that the lives of men and women and parents and children intersect, and that funerals are conducted. The domestic setting lends its imagery to every facet of social life and personal experience, and we must return to it to gain an understanding of work and love. Indeed, a translation of "work" and "love" as domestic production and reproduction would not be far off the mark for the Gusii, but it is not specific enough to capture their distinctive conceptions of production and reproduction and the ways they are experienced in adulthood.

In the case of work, we must distinguish physical labor from the Gusii conception of task performance. That conception, as embodied in the domestic group, always involves a person with authority delegating responsibility for routine tasks to someone lower in the age-sex hierarchy so that the person in authority can turn his or her attention to tasks that have not yet been delegated. Thus the husband allocates fields among his wives, gets their cultivation under way, and turns his attention to the herds and other areas of domestic production in which the wives are not involved. Having delegated responsibility to them, he exercises very slight supervisory authority during the growing season, expecting that the wives in turn will delegate tasks on a daily basis to the children in their charge.

This model of delegation was followed among the men and boys herding cattle, sheep, and goats, and continues to be followed by mothers in their infant care, that is, the infants are cared for by older children while the mother turns her daytime attention to cultivation and household work. This system means that physical labor and routine tasks are distributed downward in the age-sex hierarchy, from men to women, parents to children, and seniors to juniors, when there is someone to whom responsibility can be delegated; when there is no one, those of higher status and authority perform the tasks themselves. The Gusii do not value work for itself but are pragmatically concerned with task performance, and if the task can be delegated, then it should be. Gusii men do not consider it demeaning to do the work themselves, only confining, as it prevents them from attending to other tasks in the service of domestic expansion. It is nevertheless true that a successful Gusii man is someone who "has people" enough to permit him more leisure than anyone else in the homestead. Thus, conspicuous leisure is distinctly a prerogative of patriarchal status in the homestead and of authority that has been successfully delegated.

Contemporary Gusii men continue to see themselves as investors and supervisors of a domestic economy in which their wives and sons are the workers, with the family shop, bar, or market stall now appended to the family farm. The successful Gusii man is an entrepreneur, busily finding new ways of investing the human and financial capital he controls, and organizing new productive units, the management of which he intends to delegate to others. Yet most young men seek employment in bureaucratic jobs based on a different set of assumptions concerning the relationship between work and career. How do they integrate bureaucratic employment with entrepreneurial goals in their lives and personal experience?

The Gusii men I observed from 1974 to 1976 did not form psychosocial identifications with the occupational careers defined by their bureaucratic jobs. They saw themselves as entrepreneurs pursuing an occupational role only as one of several concurrent and future productive activities. The other activities were delegated to their wives: if they had land, it was cultivation; if not, it was a small commercial enterprise. The bureaucratic job, or in some cases the jobs of both husband and wife, were seen primarily as stable sources of investment capital rather than subsistence, on the assumption that living costs would be kept low by having most of the family in the rural home or in subsidized housing, with as much food as possible coming from home. These men spent a great deal of their time planning new investments, setting up new businesses or farms, and supervising their old ones. They took maximum advantage of the spare time provided by their employment to devote themselves to their activities as entrepreneurs, and their primary interests seemed to be in those activities. They looked forward to bureaucratic advancement but as a means to an explicitly formulated goal of entrepreneurial expansion and beyond that to early retirement and a satisfying life as supervisor of a family-run conglomerate of farms and commercial enterprises. There are numerous examples of men who had achieved these goals. Their conception of the ideal life course, then, departed from the prototype of the Gusii life plan only in the institutional settings of some of the productive activities engaged in, but not in the relation between work and role performance during the adult years.

As for love, its contemporary meanings also have their roots in domestic prototypes embedded in the Gusii life plan. Gusii culture past and present has a place for romantic and erotic ideas and activities, primarily in the context of courtship and in private departures from the prevailing puritanism of the Gusii code of marital fidelity and kin avoidance (LeVine, 1959; LeVine and LeVine, 1966). In private as well as public contexts, however, reproductive goals are paramount and are experienced as such in the marital relationships of all adults. The "love" element in Gusii marriage, while considered necessary up to a point, is seen as potentially disruptive and even dangerous if carried on beyond that point. The domestic prototype includes a man with several wives who necessarily compete for his favor. His task is to maintain an atmosphere of equity in handling them, not playing favorites among them or their children. This is known in Gusii lore to be difficult because a man will be more interested in and involved with the new bride than with the old drudges, he may continue to be more attracted personally to one of the wives than to the others, and in any event each wife will be plotting to get more for herself. He is, however, obligated to keep each wife pregnant on schedule and to maintain a modicum of congeniality in what can become a difficult set of relationships. The prototypical strategy for managing this situation is for the husband to keep his distance from all the wives, building his own house (*esaiga*) and rotating among them on a visible schedule that they all find tolerable.

This normative distance in the husband-wife relationship is experienced by many Gusii as being desirable personally as well as pragmatically. There is a fear that too close a relationship between husband and wife — too much "love" — will endanger the physical and mental well-being of the partners, particularly the husband. The polygynous situation drives some women to use "love potions" (*amaebi*), which are commercially available, to make their husband love them more than the others. But these love potions can, as a popular Gusii song warns, endanger the husband's health and even kill him. The song, composed by a young man in the area, is called *Amaebi nemechando*, "Love Potions Are Afflictions." This epitomizes the meaning of love in Gusii marriage: it must be confined to the distance prescribed by the norms of domestic relationships.

As these brief examples show, the meanings of work and love for

Gusii adults differ substantially from those in our society because they are embedded in understandings derived from prototypes of the Gusii domestic social order — prototypes which continue to organize Gusii experience in the adult life course today, though many of the conditions of life have changed. The Gusii domestic group, like that of many less differentiated societies, functioned as a basic unit of reproduction, economic production,˙ and religion, providing roles defined by sex, age, and kinship that combined these functions in a coherent life plan. An examination of this life plan shows that with control over the labor of wives and children, the Gusii patriarch assumed an entrepreneurial role rather than an occupation as we know it; with polygyny as the marital ideal, men maintained an emotional distance from their wives as they sought new unions. Work and love clearly meant something different for adults in this indigenous context than they do in modern Western society. That these meanings have retained their salience after the introduction of Western occupations and the diminution in child labor and polygyny suggests that they are rooted in Gusii representations of self more durable than the institutions that generated them. Contemporary Gusii share the aspirations of their forefathers for public validation of self in a home funeral, and their adult lives can be seen as organized toward that end. Their example indicates how much we have to learn from other cultures about the sociology and psychology of the adult years.

Notes

The 1974-1976 field work reported here was carried out with support from the National Science Foundation (BNS 77-09007). Susan Templeton made valuable comments on the first draft and assisted in the editing of the manuscript. I am also indebted to Sarah LeVine, Gary Pfeiffer, Joel Momanyi, and David Riesman for helpful criticisms of the second draft, though I bear full responsibility for this final version. For illustrative case material on Gusii married women, see Sarah LeVine (1979).

References

LeVine, Robert A. 1959. Gusii sex offenses: a study in social control. *American Anthropologist,* 61:12-59.

LeVine, Robert A., and LeVine, Barbara B. 1966. *Nyansongo: a Gusii community in Kenya.* New York: Wiley; rpt. Kreeger, 1977.

LeVine, Sarah. 1979. *Mothers and wives: Gusii women of East .Africa.* Chicago: University of Chicago Press.

FIVE

Vicissitudes of Work and Love in Anglo-American Society

———————— NEIL J. SMELSER ————————

IN THIS SPECULATIVE ESSAY I shall explore the ways work and love have been valued and institutionalized in recent Anglo-American history and then briefly consider their future. But first, a few definitions and distinctions are in order. Two modes of human action frequently distinguished in this essay are the instrumental and the affective. The instrumental mode refers to the disciplined organization of activities toward the accomplishment of designated tasks; the affective mode refers to expressive or gratificatory attachments to both human and nonhuman objects. This distinction has appeared in diverse guises in the history of philosophy, and has constituted a central basis for much contemporary thinking in social theory (Parsons, 1949; 1960; Parsons and Shils, 1951).[1] More specifically, these two modes of human action are reflected in the distinction between work and love: work is one variety of instrumental activity, and love can be regarded as one organization of affective attachments.

Analytically the distinction between the instrumental and the affective may be considered at several levels—the personality, the culture, and the social structure. At the personality level we clearly observe people at work and people in love, recognize these orientations in ourselves, and distinguish between the two easily enough. Yet I would argue that the distinction, to be useful at this level, should be regarded as identifying aspects of human action but not discrete orientations, because in fact the two orientations are often so inextricably meshed that it becomes difficult to distinguish between them. For example, one can love one's work, and one can—indeed, is well-advised to—work at love. What we call "work" invariably has some kind of expressive dimension and what we call "love" is never without an instrumental component, though they may be repressed or denied in various ways.

At the other two levels, however, the distinction can be made more clearly. Cultures and world views may value or devalue either the instrumental or the expressive mode, or both; may ignore one or the other; and may regard the two as complementary, mutually exclusive, or antipathetic. At the social-structural level, each of the two orientations may be compartmentalized in various ways. This is most clearly seen in the pervasive tendency to institutionalize the "instrumental" or "work" orientation into discrete occupational roles, governed by an array of norms in relative isolation from other arenas of life. And while the normative regulation of affective expression is perhaps less self-evident, institutionalized norms of love, marriage, kinship, and friendship clearly define the times, places, and situations in which impulses are and are not to be gratified, and feelings are and are not to be experienced (Durkheim, 1951; Davis, 1936).[2]

SEPARATION AND MUTUAL EXCLUSION

At the cultural level, modern British and American history have been characterized—in different ways, as we shall see—by the increasing intrumentalization and rationalization of life, with a corresponding split between the instrumental and expressive modes. With respect to the cultural origins of this split, I would join Weber in pointing initially to the ever-increasing rationalization of life that was symbolized but not exhausted by the ascetic wings of the Protestant Reformation (Weber, 1930). With respect to the social-structural manifestation of the split, I would point primarily to the rise of depersonalized occupational roles, especially in business and professional life, as the models for dedicated work and as the institutional realization of middle-class values. Weber stressed the religious discipline of Protestantism, but he also saw the advent of Protestantism as part of a larger movement toward the rationalization of the universe. This rationalizing impulse invaded many spheres of life other than the religious—the legal, the economic, the academic—everywhere heralding the virtues of discipline, calculation, instrumentalism, labor, and self-control. In many instances, however, the rationalizing impulse has not been explicitly religious, as it was in the case of Protestantism. In modern times, the world has witnessed efforts to transform and rationalize society under the aegis of diverse values and ideologies, including communist and socialist ideologies of progress, and including—especially in Third World countries—ideologies that envision simultaneously the restoration of traditional cultures and the revolutionary transformation of society.

Certainly in the West the commitment to the virtues of instrumentalism and rationality has meant a corresponding downplaying of expressive gratification. The Puritan strand of Protestantism was openly hostile, attempting actively to repress the sexual, aesthetic, playful, and other expressive realms of life as foreign and irrational. Relaxation and play were accepted as a part of rebuilding for the serious business of a methodically conducted life. Even when the expressive mode of action has not been the subject of direct or comprehensive attack, it has often been regarded as in the realm of "pleasure" or "entertainment," to be enjoyed only after it has been earned by the devotion of energies to the rational, workaday world.

A number of ideological trends in the nineteenth century simultaneously reflected and deepened this cultural tendency to dichotomize the instrumental and the expressive. The ideology of Victorian prudery marked the high point of the conquest of discipline, rationality, and self-control, as well as the most extreme negation of impulse gratification. That ideology involved a near-total denial of sexuality for women, and defined sexuality and its related affects as a lack of control and discipline on the part of the male — a kind of regrettable pathology. Consider also some parts of the corpus of the discipline of economics as it developed in the nineteenth century. I have in mind the fundamental distinction between production on the one hand, which involves the systematic "building up" of value by the rational organization of skills and other resources, and consumption on the other hand, which involves the "use" or "running down" of products in the gratification of individual "tastes." That distinction, however useful for analytic purposes, clearly parallels the distinction between instrumentality and expressiveness. Also, that which went into production — labor — was widely regarded as having nothing to do with enjoyment or positive affect; it was measured in units of "disutility" which had to be extracted by rewards (wages) extrinsic to the work activity itself. Consider, finally, the ideological adaptations that occurred when psychoanalysis became more or less widely accepted in the West. Without regard to the qualifications that Freud himself placed on that theory, the public came to regard sexuality and impulses generally (libido) as constituting the irrational side of man, opposed in all respects to discipline and rational control. The "irrational" aspect of the theory of psychoanalysis — as well as of the work of Schopenhauer, Nietzsche, and other "irrationalist" thinkers — tended to be exaggerated largely because these theories

were judged in terms of the values of instrumental rationalism, the
dominant perspective of the time. The fundamental cultural dicho-
tomy, in short, broke through and manifested itself in ideological
and intellectual developments of very diverse kinds.

Especially in his writings on bureaucracy, Weber emphasized
the depersonalizing and dehumanizing effects of the trend toward
the greater rationalization of life, and regarded certain modern
charismatic trends as a "reassertion" of the irrational (Weber, 1948).
When efforts are made to resist rationality and its associated values,
those values are discovered to be so powerful that they can be at-
tacked only by completely denying them and asserting the overwhelming importance of their negations—that is, pure and unadul-
terated affect, irrationality, indiscipline, and the like. In other
words, because of the strength of the values of instrumental rationality, suggested solutions for the dilemmas of the human condition
have tended to assume as extremist either-or character. It has proved
difficult to generate belief systems that are a genuine synthesis of rational or irrational—or, if you will, instrumental and expressive, or
work and love—ingredients. Rather, the relationship has tended to
be a dialectic one. Critics of the rationalist tendencies are driven into
constructing denials and negations, which take the form of romanti-
cism, irrationalism, expressionism, and hedonism. Consequently the
cultural dynamics of the modern West have tended to put work and
related instrumental activities into one joyless category and love and
related affects into a separate category, and then to represent them
as mutually exclusive. This cultural opposition has dominated the
structure of Western thought for several centuries and has limited the
number of moral and psychological solutions for the dilemmas of
human existence.

A number of recent cultural phenomena have involved a rejection of the instrumentalist work ethic and a glorification of expression. Many of the movements of the aesthetic left, including
bohemianism, the hippie movement, and others, involve sharp critical reactions against the dominant values of instrumentalism,
whether these be characterized as "bourgeois," "decadent," or
"square." Yet such protest movements have found it difficult to develop substantive and positive ideologies of their own. Similarly, the
hedonistic ethic as manifested in the "sensuous life" ideology of *Playboy* magazine and related publications involves a rejection of discipline and work. (Indeed, the word "playboy" has historically referred to a man who does not work but spends his life playing; by and
large the term has had negative connotations.) Yet that movement,

like the broader pornographic revolution of which it may be considered a part, has also failed to develop an ideological position that goes beyond the negation of discipline and the positive stress on sensuality, which is considered to be the opposite of discipline.

These intellectual and ideological trends illustrate the fundamental opposition between instrumentalism and affect that is so deeply rooted in the modern Western tradition. They also suggest that even when individuals and groups try to break out of what Weber called the "iron cage" of rationality, they find themselves still caged, because they are again constricted by the narrowness of the alternatives they envision.

Moving back to the individual, this extreme split between the instrumental and affective can be regarded as cultural encouragement for two types of adaptation that are commonly described as neurotic. Each adaptation involves an effort to deny the individual's connection with some aspect of psychic reality that is intrinsically associated with the human condition. On the one side there is a temptation to repress the affective, emotional, loving side of life altogether. This is the classic solution of the methodical rationalist as depicted by Weber. This temptation is probably the dominant one, even today. It is an invitation to clothe oneself in the garments of the obsessive-compulsive and to push down, as obsessive-compulsives do, the expressive side of life. For the minority, protesting segment, the temptation is to act out the negation of the dominant values. By fostering the notion that affect and the actions associated with it constitute the whole of human existence, proponents of this position encourage people to live out their lives without reference even to the instrumental, disciplined dimensions that are part of affective attachments and expression. Insofar as both adaptations deny a proper mix of the instrumental and affective modes, the living of social life becomes correspondingly impoverished and alienating.

SOME SOCIAL-STRUCTURAL COMPLICATIONS AND VARIATIONS

The account just given of the two trends in Western cultures is overly simple for two reasons. First, it ignores variations in the ways in which instrumental rationality is valued and ignores the contrapuntal interplay between this mode of action and other cultural forces. Second, this simplistic account suggests that the relation of the two to the societies they have influenced has been one of simple conquest. That is clearly not the case. Any cultural trend, however powerful, takes root in the historical context of the societies it affects and is modified accordingly. This two-way influence may be illustrated by tracing the different courses taken by these two cultural trends in Great Britain and America during the nineteenth century and examining the way those trends have affected the social structuring of work and love relationships in the two countries.

The chief difference in historical context between Great Britain and America is that in Great Britain the values of instrumental rationality were carried by a religious tradition (Nonconformism) that was from the beginning subordinate in power to the established Church of England, and by a group (the middle class) that was subordinate in status to the landed aristocracy. America lacked both a formally established church—though Puritanism and its variants were dominant culturally—and, especially after the Jacksonian era, anything approaching a landed aristocracy. In England, furthermore, the aristocracy had developed according to a "gentlemanly" ethic in which one of the positive virtues was *not* to work, either in a formal occupation or at home, where personal servants did the work and symbolized the status of the family. America lacked both the tradition of aristocratic disdain for work and the corresponding division of society into a small "leisured" and a large "working" class. Thus, when the middle classes came to consolidate themselves in both societies, they did so in a very different class context.

Matthew Arnold, England's sensitive mid-nineteenth-century sociological observer of many nations, undertook to characterize British and American society in his *Culture and Anarchy*. In a somewhat whimsical moment, he announced that it was "awkward and tiresome" to refer always to "the aristocratic class, the middle-class, and the working-class" in Great Britain. Instead, he wished to call the aristocracy the "Barbarians," a class which had descended from that stock and which stressed, in its contemporary manifestation, personal liberty, honors and consideration, field-sports and pleasure. To the middle classes he attached the label, "Philistines," suggesting business, money lending, religion, propriety, and sobriety (and the values of instrumental rationality, I might add). The working class he described as "Populace," which "raw and half-developed, has long lain half-hidden amidst its poverty and squalor, and is now issuing from its hiding-place to assert an Englishman's heaven-born privilege of doing what it likes." English life, he maintained, could not be understood without continuous reference to these three great orders. He went on to say, "America is just like ourselves, with the Barbarians quite left out, and the Populace nearly. This leaves the Philistines for the great bulk of the nation; —a livelier sort of Philistine than ours

. . . but left all the more to himself and to have his whole swing. And as we have found that the strongest and most vital part of English Philistinism was the Puritan . . . middle-class . . . so it is notorious that the people of the United States issues from this class, and reproduces its tendencies", (Arnold, 1869, pp. xxx-xxxi). Arnold's observation is not entirely original; other observers (notably Tocqueville) had noted the absence of a feudal tradition in America; and still others (notably Marx) had noted the weakness of a genuine working class. And his observation also appears to be exaggerated. Nevertheless, following through some of its implications leads to insights on the social structuring of work and love in the two societies.

BRITISH MIDDLE CLASSES

By "the middle classes" I refer to that wide band of families in Great Britain sustained by a husband-father in professional (law, medicine, clergy, and civil-service) occupations, business and mercantile positions, and—toward the lower end—roles such as schoolteacher and clerk, which began to appear in greater numbers in the latter part of the nineteenth century. Insofar as this class propounded the values assigned to them by Arnold, they deviated from the aristocratic ideal by stressing the value of rationality, work, and discipline. As these classes consolidated their gains in the early part of the nineteenth century, there developed simultaneously a powerful ideological movement that split the world of work from the world of sentiment, giving the former to men and the latter to women. This movement, associated with the early Victorian family, extolled the womanly virtues of gentleness, kindness, softness, radiance, purity, and devotion—virtues to sustain a happy home and family. Since the worlds of business, politics, and community were foreign to women's nature, women ought to remain as the spiritual and emotional center of the home and not partake of the workaday world. In fact, the participation of middle-class women in the labor force in the first half of the nineteenth century was negligible. As a result of these ideological and economic developments, British middle-class society effected a split between the rational, instrumental world and the sentimental, affective world strictly along sexual lines.

Though deviating from the aristocratic ideal with respect to attitudes toward work, the middle classes nevertheless accepted certain values of gentility and respectability and incorporated many status symbols from the aristocratic model. In particular, the increasingly prosperous middle classes in the middle and late nineteenth century began to adopt a life-style that included an education for one's children in an appropriate private school, a respectable material position, frequent social entertainment, and above all personal household servants for cleaning, cooking, serving, and caring for and educating one's children. This life-style represented respectability and gentility throughout the middle-class ranks, and was adopted to the degree that the family income would permit. From the standpoint of the role of women, however, the main implication of the inherited tradition was that it was neither respectable nor genteel to work in a paid occupation. Virtually no women in the middle classes nor any women aspiring to middle-class respectability participated in the labor force until new occupations, such as schoolteaching and clerical work, began to open to women later in the nineteenth century.

One of the fascinating ramifications of the life-style of the middle classes was that the traditional obligations associated with the role of women — relating to work and, to some extent, love as well — began to "empty out," with little emerging to take their place. Because of the taboo on working, women were excluded from the paid labor force. By hiring paid servants, women were progressively relieved of domestic labor as well. And, particularly in the wealthier reaches of the middle classes, the hiring of nurses and governesses meant that the middle-class woman was losing some of her childrearing responsibilities. What remained was the actual bearing of the children, the (sometimes difficult) managerial responsibility for a number of servants, and the status-maintaining functions of visiting and entertaining in a proper style.

Another feature of the role of the middle-class woman in the mid-nineteenth century was that virtually the only career positively sanctioned and designed for her was marriage and family. Girls participated minimally in the secondary educational system of the day — the middle-class schools and great public schools — and were oriented to no particular occupational role. What education they received was either from parents or from governesses, and stress was laid on genteel but impractical subjects such as singing, dancing, and modern European languages. Virtually no preparation for the world of occupational work was available.

Despite the fact that marriage was virtually the only career available to women, many of them were unable to find eligible men to marry. This unfortunate circumstance came about because so many men emigrated from Great Britain during this era, and because in the middle classes it was not respectable for a man to marry before he was earning an income sufficient to support a family according to an appropriate middle-class standard. Thus many women faced the prospect of entering late—or perhaps not at all—the only viable adult role that society had designed for them.

This complicated confluence of forces—changing middle-class attitudes toward work, the exclusion of women from the world of work and from preparation for it, the reliance on personal servants as a mark of gentility and respectability, and demographic developments—can hardly be regarded as a deliberate creation of British society at the time. Taken together, nevertheless, they tended to exclude women from virtually all instrumental and many expressive activities and to create an unviable personal situation for many. It was from this confluence, moreover, that the first significant stirrings of feminism arose in the mid-nineteenth century. By and large, women appeared to accept the assignment to the predominantly domestic realm. Except for a modest protest against the asymmetrical divorce laws, few voices were heard complaining about the position of women *within* the middle-class family. It was, rather, on behalf of the women who were excluded from that family—the unmarried and the widowed—that feminist protests first were heard. There was a minor movement to encourage single women to emigrate, primarily to become wives of men who had already emigrated. The more significant stirrings, however, were on the part of groups of women concerned mainly with generating opportunities for unmarried women. It was from this source that the early agitation for improving women's secondary education and providing colleges for women arose in the mid-nineteenth century, and from which philanthropic and reformist activity also developed (Banks and Banks, 1964; Banks, 1954).

British Working Classes

Generally speaking, before the onset of industrial production, the working family itself constituted an economically productive unit—the peasant family and the household craft family are prototypes. This social structure permitted a fusion between the instrumental and affective facets of family relationships because the family members worked together. Industrialization, with the economic efficiencies that arose from its rational organization, put these families out of business as productive units and generated the system of wage labor. Under this system, a member of the family—usually the husband-father but sometimes others as well—left the premises of the household and worked for a large portion of the day for wages which were brought home to cover expenditures that maintained the family as a social unit. The working-class family became more specialized, focusing on the emotional and child-rearing side and giving up its role as an economically productive social unit and as the organizing base for many of the instrumental activities of its members.

Of course individual families often deviated considerably from this general model. The family's adoption of this wage-earning organization was gradual in Great Britain; in many cases the family as a whole retained its instrumental involvement in the economy. For example, early in the industrial revolution the family as a production unit in the home survived in some industries, particularly in textiles; and even in the factory, workers were permitted to hire wives and children to help tend machines and perform ancillary tasks (Smelser, 1959).

But beyond the limited practice of family hiring, the distinctive feature of the British experience during the industrial transition — in contrast with the American experience — was that a very high proportion of the working-class women and children continued to be active wage earners in the labor force. The continued involvement of women is partly explained by the fact that the British industrial revolution was dominated by the cotton and woolen textile industries, where the work was light enough for women to be efficiently employed. This was not the entire story, however, for large numbers of women were employed in arduous jobs as well — in mining, for instance — which suggests that manufacturers were motivated to utilize female labor wherever they could, because of the relatively lower wages it commanded. Another distinctively British feature contributing to the high utilization of female labor lay in the importance of personal servants (maids, cooks, ladies-in-waiting, and so on) as an ingredient in the upper class genteel life-style. The great majority of these servants were drawn from agricultural and working-class families.

At the same time, the expectation that women would continue to maintain primary expressive responsibilities as wife and mother in the family did not diminish. Fertility remained high among the working classes until very late in the nineteenth century. Their families were large, and workers, many of whom remained near the poverty line, could seldom afford paid domestic labor to care for children. For the woman who chose to stop working during the period when her children were young, there was a decline in family earnings at a phase in the life cycle when material demands were heaviest. This period of deprivation was likely to continue until the older children were able to augment family earnings by taking employment—at about age twelve or thirteen—or until the mother could resume working, relying on the older children to care for the younger.

The children of the working classes contributed to the family's economic welfare from a very early age. Various parliamentary inquiries into popular education in the first three-quarters of the nineteenth century produced consistent evidence that, by and large, when children were able to contribute anything, however small, to the family income, they were put to work. The age at which children began to work varied from industry to industry, but it ranged from seven to eleven. Child labor constituted one of the principal barriers to the spread of popular education in Great Britain, as families would terminate or interrupt their children's education when they could begin to earn. The children's wages were generally turned over to the parents, with bits returned to the children as pocket money; in later years they retained their wages and paid for their keep.

This "instrumentalization" of the British working-class family clearly overloaded the wife-mother's role with both work and affective responsibilities and taxed the family's capacity as a viable affective unit. One response was to diffuse affective responsibility by relying on extended kinspeople, especially grandmothers, and older children, especially daughters, to care for the younger children when the mother worked outside the home. Sometimes, too, the child's principal affective ties were with peers, and the large numbers of children in street gangs became a menacing problem in the eyes of reformers.

THE AMERICAN FAMILY IN THE EARLY INDUSTRIAL PERIOD

During the early years of America's industrial revolution the split between the world of work and the family was generally sharper and more widespread than in Great Britain, and the instrumental—affective split along sex-role lines was correspondingly more extreme.

The circumstances accounting for this difference are rooted in economic, religious, and class differences. The first important industrial developments in the United States occurred mainly in the 1820s and 1830s—though there were some small stirrings earlier—in the textile industry in New England and in a number of other industries in the Middle Atlantic states. In contrast with the British experience, however, this industrial development did not involve a massive incorporation of working-class women into the ranks of factory labor. Women were employed, to be sure, but in smaller proportions. Furthermore, those women employed in the mills increasingly tended to be immigrants rather than women of Anglo-Saxon stock. Finally, demand for domestic servants was generally low, partly because service was not so conspicuous a feature of American middle-class life. Thus, American working-class women were less involved than British in the world of work — occupationally defined — though they were heavily involved in the instrumental side of maintaining a household and family.

At the same time, in the 1820s and 1830s, there developed a vigorous ideological movement that rationalized women's nonparticipation in economic life and glorified a more or less exclusively domestic role for the wife and mother. This movement has been termed the "cult of true womanhood," and resembles in large measure the dominant early Victorian attitude toward middle-class women in Great Britain. The same domestic virtues were extolled, and the same consignment to the hearth and home was made. But in certain respects the American experience offers contrasts with the British. In both early industrial America and early Victorian England, ideologists extolled the sanctity and the purity of women and called for their protection from the ruder aspects of the profane world. But in England the admonition against work for pay was based not only on this Puritan theme but also on the class-related theme that it was not *respectable* to do so; this value of respectability was rooted in the traditional aristocratic emphasis on leisure as an essential part of a life-style appropriate to the higher ranks. By contrast, the American ideologists of true womanhood did not denigrate work as such. Rather, they rationalized woman's domesticity in a more typically Puritan style. Women represented the highest and most spiritual emotions, and these should be protected from harsh reality, and above all from sexuality. For accompanying the focus on true womanhood was a second ideological strand, which has come to be known as the "prudery" movement. This movement portrayed men as base, sensual, and depraved, and women as pure and without low passion. Its mission was to protect women from the menace of sex, and even to stamp it out altogether, except for narrowly reproductive purposes. So while the dominant British ideology on women was rooted in both class and sexual symbolism, the American ideology was more nearly exclusively Puritan in character.

The experience of women in America did not show the same discontinuity between the middle and working classes as existed in Great Britain. In England, the values of respectability and gentility tended to filter down from the upper through the middle classes, stopping only at the working class, for whom respectability did not include an extreme split between the instrumental and the expressive modes of behavior along sex lines. By contrast, the American deification of the purity of women was a Puritan, middle-class movement that tended to diffuse more generally throughout the community, including the working class, as might be expected in a young society in which class lines were relatively indistinct.

I have stressed the different historical routes taken by British and American society in the period of their early industrialization, and indeed one should not lose sight of those differences. But it should also be emphasized that both countries succeeded in accomplishing a radical split between the sexes — in America perhaps more generally so than in Great Britain, since in the British working classes the split between the family (female domain) and workplace (male domain) was never so clear. The period of early industrialization, moreover, generated and consolidated the division of roles between the sexes in both countries that has constituted the basis for all feminist protest, right up to the contemporary "women's liberation" movement. Feminism has defined its mission as opposing the historical heritage of a structural division between the instrumental and the affective along sex lines and its attendant inequalities.

A GLIMPSE INTO THE FUTURE

There is reason to believe that the process of isolating the affective dimension of life is not complete, though the future will not bring a simple extension of the assignment of the expressive realm to women. The increasing isolation of affectivity, rather, will occur as the result of a new set of arrangements in the family which are now developing. These new arrangements involve the increasing structural separation of the marital relationship from the parental relationship. This separation might be regarded as building on and extending the earlier process of differentiation that tended to remove much of the instrumental mode from the family, leaving it primarily responsible only for the affective relations between and among parents and children. In the United States and to some extent more generally in the developed societies a number of trends are resulting in the progressive removal of the child-bearing and child-rearing functions from the affective relations between the adult man and woman. These trends include an increasing rate of illegitimacy, which means a larger proportion of single-parent homes; an increasing divorce rate, also resulting in a greater proportion of single-parent homes; the growing participation of women in the labor force, which separates them from their children, even at an early age; an increasing growth of nursery schools, prenursery schools, playgroups, and the like, which augments the separation from the parent or parents at early ages.

Such trends—all of which probably will continue into the future—suggest that the relationship between adults and children is becoming more specialized, more formally organized, and more instrumental. Furthermore, affective attachments between adults are moving away from simultaneous responsibility, for the rearing of children. Put another way, the affective relations between adults— whether married or unmarried— are in the process of becoming more isolated and less intertwined with other dimensions of social life. I would observe that the very recent trend toward greater toleration of "alternative" marital forms—for example, communal marriages, gay marriages, sexual liaisons without marriage—rests at least in part on the fact that the marital relationship has become relatively isolated from the rest of social life; accordingly, experimenting with marriage forms affects much less of the rest of life than it has in the past. There is also reason to believe that in the future more and more people will question the necessity of the legal marital bond as the dominant institutional basis for adult affective relationships, largely because the social realities that once necessitated and shored up that legal bond will have so weakened. Insofar as that occurs, we will likely witness the simultaneous emergence of a vast range of new experiments in personal intimacy that will make the experiments of the 1960s and 1970s appear modest by comparison.

Notes

1. Talcott Parsons returned to the distinction repeatedly in his theoretical formulations, for example, in his early distinction between the "instrumental" and various kinds of "situational" modes as fundamental orientations of action; in his formulation of the pattern-variables, particularly the distinction between affective neutrality and affectivity; and in his formulation of the functional system-problems facing any system of action.

2. In his discussion of anomie, Durkheim portrayed the family as an institutional contrivance for limiting and regulating desires (pp. 259-276).

References

ARNOLD, MATTHEW. 1869. *Culture and anarchy: an essay in political and social criticism.* London: Smith, Elder.

BANKS, J.A. 1954. *Prosperity and parenthood: a study of family planning among the Victorian middle classes.* London: Routledge and Kegan Paul.

BANKS, J. A., AND OLIVE BANKS. 1964. *Feminism and family planning in Victorian England*. Liverpool: Liverpool University Press.

DAVIS, KINGSLEY. 1936. Jealousy and sexual property. *Social Forces,* 14:395-405.

DURKHEIM, EMILE. 1951. *Suicide.* Glencoe, Ill.: Free Press.

PARSONS, TALCOTT. 1960. Pattern variables revisited. *American Sociological Review,* 25:467-483.

———. 1949. Toward a common language for the area of social science. In *Essays in sociological theory, pure and applied.* Glencoe, Ill.: Free Press.

PARSONS, TALCOTT, AND EDWARD A. SHILS. 1951. Values, motives, and systems of action. In *Toward a general theory of action,* ed. T. Parsons, G.M. Platt, and E.A. Shils. Cambridge: Harvard University Press.

SMELSER, NEIL J. 1959. *Social change in the industrial revolution.* Chicago: University of Chicago Press.

WEBER, MAX. 1948. *From Max Weber,* ed. H.H. Gerth and C. Wright Mills. London: Routledge and Kegan Paul.

———. 1930. *The Protestant ethic and the spirit of capitalism,* tr. Talcott Parsons. London: George Allen and Unwin.

SIX

Love and Adulthood
in American Culture

ANN SWIDLER

ADULTHOOD, WHICH ONCE SEEMED an uneventful, predictable time of life, has more recently come to seem problematic and mysterious. We find ourselves asking whether adulthood is a period of stability or of change, whether adults "develop" or only drift, whether there are patterned "stages" of adult development or only more and less successful responses to external pressures. The answers to these questions depend in large part on emerging shifts in the way our culture patterns adulthood. By examining the ideology of love, one of the central anchors of our culture's view of adult life, I will explore the changing structure of meaning that shapes the contemporary adult life course.

Love in our culture is both an experience and an ideal, richly arrayed in symbol and myth. These myths outline the shape of adulthood, and the rituals of love mark its moments of transition. Like religious experience, the culturally grounded experience of love links the lives of individuals — their private struggles and triumphs — to larger issues, framing the meaning of adult life. Thus Freud's statement that an adult must be able "to love and to work" is a moral as well as a psychological ideal. If this ideal is undermined, if love and work no longer seem to be significant achievements, the integrity and meaning of adult life are undermined as well.

As Erik Erikson's work has made us aware, ideological and religious images provide symbolic resources which structure individual developmental crises and make possible their resolution. Although love in real life is not like love in literature or in the movies, our culture's images of love provide a background, a language, and a set of

120

symbols within which people enact their own lives. In loving and being loved, people give themselves over, at least for brief periods, to intensely moving experiences through which they achieve new awareness of self and others. Love can make possible periods of crystallization or reformulation of the self and the self's relationship to the world. Beliefs about love permeate people's hopes for themselves, their evaluations of experience, and their sense of achievement in the world.[1]

While love is only one part of adulthood, its symbolic richness makes it an ideal place to examine the cultural dilemmas of contemporary adulthood. We may ask both what resources our culture provides for building a satisfactory adulthood, and what new models and images of adulthood are developing to give meaning to emerging challenges in adult life.

THE TRADITIONAL CULTURE OF LOVE

In the West the ideal of love became infused with moral meaning. While the heroes of most societies are great warriors, or leaders who dedicate themselves to their people, in our culture the drama of love embodies a struggle for moral perfection and social commitment. This symbolic link between love and moral life is the legacy of courtly love.[2]

Courtly love, from which our modern love mythology derives, grew out of the crisis of feudal loyalty in twelfth- and thirteenth-century Europe (Lewis, 1958; Bloch, 1964). The moral ideal of the vassal's devotion to his lord came under strain as vassal warriors became hereditary aristocrats whose interests conflicted with those of the lords they served. Emergent states established wider principles of moral and legal order which competed with feudal traditions of personal loyalty and perpetual warfare (Bloch, 1977). In courtly love the feudal ideals of service and devotion were transferred from the noble lord to the lady, and the knightly virtue of courage in battle was transmuted into the display of heroism and moral worth in the quest for love. Courtly love articulated a new conception of individual moral autonomy, expressed in the conflicts of choices faced by the courtly lovers. Originating in southern France at the end of the eleventh century, courtly poetry and the games of courtly love spread rapidly throughout the courts of Europe, providing the central motifs of aristocratic culture for the next six-hundred years.

While courtly love and its associated code of chivalry remained the status-ethic of a narrow class, they gave a distinctive orientation to Western ideals of love. Broadened and popularized, courtly love provided the images and symbols underlying the bourgeois love ethic that is ours today. Most important among these ideals is that love ennobles and transforms the lover. As Andreas Capellanus, the twelfth-century codifier of the "rules of love," wrote in *The Art of Courtly Love* (cited in Stephens, 1968, p. 41): "Now it is the effect of love that a true lover cannot be degraded with any avarice. Love causes a rough and uncouth man to be distinguished for his handsomeness; it can endow a man even of the humblest birth with nobility of character; it blesses the proud with humility; and the man in love becomes accustomed to performing many services gracefully for everyone. O what a wonderful thing is love, which makes a man shine with so many virtues and teaches everyone, no matter who he is, so many good traits of character!" Through an elaborate code of sexual flirtation combined with sexual restraint, courtly love heightened self-control, so that passion could inspire virtue, putting the power of sexual feeling behind the demands of self-perfection.

But courtly love had a second side — a side of treachery, suffering, and death. As Denis de Rougemont (1956) has emphasized, the great love stories, from Tristan and Iseult to Romeo and Juliet, are of forbidden love which ends in tragedy and death. The great chivalric romances, like the stories of Lancelot and Guinevere or Tristan and Iseult, are tales of adultery — of a terrible conflict between love of a lady and loyalty to the lord to whom she is married. Thus in the crisis of feudal loyalty, courtly love sustained the traditional virtues of devotion and courage, and added to them more refined qualities such as "courtesy," humility, and a willingness to protect the weak and helpless. But it was also a code of adulterous love, mythicizing a rebellion against social obligations. Love was both virtue and sin; while it ennobled, it also led to betrayal, and ultimately to tragedy and death. This duality of the courtly love, its fusion of moral striving and social rebellion, has deeply influenced our own love mythology.

Although courtly love provides the basic ingredients of our view of love, in courtly love these elements still lack their modern shape. Only in the eighteenth century did the emerging middle class, influenced by Protestant conceptions of individual destiny and faced with the dilemmas of social life in a market economy, reappropriate the aristocratic love myth, using it to formulate a new relationship between individual identity and social life and a new conception of the shape of the adult life course. Now the power of love would sustain and glorify the individual's attempt to forge his identity, to know himself, and to find his place in the social world.

The novel was the new literary form whose emergence in eighteenth-century England marked the triumph of a bourgeois conception of love and a new interpretation of society and the self. This literary evidence is important because the mythic themes of the novel still dominate popular culture, and because the basic structure of the novel — its description of life as a plot, with a beginning, middle, and end, linked by comprehensive unity of character and action — is such a perfect embodiment of our culture's view of the adult life course.

In *The Rise of the Novel,* Ian Watt (1957) argues that the novel's characteristic themes, structure, and formal properties reflected the needs of an emerging middle class — involved in market exchange, individualized, and anxious in a new way about achieving success. To crystallize the novel as a literary form (in contrast to loosely organized prose narratives such as the rogue biographies or dramatic genres with fewer claims to "realism"), a satisfactory ending was required — an ending that could believably bring dramatic closure to the lives of ordinary individuals. The event that could serve as a resolution for complex problems of character and action in a realistic social setting was marriage. As a symbolic turning point in the lives of individuals, marriage fused together important themes in middle-class life with the formal needs of the novel.

Especially for the women who predominated among the early novel-reading public, marriage concentrated into one critical event all the questions about livelihood, mobility, and achievement that were becoming critical for the middle class. The increasing separation of work and home in the seventeenth and eighteenth centuries denied women their traditional role in the domestic economy and made middle-class women who did not marry — the "maiden aunts" and "spinster" daughters or sisters — dependent on the charity of others. Women had to marry, and whom they married was the major determinant of their life chances. So Samuel Richardson's Pamela, the virtuous maidservant who became wife of the master, was the epitome of female success. Marriage, linking questions of class, mobility, and money to the most intimate aspects of private experience, could symbolize the new middle-class concern with individual merit and achievement (Watt, 1957, pp. 144-151). The Protestant view of the self as having a single, unified inner essence decisive for the individual's fate was, in the love myth, linked to a single moment in the adult life course when a person could find out who she (or he) was, and what her fate was to be.

But themes of love and marriage in the bourgeois novel (as opposed to the courtly depiction of adulterous love) also tied the problems of inner experience, the search for the "true self," to the quest for one's proper place in the social world. The innovation of the novel, when it placed love, money, and marriage at the center of its dramatic structure, was to link the quest for personal and social identity. The courtly theme of love as rebellion against social life was retained, but now the individual rebelled to assert his identity against society and to carve out a unique place in the social world. In our love mythology, love conquers all. Identity is symbolized through choosing whom to love and remaining true to one's choice against all opposition. The love relationship that defies convention, family, or class barriers asserts the autonomy of the individual.

While love in the novel's mythology can motivate individuals to assert their will against society, it also allows them to find their true selves, to measure their own worth, and to achieve just reward for their real merits. The novel's concern with market exchange is exemplified by Robinson Crusoe, whose greatest joy was building up his fortune through exchange, but also by Pamela, who surrendered her virtue only in return for marriage (Watt, 1957, pp. 60-70). Although the "virtue rewarded" theme of *Pamela* was banished to the realm of bad literature almost as soon as it was invented, its underlying assumption that love will reveal and reward true merit is deeply imbedded in our culture's view of love.

The concern with fair exchange and just rewards is linked, finally, to what is perhaps our culture's most profound assumption about love — that love can both transform and reveal character. Love gives the power to see through surface appearances, so that the lover recognizes the true value of the beloved. But love is also a moral test in which one discovers his own true worth. Thus in the perfectly balanced novels of Jane Austen, recognition of self and other coincide: by loving, the heroine reveals her own character, which only her lover has been able to see, and her mature virtue develops as she recognizes his true merit. Because the two lovers have become worthy by loving each other, in marriage each receives a fair exchange. The love myth has it that, in a world where people are often profoundly alone, love can break through the superficial and penetrate to the true self — so that in loving one can know and be known by another person, and in doing so come to know oneself.

Love also motivates character development and marks major turning points in the development of the self. Clarissa, another Richardson heroine, succeeds through her death in transforming and redeeming Lovelace, her seducer. Even when the changes wrought by love are not "good" in the moral sense, or when the choice of a lover is not good in a practical sense (Adam Bede's choice of Hetty; Anna Karenina's love for Vronsky), the powerful heat of emotion engendered by love can, nonetheless, temper and forge character into stronger and better stuff.

AMERICAN CULTURE AS A FRAMEWORK FOR ADULTHOOD

The way adulthood is experienced is shaped by the way a culture organizes and frames adult life. In Western culture love has played a central symbolic role in integrating the issues of individual identity, moral choice, and social commitment. Courtly tradition made love a moral matter, ennobling and disciplining the self; bourgeois culture made love a central symbol of the individual quest for identity, integrity, and fulfillment.

In the traditional love myth, individuals rebelled against society (family, convention, tradition), but in loving they simultaneously sought new commitments and found their own place in the social world. The search for love and the search for a way to deal with society were inextricably linked. But American culture dealt differently with the symbolism of adulthood. What does the love myth tell us about the attitude of our culture toward adulthood, toward the nexus of individual identity with social commitment? How is this attitude changing? By examining the peculiar form the love myth has taken in American culture, and exploring contemporary changes in the ideology of love, we will see how adulthood itself is changing. In doing so we will better understand whether our culture can infuse the tasks of adulthood — the achievement of fidelity, love, care, and wisdom — with richness and meaning.

The traditional American attitude toward adulthood has been one of fear, and along with this fear has gone great uncertainty about love. The power of the love myth has always come from its ability to bind together contradictory elements — ennobling passion and adulterous betrayal in courtly love; individual rebellion and social commitment in bourgeois romantic love. These conflicting images embody the tension between individual and social demands, and the love myth promises their resolution. But in America the relation between the individual and society has been particularly problematic, and thus the attitude toward love peculiarly ambivalent.

While the traditional love myth has always had a strong place in American popular culture, particularly in "women's literature" (romantic novels, women's magazine fiction, and Gothic romances), Leslie Fiedler (1966) noted some time ago that the greatest American novels, from *The Last of the Mohicans, Huckleberry Finn,* and *Moby Dick* to the modern novels of Faulkner or Nathaniel West, avoid passionate love as a central theme, their male heroes seeking self-definition against nature or Gothic terror and seeking intimacy in the companionship of other men. In the American myth, women and love represent the entangling bonds of social obligation, and the only real self-definition comes from a Faustian quest to face inner and outer evil alone (Fiedler, 1966). Even in popular culture, our traditional heroes are the cowboy and the private eye, men pursuing their own self-created image of freedom and justice outside the corrupting ties of social life (Cawelti, 1976).[3]

Americans have also been criticized, by themselves and others, for a sort of premature closing-off of the self. Kenneth Keniston (1968) has written of an adolescence in which inner conflict is submerged in conformity to the peer group and an adult identity achieved by reluctant submission to the demands of work and marriage. The irony of American identity formation, as Erikson (1963, p. 286) has written, is that it "seems to support an individual's ego identity as long as he can preserve a certain element of deliberate tentativeness of autonomous choice. The individual must be able to convince himself that the next step is up to him and that no matter where he is staying or going he always has the choice of leaving or turning in the opposite direction if he chooses to do." In fantasy Americans remain perpetual adolescents, while adult commitments represent the defeat rather than the fulfillment of the quest for identity. People are "trapped" into marriage;[4] work is a loss of freedom, a shameful "settling down."

Americans have, perhaps, a more passionately developed sense of individuality and selfhood than members of most other cultures, but this individuality remains forever locked in a sort of childish wish not to become adult, a cultural rejection of adulthood itself. The love myth has always had a place in American culture, but a degraded one. While it promised individuality, integrity, and independence, these were compromised by the danger of a confining, settled adulthood. What American culture could not do was to make the achievement of adult commitment, fidelity, intimacy, and care themselves seem heroic, meaningful achievements. In the current period the love myth is undergoing a change. The historic oppositions which traditionally gave the love myth its emotional appeal and cultural dynamism are being intensified, while the balance of elements in the myth is shifting. These changes have important consequences for the definition and meaning of adulthood.

The emerging love ethic reemphasizes the rebellious, free, individualistic side of the love myth. In some ways the values of permanence and commitment have been undermined even further, while the adolescent-fantasy core of American culture has strengthened its hold. On the other hand, the emerging love ideology, because it endorses flexibility and eschews permanence, also sees love more as a continuing process than as a once-and-for-all culmination of life, after which people need only live happily ever after. The central elements of the love myth remain; people still seek moral self-definition, fulfilling intimacy, and a meaningful identity. But the framework of expectations about what it means to achieve these things, and thus the cultural definition of adulthood itself, is changing.

Changes in the cultural meaning of love are grounded on the one hand in changing definitions of the self (and thus implicitly of adulthood as a whole) and on the other hand in changing social-structural demands on the life course. There are four distinguishable oppositions within our culture's love mythology, tensions which have given the myth its richness, its seeming power to reconcile divergent needs and opposing parts of the self. Each of these four oppositions links the lives of individuals to aspects of the social world and thus to specific changes in contemporary society. The tension between choice and commitment embodies the problem of moral self-definition and the achievement of identity. Choice of a marriage partner and its implication of permanent commitment have provided the structural foundation of this aspect of the love myth. The second important symbolic tension in the love myth is that between rebellion against social obligation versus attachment to the social world, particularly the world of work. The third opposition is that between self-realization and self-sacrifice. Love traditionally promised self-realization, yet required self-sacrifice, especially when love led to children and the full burdens of family life. Finally, libidinal expression through love is in tension with the libidinal restraint required by the traditional norm of fidelity and the related problem of the sources and grounds of intimacy.

CHOICE VERSUS COMMITMENT

The tension between choice and commitment involves the problem of identity. If identity is something that must be won only once, if the self is a stable achievement, remaining constant despite superficial flux, then the choice that symbolically consolidates identity forecloses further possibilities of or needs for choice. But when the fixity of the self cannot be taken for granted, the tensions implicit in the love myth's treatment of choice and commitment become more apparent.

The love myth describes the attempt to define one's self by the free choice of a love partner, fusing the problem of the search for one's true self with the quest for one's right mate. The correlate of such self-definition is identity and, in Erikson's terms, fidelity. Faithfulness to one's choice becomes faithfulness to one's self. The capacity to make a commitment and stick to it is the measure of successful identity formation. Yet the traditional model of choice and commitment implies a relatively static notion of both love and identity. While a process of liberating personal growth culminates in choice of the "right" partner, the choice consolidates that growth while prohibiting further change. One chooses only once, after which commitment closes off alternative choices and alternative identities.

Here we can see a profound shift in the ideology of love — an attempt to preserve its ennobling moral quality and its power of defining identity, while giving up the ideal of commitment which was traditionally the hallmark of both moral achievement and secure identity. Modern moral ideals for the self, in particular the emphasis on self-actualization and the demand for continuing growth and change in adulthood, clash head on with the traditional ideal of love as commitment.

New ideologies of love attempt to preserve the heroic myth of the struggle for identity by giving it a new content. The discovery of self and other through love, the culminating moment of the traditional love myth, is absorbed into a new ideal of continuing mutual revelation. "Struggle" becomes a sign of virtue in a relationship, and loving comes to mean facing one crisis after another in which two autonomous, growing people work to deepen communication, to understand each other, and to rediscover themselves. Here the whole valence of the love myth is changed. And these changes affect our moral perceptions, fantasies, and intuitive feelings about what is a meaningful, satisfying, or profound love relationship. Even the terms of evaluation change. Whereas once we might have spoken of "true love" or of a love one would die for (or die without), now "deep," "meaningful," or "alive" seem more appropriate terms for praising a love relationship. Even where the new ideology seems most flat and without conviction we can see disconnected threads of an emerging mythology of love, not yet woven into a unified fabric. We can also follow the strands of such developing ideologies, listen to the changing language in which ideals of love and selfhood are expressed, and think about what they imply for the course of adulthood in the contemporary period.

The search for self-knowledge and identity is still central, but that search can no longer be defined by a single decisive choice, a struggle against external obstacles to assert the self against the world. Now the obstacles to love are internal to the self and to the relationship (as, for example, in Ingmar Bergman's "Scenes from a Marriage"), and one can love most fully by deepening the honesty and communication in a relationship, even if the relationship ends as a consequence. True love is not a love to which one is committed, so much as a love in which one can have complete communication. And communication is difficult; it requires heroic struggle with the self and the lover. By the same token, a love relationship that does not require painful change no longer performs its function. The value of love, and its challenge, is that it must stimulate and absorb perpetual change.

New images of love do not reject the core elements of the traditional love myth — that love is a moral achievement, capable of defining and transforming the self. But what the self is, and how it is to be defined and enshrined, is differently conceived. Ralph Turner (1976) has argued that there are two fundamentally opposed ways of viewing the self, which he calls "institution" and "impulse." People who locate the "true self" institutionally define themselves by acts of choice and will, in the institutionalized roles to which they commit themselves. People who define their real selves by impulse see as true only what wells up outside institutional roles. "The outburst or desire is recognized — fearfully or enthusiastically — as an indication that the real self is breaking through a deceptive crust of institutional behavior. Institutional motivations are external, artificial constraints and superimpositions that bridle manifestations of the real self" (pp. 991-992). What the traditional ideal of love accomplished was to fuse these two conceptions of self together into one overriding achievement. One could follow his deepest impulses to find his true self, and imbed that self in an institutional commitment. Will and desire could merge in the achievement of identity. In the shifting structure of the love myth, the impulsive sides of the self are given greater emphasis, and the ideal of permanence is undermined. What is good about a relationship is not the commitment it embodies, but how much a person learns about himself from the relationship. Love is not the emblem of a crystallized identity but the mandate for continuing self-exploration.

In the traditional view, a love that ended was a failure, a sign of some terrible mistake in the search for self and identity. But the new love imagery can claim great gains from failed relationships. Each person can grow and learn, even from loss and disappointment. Indeed permanence, which was the hallmark of success in the earlier model of identity formation, becomes almost a sign of failure. After all, is it likely that one can keep growing and changing with the same partner? Doesn't permanence in a relationship necessarily require some compromise of individual possibilities for growth? And even for those who value permanent commitment, its meaning is changed. Enduring relationships mean a deeper challenge and even more profound opportunities for growth than do short-term relationships. So both those who value long-term and short-term relationships increasingly justify relationships by the opportunities they offer for challenge and change. The greatest sin a lover can commit is not betrayal, renegging on a commitment, but obstruction, trying to thwart, hamper, or limit another's freedom to grow.

In recent films — "Annie Hall" and "Scenes from a Marriage," for example — we are asked to feel that the relationship between two lovers must end because staying in the relationship would mean stagnation, while the end of the relationship forces valuable if painful growth. These films also converge in the view that in some ways one can really love — that is, understand, appreciate, communicate with another — only after a love relationship is over, freeing love from the stifling obligations of day-to-day contact. Another easily idealized love relationship is that of *Love Story* or "Harold and Maude," where the loved one gives the hero strength and helps him grow toward a new joy in living, and then, conveniently, dies, so there is no possibility of constraining further growth. A modified version of this new pattern is the found-lost-found relationship among adults where, by leaving each other, two people discover new possibilities, new facets of themselves, new strengths and vulnerabilities, and then come together again to rebuild their relationship on new terms. This story, in *The War between the Tates*, for example, allows incorporation of the new image of love as a perpetual quest for self and identity without completely abandoning the older ideal of a love that lasts a lifetime.

While the new mythology of love and the new ideal of the self have been criticized as examples of the "new narcissism" (Lasch, 1976), the new ideology is also a shift in the direction of adulthood. In keeping alive the image of love as a crucible for identity, but making the quest for identity and the quest for love continuing preoccupations, the emerging love mythology validates adulthood as a period of continuing crisis, challenge, and change. It rejects the notion that life's dilemmas are resolved at one crucial moment of choice and commitment, after which one must only live happily ever after.

Both Robert Lifton (1971) and Kenneth Keniston (1968) have argued that modern society changes the nature of identity, making it more flexible, less fixed, and less permanent than traditional models of personal development allowed. What we see in the contemporary culture of love is an attempt to give moral content, added meaning, to this new model of development. By drawing on the rich symbolic resources of the Western love mythology, contemporary culture redefines the morally significant elements of love, focuses attention on new frontiers of the quest for identity (communication and understanding rather than permanence and commitment), and enshrines a new image of the self. While in some ways it means abandonment of central aspects of the love myth in our culture, it also opens up new possibilities for exploring the meanings of adult life. By reappropriating elements of the love ideology, it offers the possibility of new cultural grounding for the adult life course.

REBELLION VERSUS ATTACHMENT

Love justifies rebellion against family and society; it legitimates the rejection of social demands. In searching for his own destiny, for his own place in the social world, a person "marries for love" — rejecting the claims of family, defying the prejudices of class. Yet love, like religion, has a profoundly dual aspect. It creates an alternative in contrast to "this world," and it justifies conformity to the world and its demands. In the bourgeois tradition, love leads to marriage, and thereby to social attachment and obligation.

One of the great justifications for conformity to the world of work, for acceptance of social limitations, for "settling down" and "toeing the line" is love. Women are told that washing socks, cooking, and cleaning are morally fulfilling because they express love. Men feel that going off to work every day is meaningful because it supports the wives and children they love. Love elevates and transforms the mundane activities of life, but in doing so it also binds people to that life.

The issue of rebellion versus attachment is linked sociologically to the world of work. While the traditional ideology of love justified rebellion against social constraint, it was rebellion in behalf of a sense of meaning which, ultimately, had to be confirmed by the social world. The love myth was concerned with whether individuals could force from the social world recognition of their true selves and of their real worth. Pamela was successful: her virtue was rewarded with a social position equal to her true merits. But even in tragic love stories, love symbolizes the ability of the individual to struggle against the social world, to confront it on even terms. The significance of rebellion is found only in dialectical tension with the aspiration for meaningful social attachment.

As social attachment comes to seem either dangerous or destructive, love loses some of its appeal. Diana Trilling (1964) has noted that in "good" contemporary literature both love and society itself (that is, money, work, class, or concrete social settings) have all but disappeared. "If we think of Hemingway as the last writer to give us love stories, we realize that he was also the last significant novelist to engage in anything like an equal dialogue with society; we begin to realize that where there is no dialogue between society and the individual there can be very little dialogue between individuals" (pp. 61-62). Society becomes, in Trilling's terms, "a giant implacable power" able to overwhelm and destroy the individual. In place of the individual's struggle with society is an obsession with the isolated self, in which self-exploration replaces social purpose, and "proper awareness of self is equated with social morality" (p. 60). Here the hero is the madcap loner, careening along in a disordered social world. The only escape from society is to turn inward into madness or outward in frenzied, hopeless rebellion.

While the theme of a world of men freed of the entangling demands of women has always had great appeal in American culture, there is nonetheless a remarkable change in both high and popular treatments of rebellion and attachment in recent years. In the traditional romantic myth, even in America, the hero, however much of an individualist, might finally settle down if only he found a girl whose individualism of spirit matched his own. In cowboy movies, for example, though the hero had to fight alone, he could ultimately join society, perhaps marrying the town's schoolteacher. Even when the cowboy hero rode off into the sunset alone, he went with the gratitude and acceptance of society (Wright, 1975). But since the 1960s cowboy movies have shifted from the "classical plot," where the hero used his uniqueness to be accepted by society, to the "professional plot," in which a group of heroes remain outside a corrupt and undesirable society. Whether the heroes live or die, they do it together. The only people they respect are the "bad guys" who are also professionals, with their own skills and code of loyalty. The heroes do not wish to enter society, and they do not do so. Finding a place in society is not at issue (Wright, 1975). In this transformed myth, love also becomes possible again. Since the heroes are building a new society and are totally rejecting conventional society, a woman who joins the "outlaws" can be as much a part of the rebellion as men can (Wright, 1975).

But in "higher" culture the scenario is not quite so optimistic. Here heroes refuse to join society, but they cannot quite escape it either. Indeed, even the hero of Vonnegut's *Slaughterhouse Five* escapes his sordid earth life only to find himself a caged pet of beings from another planet. In *One Flew over the Cuckoo's Nest,* while the hero creates a band of buddies who defy the head nurse (now the paradigm of the overwhelming, repressive, female social force), their triumph is ambiguous. The men recover their masculinity and their will to resist, but the hero is destroyed as a person, though his spirit lives on. And in high culture—the novels of Saul Bellow or Thomas Pynchon, for example—unstrung heroes, with no social attachment anywhere, twist and turn through a world which has disintegrated around them. Madness makes the world incomprehensible and real contact with anyone in it impossible. Society, and the world of love and of women, has become positively sinister—a senseless, overpowering juggernaut. The individual must defy society, but he can never hope to overcome it.

Thus contemporary culture has undermined the romance of rebellion, while it has also made attachment inconceivable. But why has this desolate picture of the possibilities for individual expression come into vogue in contemporary fiction? Why is there now such a terror of forces which can bind or strangle the individual? The implicit claim, found in Trilling and other critics of contemporary culture (Lasch, 1976), is that the death of love in modern literature and the rise of narcissism in contemporary culture reflect the power of modern society to overwhelm the isolated individual. Yet I am not at all convinced that modern work or modern institutions allow fewer possibilities for individual expression, freedom, or achievement than did those of a few generations ago. Our literature speaks of the victory of implacable social power. But I think there are other reasons why individuals resist the social commitment that can be expressed in work, and extend this attitude back into a rejection of confining love relationships.

In the modern economy, those occupations with the greatest prestige and interest are also those which require the greatest readiness for continuing change. Innovation in the economy requires flexibility in elite workers; an occupation in which one can "settle down" is an occupation which represents a "dead end." Only the person who is always ready with a new idea, who can move from one organization or role to another, can succeed.[5] We therefore find a new tentativeness about the meaning of work. Finding one's "right place" in the social world—one of the core meanings of the love myth—now becomes a contradiction in terms. The right place is inevitably wrong, a chimera. The only right solution is to have a set of ideas and talents, completely contained within the self, perpetually renewed, continually shifting into original patterns. One's self is one's only resource, but that self cannot look for "proof" of its worth, either in a fixed calling or in a single love relationship. This emphasis on keeping one's options open weakens the mythic appeal of a rebellious struggle to mold a social destiny. Rebellion is still essential, but not in the service of a new social attachment. Keeping one's inner self vibrant and flexible means remaining in a state of perpetual rebellion, rather than using the capacity to rebel, which the imagery of love contains, in the service of finding one's right place in social life.

In this renegotiation of the balance between rebellion and attachment, the meaning of adulthood changes. The need to be continually ready for new demands creates a wary avoidance of entanglement in love and work, an eagerness to keep the self free and unconstrained. This means that adulthood provides no resting place from demands on the self, and perhaps this is why the demanding society and the demanding lover are such ominous forces in contemporary fiction. Yet the fear of binding attachments which may constrain the self is not necessarily a rejection of adulthood so much as a redefinition of it, and a redirection of emotional and moral energy toward new challenges.

These new challenges create a new relationship between work and love in adulthood. Smelser argues that there is an increasing separation between instrumental and affective realms in modern life, between work and love. At the cultural level there does seem to be a growing rejection of the romantic myth that love both transcends and resolves problems of career and livelihood. The worldly young today believe that finding someone to love is no solution to life's difficulties; you still have to decide who you are and what you want to do. And they also see that work commitments may compete with emotional attachments; two conflicting career trajectories, for example, may destroy a relationship. When people follow their own destinies, they may be driven apart.

But in other ways contemporary culture fuses together rather than separates the issues of work and love. Instead of two separate questions — one of internal identity and the other of social destiny — which must be resolved together, both problems become the same problem, that of the restless self. One pattern in the contemporary popular view of love turns love itself into a kind of work. For some people in modern society the continual negotiation and renegotiation of personal relationships becomes the major sphere of accomplishment in daily life. People take on "struggle" in their relationships with a vengeance, "working at" their relationships, putting in the effort to "make them work." Rather than symbolize social commitments through love, they substitute personal relationships for social commitments. There grows up a new moralism in personal relationships — not the old concern with personal virtue but a new passion for honesty, fairness, equality, and communication. Sometimes the intensity of concern with the self-conscious negotiation of terms, rights, and responsibilities in relationships makes their activities sound like those of a workshop or a battlefield rather than a domestic circle.

Work and love also converge in a second pattern marked by fear of emotional engagement and by the effort to create relationships that demand nothing, threaten nothing, and commit nothing of the self (Hendin, 1975). The self is vulnerable, and its integrity must be protected by clear understanding — no expectations, no strings, no demands for involvement. Relationships are required to have an explicit constitution in which nothing is left to chance, no tentacles of unrecognized attachment can reach out to strangle, no illegitimate expectations can develop. This self-protective openness makes the relationship serious business, but it denies the irrationality and dependence that were part of the traditional myth of commitment, in which one bound oneself to another without bargaining for specific terms (Cagle, 1975). Contemporary ideology, with its serious attention to the work of loving, also reflects a fear of dependency, an assertion that people are bound only to what they have agreed to. Good lovers, like good workers, cannot afford unlimited attachments. They may stay on, but only if the terms are right, if the job or the relationship permits them continued development.

If neither rebellion against nor attachment to the social world can adequately define the self, if work on the self has become the essential and most gratifying form of work (expanding one's capital in an era when the self is one's major capital), then love takes on a new and more somber set of meanings. While it may still appear occasionally as the stimulus to a great rebellion ("The Graduate" or *Love Story*), that fantasy seems to have run aground. There is nowhere for rebellion to go without again becoming binding attachment. Hence the pessimism of much contemporary fiction in which the plot seems to die for want of a satisfactory ending. There is no decisive event which can resolve life's difficulties. However, there is also a new respect for the seriousness and significance of living as an ongoing, day-to-day challenge. The crucial question might be seen as how to give life meaning, how to live it with richness and depth, without requiring that the present be given significance by binding the future. While one aspect of this change in ideology is simply an escape from strong feeling or deep involvement which might threaten individual autonomy, there is also a new attention to adult experience, to making it gratifying, stimulating, and meaningful in its own terms.

SELF-REALIZATION VERSUS SELF-SACRIFICE

How much to give and what one will be allowed to take, the balance between satisfaction and sacrifice, has been a continuing theme in stories of love. In the traditional mythology the lover seeks his own happiness, fights for his own gratification, and yet the highest form of love is selfless giving. In the traditional imagery of love, the ecstasy of possessing another merges with the altruistic wish to sacrifice oneself for the other's well-being.

As long as we believe that a person can fulfill himself only through love of another, the tension between self-realization and self-sacrifice is minimized. One realizes himself *through* self-sacrifice. But with changes in the kinds of self-definition people expect from love goes a change in the norms and language of love. While these shifts may sound like simple cloaks for self-indulgence, they contain deeper meanings. The obligation to sacrifice oneself for another is replaced by the duty to respect the other person's separateness, to recognize the other's needs for growth and change, to give to the other in return for what one receives.

Marcia Millman (1972), in a study of experimental small groups, has written of two contrasting sets of metaphors with which group relationships are described, which she calls "exchange" and "tragic-mythic." Exchange imagery describes what people "get out of a relationship," how much they will "take" from one another, who will "dump" what onto the group. Tragic-mythic imagery, on the other hand, imbeds the relationship in a dramatic structure: "The group member who uses 'tragic-mythic' imagery frequently describes his relationships in the group in terms of his search for identity, of recalling certain things from his past and rediscovering himself, and of his downfall in the group. He is concerned with the issues of free will and destiny, and his attention is on action. He understands the other characters in terms of their origins and culminations, and he views his present relationships as the reenactment of old stories" (p. 9). The traditional love myth is a "tragic-mythic" organization of self and experience, in which life can be given meaning by its "culmination," the climax of the novel's (or of life's) story. The emerging cultural view of love, on the other hand, emphasizes exchange. What is valuable about a relationship is "what one gets out of it." One values what one can learn from another person, what one can take away from the experience. One is valued in turn for what he gives in exchange. Rather than a relationship standing as the culmination of a drama of self-discovery, the partners in a relationship remain autonomous and separate, each concerned about what he will have gained, what he will take away, when the relationship is over.

Exchange metaphors, indeed, imply impermanence. In a successful exchange each person is enhanced so that each is more complete, more autonomous, and more self-aware than before. Rather than becoming part of a whole, a couple, whose meaning is complete only when both are together, each person becomes stronger; each gains the skills he was without and, thus strengthened, is more "whole." If we enter love relationships to complete the missing sides of ourselves, then in some sense when the exchange is successful, we have learned to get along without the capacities the other person had supplied.

Exchange metaphors and the ideal of the autonomous individual are closely linked. We can see the image in changing ideals of male-female relations, for example, where the demand is for two people who can each be "whole people" with a balance of instrumental and affective capacities, rather than two people who are each specialized halves of a couple but inadequate as individual human beings. This imagery is used explicitly by Philip Slater (1970), and it underlies much of the rhetoric of the women's movement. The moral ideal is the person who is complete in himself or herself, who is able to stand alone, whether or not she chooses to do so.

The hidden message in modern treatments of love is, then, not self-sacrifice but self-development. A good relationship is one in which one has learned something and can leave it a stronger or better person. Most profoundly, the emphasis in love stories is on survival, on a person's need to be reassured that he can endure any loss, can get along without anyone. So in one of the most popular love stories of our recent history, *Love Story*, the essential drama was not that Oliver and Jenny won each other, but rather that Jenny gave Oliver a great lesson in survival. She helped him learn to love and to forgive his parents and to win greater control over himself before she died, leaving him unencumbered yet strong. In a similar way, the theme of movies such as "Alice Doesn't Live Here Anymore" or "An Unmarried Woman" is that people can learn to survive alone, and indeed to prefer their hard-won autonomy to renewed ties of dependence.

This anxiety about the wholeness and integrity of the self also shows up as a new concern with self-realization and a denunciation of self-sacrifice. Of course in social-structural terms, the most significant sacrifice to which one can be committed by loving is the sacrifice one makes for one's children. While one marries for love, for the fulfillment of one's own needs, marrying commits one to a life of serving others — one's spouse and especially one's children.

But in contemporary literature even the sacrifice of parents for their children has been brought into question. Several modern novels portray a conflict between sacrifice for anyone else, including children, and the necessary attention to the imperiled self. Novelists can now portray children as predators or enemies who demand without giving, who threaten the necessary self-nurture of their parents. Recent women's literature, of course, takes up this theme, though in most feminist literature the husband-lover is the enemy who robs women of the energy they need for themselves. But in novels such as *The War between the Tates* children are portrayed as sullen strangers, and in Joseph Heller's *Something Happened*, the demanding child is an enemy to be outsmarted, the retarded child a symbol of hopelessness, and the bright, good child an emblem of the father's guilt.

Self-sacrifice, which once seemed the ultimate proof of love, now seems suspect. For people to try to realize themselves through the sacrifices they make for others comes to seem not nobility but parasitism. We fear clinging wives and smothering mothers and we condemn the man or woman who cannot stand up for his or her own needs. The drama in many modern love stories is whether people will be able to resist the temptations of love and surrender in order to perform the more difficult task of finding themselves.

This cultural legitimation of "selfishness" is in many ways a claim on behalf of adulthood. We no longer believe that an adult's life can be meaningfully defined by the sacrifice he or she makes for spouse or children. Current ideologies of child rearing emphasize that parents have rights also, that it is not enough to use up each adult life in nurturing the lives that come after it. Adulthood is viewed as a period with its own tasks and demands. Just as husbands and wives cannot submerge their own needs in those of their partners, so adults cannot sacrifice themselves completely to their children.

We can cite demographic changes that have intensified the problem of how to live as an adult, particularly for women: the reduced period of child rearing and the prolonged period of the "empty nest" when parental roles no longer define the meaning of a couple's relationship; widowhood and divorce which force women, and men as well, to face the question of what to make of their own lives; and delayed marriage which allows adults to be more fully formed before they undertake marriage at all. But accompanying these demographic challenges to old models of adulthood are new cultural values—a new concern with the survival, wholeness, and autonomy of the self that makes self-sacrifice seem weakness, and self-realization seem a moral duty. In this context the very meaning of love changes. In the attempt to legitimate a concern with adult life on its own terms, our culture also holds up a model of human relatedness that makes the sufficiently complete self a precondition for relations with others. Other people can be only a stimulus to our own growth and development, not a source of the meaning of our lives. We are mistrustful of those who seek to find themselves through love, rather than loving from a position of strength, fully in possession of themselves.

LIBIDINAL EXPRESSION VERSUS RESTRAINT

In the traditional love myth the tension between sexual expression and restraint worked to intensify and strengthen commitment. Love offered the fulfillment of libidinal aspirations, but the ideals of virginity before marriage and fidelity afterward demanded sexual restraint. Sexuality sealed the intimacy of lovers; sexual restraint made their bond exclusive and inviolable.

But there is another layer of significance in the symbolism of sexual restraint. Watt points out that Clarissa's defense of her virtue was ultimately a defense of the integrity of the self; "she proves that no individual and no institution can destroy the inner inviolability of the human personality" (Watt, 1957, p. 225). The integrity of the self is demonstrated by its capacity for unified devotion, for fidelity. Just as there is one right choice in marriage, there is one right self which, when correctly bestowed, can remain true forever. This faith in the wholeness and unity of the self gave special depth and resonance to the experience of intimacy.

In the contemporary period the ideal of sexual restraint has weakened, and the possibilities for sexual expression have been broadened. The ideology of individual development has entered the sexual sphere, condemning relationships that limit individual growth or possibilities for exploring new experiences. In this view jealousy is bad, a possessive attempt to own another person and limit that person's freedom to grow. Sexual restraints are rejected as artificial restrictions on experience, and sexual experimentation is valued because it opens the self to new experiences.

Michael McCall (1966) and Randall Collins (1971) have each provided social-structural explanations of these shifts in sexual ethics. Both see a crucial change in the social functions of marriage. McCall argues that as marriages no longer cement broader alliances between families, as women are less dependent economically on marriage, and as marriages become less stable, the older pattern of courtship bargaining no longer makes sense. Now women and men bargain about the terms of an ongoing relationship, rather than maneuvering to make the best possible marriage. There is no single decisive event that is worth "saving oneself" for; and current pleasures become more important than either future rewards or past commitments. Collins draws a similar link between the traditional morality of sexual restraint and courtship bargaining. However, he emphasizes the conflicting interests of women and men and the role of sex in the battle between them. For women in a market economy, sexual restraint can be used to force men into marriage. Then women, having enforced chastity on each other to improve their collective position in marriage bargaining, can use their increased power (further enhanced by restraints on violent domination by men and the female monopoly of intimacy and emotional support in the household) to extend "sexual property norms" to men (Collins, 1971, pp. 13-14). In the "advanced market economy," with the spread of female employment, "the greater freedom of women from economic dependence on men means that sexual bargains can be less concerned with marriage; dating can go on as a form of short-run bargaining, in which both men and women trade on their own attractiveness or capacity to entertain in return for sexual favors and/or being entertained" (p.17).

While on a cultural level these structural shifts undermine the unique significance of the marriage tie, in another sense they are part of an attempt to deepen the adult experience of love. As with most of the other issues we have examined here, the resolution of the tension between sexual expression and restraint has traditionally been designed to heighten the initial experience of discovery, choice, and commitment in love, while giving scant attention to the further development of a love relationship. Launching people into commitment was more important than sustaining a continuing capacity for intimacy. Indeed, part of what is reflected in the changed attitude toward sexual expression is a changed understanding of intimacy.

While on the one hand the new ideology encourages a shallow, exploitative approach to human relationships, it can also encourage couples to be more attentive to the gratifications each derives from the relationship. Both men and women make conscious attempts to enhance the enjoyment of their adult sexual lives. While all of this is often criticized as having become a burdensome obsession rather than a source of pleasure, it is once again clear that the needs of adult life are being given greater attention. Sexuality must do more than motivate people to form relationships; it must also sustain satisfaction and closeness within those relationships. Traditionally in American culture adulthood has meant a renunciation of the aspirations of youth, so that sexuality belongs to the young and is abandoned in adulthood. The new "clinical" approach to sexual fulfillment, which seems so lacking in romance, may be seen as an attempt to keep sexual experience gratifying for people who are not in the first blush of romantic involvement.

Here again, structural change and shifting cultural preoccupations are linked. Postponement of marriage, effective contraception, and female independence, which may be seen as the social bases for the "sexual revolution," also give young people enough sexual experience so that sex is no longer an elusive prize and becomes a normal human experience that may be enjoyed, but also improved. This demythologization of sex does not 'mean the loss of social and moral meaning. If sexual restraint symbolized preservation of the integrity and moral definition of the self, sexual experience has come to symbolize the expansion and fulfillment of the self—the continuing capacity to grow, learn, and appreciate experience.[6]

But sexuality has also been a symbol of intimacy, and sexual exclusivity was a seal of emotional bondedness. In some ways the new ideology, by legitimating a continuing attention to libidinal needs, encourages a deepening of intimacy and mutuality, both sexual and emotional. On the other hand, by undermining the norm of fidelity, the new ethics may also undermine the trust and continuity necessary for real intimacy. But at least these are genuinely adult dilemmas. To want more from adult life may also be to take greater risks.

In Western culture the experience of love is imbedded in a matrix of moral ideas which have given shape, definition, and meaning to the individual life course. Rich in ritual, myth, and symbols, love has provided an element of broader meaning at the core of the life experience. But the love myth contains tensions between opposing elements, oppositions that account in part for the depth and resonance of the myth. By arousing contradictory impulses, by fusing together divergent aspects of individual experience, love acquires great power as an experience and as a symbolic consolidation of life.

Choice versus commitment, rebellion versus attachment, self-realization versus self-sacrifice, and libidinal expression versus restraint — these are contradictions not in the sense that they present people with irreconcilable alternatives in their practical life arrangements, but in the sense that they permeate the cultural meaning of love with contradictory expectations. The great power of the love myth is that it promises to resolve those contradictions, to fulfill both sides of the duality at once: Love provides the opportunity for profound choice, the choice of a life-long commitment; love sanctions rebellion against social ties in the service of attaching oneself to society; love inspires self-realization through sacrifice of oneself for another; and love intensifies and deepens sexual expression by channeling it through sexual restraint. These paradoxical promises are not accidents or cultural "mistakes" — quite the opposite. The reason love can provide a crucible for identity formation, a symbol of achievement of a place in the social world, a capacity for dedication to something outside oneself, and a potent consolidation of one's deepest emotional urges is precisely because it can embody these dual meanings.

But in American culture the balance of these tensions has been unequal, and hence their power diminished, because of the central importance Americans give to individuality and the low value they place on social connectedness. While the romantic myth has upheld the ideals of attachment, commitment, and intimacy, it has been on the defensive against the culture's dominant individualism. Abandoned on the whole by high culture, the love myth was weakened, so that the "conservative" set of meanings it embodied — love as commitment, acceptance of social attachment, self-sacrifice, and libidinal restraint — predominated, no longer complemented by the sense of passionate choice and rebellious assertion of identity that gave depth and power to the English and European forms of the love myth. All women were mothers, not mistresses or lovers, and all love implied being trapped into congealed domesticity.

In the contemporary period, complex changes are occurring in our love ideology, with important implications for adulthood. The traditional oppositions in the love myth fused together aspirations of youth and adulthood; the myth sanctioned youthful rebellion in the service of finding adult commitments. But in this fusion one moment was given moral meaning — the moment of transition from youth to adulthood. The power of the myth came from glorifying and intensifying the period when identity was crystallized, attachment discovered, aspirations for fulfillment realized, and intimacy achieved. But this left the "adult" sides of the love myth without sustaining meaning. Identity, commitment, self-realization, and intimacy, once achieved, were simply supposed to last a lifetime. Moral meaning lay in being able to stick to what one had chosen, to continue to be animated by the commitments one had made. But in the contemporary period, the valence of the love myth is shifting—in ways which often seem regressive. These "youthful" aspirations for rebellion, choice, self-realization, and sexual expression are being idealized all over again. That is, our culture now seeks moral significance in acts of choice, in attempts to discover, clarify, or deepen the self, whether or not these choices lead to or remain within a commitment. The ideology of love is being partially reworked, so that elements of the love myth—that love transforms, that love allows one to know his true self, that love is a crucible for self-development—are being incorporated into a new structure.

The fate of these shifts in cultural emphasis is still obscure. What is clear, however, is that our culture's view of adulthood is changing. What once seemed a secure if difficult accomplishment, a once-and-for-all achievement, has come to seem much less secure. Pressures for flexibility in adult love and work have cut loose the anchors for many of the old definitions of successful, meaningful, morally integrated adulthood. It is hard for us to find metaphors to express the meaning of love that is not forever and work that is not a lifetime commitment. Much of our cultural response to the uncertainties of modern adulthood has been a kind of empty despair in high culture, abandoning hope for meaning, and in popular culture a shallow and somewhat hysterical emphasis on protecting a childish version of the self.

But there are also signs of hope. As moral emphasis shifts from life-long commitments to a lifetime of choices, there is the possibility of rejoining the fractured elements of the love myth, but on new terms. An identity developed through continuing choice may be a fuller and richer achievement than a single, climactic consolidation of the self. Social attachments may also be more gratifying and less terrifying if they do not mean stifling closure in work or love, but can continue to embody a rebellious streak, a search for new constellations in the relationship of self to the social world. Intimacy can certainly be deeper if there is openness to continuing mutual exploration. A commitment to another person may go beyond loyalty, to an understanding of shared responsibility for the quality of a continuing relationship. And even self-sacrifice, or the possibility of generative giving to others, can perhaps be made richer if it is matched by recognition of one's own incompleteness, one's own capacities for continuing growth and change.

In some ways the most crucial shift in our culture is a change in the symbolic and moral grounding of the self in modern society. If the self can no longer find definition in a single set of adult commitments, a set of roles which consolidate identity, what can the self be? If it must be defined, as seems implicit in the modern culture of love, by its ability to resist attachment, by its ability to go through changes without being fundamentally changed, then we have an ideal of the self cut off from meaningful connection to others, from any danger of commitment, attachment, sacrifice, or self-restraint. This is a model of human relationships in which people are not willing to take the risks of disappointment and defeat that inevitably accompany meaningful love or work.

And yet, there is strength in the recognition that "the capacity to love and to work" is not a one-time accomplishment that settles the adult life course once and for all. Further risks, further choices, further efforts are demanded, and further opportunities for self-knowledge, intimacy, and joy await us. In the past our love ideology has dealt largely with the problems of becoming an adult, as if after the adult course was set there was nothing left to worry about — people did not have to keep living together after they won each other, work did not continue to be problematic after one had settled on an identity. Now we have a cultural attempt to deal with adulthood, to develop a set of myths and images that can give moral meaning and purpose to a life that has no fixed end, no dramatic conclusion. In some ways the reaction to this challenge seems to be a culture of narcissism, in which the self and its perpetuation become all, in which the trick is to remain alive and whole without risking attachments or making binding choices. But the other side of these cultural explorations is a search for models of self and models of love that are compatible with continuing growth and change, that permeate with moral significance the ups and downs of daily life, the struggle to live well, rather than giving moral meaning only to the dramatic moment of the shift from youth to adulthood.

Notes

For helpful comments, I would like to thank Fred Block, Patricia Bourne, Claude Fischer, Arlie Hochschild, Anne Peplau, Theda Skocpol, and the editors of this volume. I would also like to thank Melvin M. Webber and the Institute of Urban and Regional Development, University of California, Berkeley, for support during the later phases of the preparation of this paper.

1. Geertz (1965, p. 8) has said that religious symbols provide "models of" and "models for" reality. "Culture patterns . . . give meaning, i.e., ob-

jective conceptual form, to social and psychological reality both by shaping themselves to it and by shaping it to themselves." While for many people in modern society religious symbols and rituals have lost their vividness and their direct applicability to daily life, love is still an experience to which people give themselves, and which allows at least a partial experience of transcendence. Like religious experience, culturally grounded experiences of love do not dominate every moment of daily life. As Geertz (1968, p. 110) says, "The key to the question of how religion shapes social behavior, is that much of religion's practical effect, like much of dreaming's, comes in terms of a kind of pale, remembered reflection of religious experience proper, in the midst of everyday life." It is in part through moments of heightened experience and its "pale, remembered reflection" in everyday life that our culture's myths about love shape the experience of adulthood.

2. C. S. Lewis (1958, pp. 3-4) writes: "It seems to us natural that love should be the commonest theme of serious imaginative literature: but a glance at classical antiquity or at the Dark Ages at once shows us that what we took for 'nature' is really a special state of affairs, which will probably have an end, and which certainly had a beginning in eleventh-century Provence . . . [The French poets] effected a change which has left no corner of our ethics, our imagination, or our daily life untouched, and they erected impassable barriers between us and the classical past or the Oriental present. Compared with this revolution, the Renaissance is a mere ripple on the surface of literature."

3. While the mythic structure of American culture is not the exclusive property of either sex, the love myth is, at least symbolically, differently shaped for men and women. In women's literature the happy ending is still marriage, and love still allows people to find themselves as they find each other. High culture, on the whole, is dominated by men and by the male version of the myth, in which the man escapes both women and society in his lonely quest for selfhood. Of course there can be Faustian heroes who are women (Hester Prynne in *The Scarlet Letter*) and men can fight for love and commitment. But in general, the polarization of the sexes around the different sides of the love myth, while it accounts in large part for the tone of aggressive warfare in America's cultural treatment of the "battle of the sexes" (from Blondie and Dagwood or Little Abner and Daisy Mae to the head nurse in *One Flew over the Cuckoo's Nest*, women tie men down, curtailing their quest for freedom and self-definition), both men and women are caught by the conflict about social commitment expressed in America's treatment of love.

· 4. Lillian Rubin (1976) and Mirra Komarovsky (1962) have both pointed out how unwillingly many working-class men claim to marry. A high proportion of marriages are precipitated by a pregnancy, so that both men and women marry without having fully chosen to do so. The only way to develop social commitments is to be "trapped." This pattern corresponds to the fantasy Martha Wolfenstein and Nathan Leites (1950) found in their study of American movies. Men and women are thrown together on a train, or forced together by some accident, so that their involvement occurs in spite of, not because of, their wishes in the matter.

5. The argument that the economy requires autonomy and flexibility in elite workers has been around for some time. It can be found in Bennis and Slater, 1968; Berkeley, 1971; Hirschhorn, 1976; and Sarason, 1977, as well as implicitly in those who examine various aspects of "post-industrial" society and politics (Bell, 1973; Inglehart, 1977). There is, so far as I know, little hard evidence of the link between technologically advanced employment and personal flexibility, though see Kohn, 1971. For a negative argument, see Braverman, 1974.

6. For an analysis of sexual fulfillment as a central image of moral transcendence in contemporary novels (those of Irving Wallace, Harold Robbins, or Jacqueline Susann, for example), see John Cawelti (1976, pp. 280-295).

References

BELL, DANIEL. 1973. *The coming of post-industrial society: a venture in social forecasting*. New York: Basic Books.

BENNIS, WARREN G., AND PHILIP E. SLATER. 1968. *The temporary society*. New York: Harper and Row.

BERKELEY, GEORGE E. 1971. *The administrative revolution: notes on the passing of organization man*. Englewood Cliffs, N.J.: Prentice-Hall.

BLOCH, MARC. 1964. *Feudal society*, tr. L. A. Manyon. Chicago: University of Chicago Press.

BLOCH, R. HOWARD. 1977. *Medieval French literature and law*. Berkeley: University of California Press.

BLOCK, FRED, AND LARRY HIRSCHHORN. 1979. New productive forces and the contradictions of contemporary capitalism: a post-industrial perspective. *Theory and Society*, 7:363-395.

BRAVERMAN, HARRY. 1974. *Labor and monopoly capital*. New York: Monthly Review Press.

CAGLE, LAURENCE T. 1975. Exchange and romantic love norms. Paper presented at the Annual Meeting of the American Sociological Association, San Francisco (August).

CAWELTI, JOHN G. 1976. *Adventure, mystery, and romance*. Chicago: University of Chicago Press.

COLLINS, RANDALL. 1971. A conflict theory of sexual stratification. *Social Problems*, 19:3-21.

DE ROUGEMONT, DENIS. 1956. *Love in the western world*. New York: Pantheon.

ERIKSON, ERIK H. 1963. *Childhood and society*, 2nd ed. New York: Norton.

FIEDLER, LESLIE. 1966. *Love and death in the American novel*, rev. ed. New York: Stein and Day.

GEERTZ, CLIFFORD. 1968. *Islam observed: religious development in Morocco and Indonesia*. New Haven: Yale University Press.

————. 1965. Religion as a cultural system. In *Anthropological approaches to the study of religion,* ed. Michael Banton. New York: Praeger.

HENDIN, HERBERT. 1975. *The age of sensation.* New York: McGraw-Hill.

INGLEHART, RONALD. 1977. *The silent revolution.* Princeton: Princeton University Press.

KENISTON, KENNETH. 1968. *Young radicals: notes on committed youth.* New York: Harcourt, Brace and World.

KOHN, MELVIN. 1971. Bureaucratic man: a portrait and an interpretation. *American Sociological Review,* 36:461-474.

KOMAROVSKY, MIRRA. 1962. *Blue-collar marriage.* New York: Random House.

LASCH, CHRISTOPHER. 1976. The narcissist society. *New York Review of Books,* 23 (Sept. 30):5-13

LEWIS, C.S. 1958. *The allegory of love: a study in medieval tradition.* New York: Oxford University Press.

LIFTON, ROBERT JAY. 1971. Protean man. In *History and human survival.* New York: Random House.

MCCALL, MICHAEL M. 1966. Courtship as social exchange: some historical comparisons. In *Kinship and family organization,* ed. Bernard Farber. New York: Wiley.

MILLMAN, MARCIA. 1972. Tragedy and exchange: metaphoric understandings of interpersonal relationships. Ph.d. diss.: Brandeis University.

RUBIN, LILLIAN B. 1976. *Worlds of pain: life in the working-class family.* New York: Basic Books.

SARASON, SEYMOUR. 1977. *Work, aging and social change.* New York: Free Press.

SLATER, PHILIP. 1970. *The pursuit of loneliness: American culture at the breaking point.* Boston: Beacon Press.

STEPHENS, WILLIAM N., ed. 1968. *Reflections on marriage.* New York: Thomas Y. Crowell.

TRILLING, DIANA. 1964. The image of women in contemporary literature. In *The woman in America,* ed. Robert Jay Lifton. Boston: Beacon Press.

TURNER, RALPH H. 1976. The real self: from institution to impulse. *American Journal of Sociology,* 81:989-1016.

WATT, IAN. 1957. *The rise of the novel.* Berkeley: University of California Press.

WOLFENSTEIN, MARTHA, AND NATHAN LEITES. 1950. *Movies: a psychological study.* New York: Free Press.

WRIGHT, WILL. 1975. *Sixguns and society: a structural study of the western.* Berkeley: University of California Press.

PART THREE

The Sociocultural Patterning of Adult Life

SEVEN

Adulthood as Transcendence of Age and Sex

JANET ZOLLINGER GIELE

IN EVERYONE'S LIFE there are some things that cannot be changed. Two classic examples have been age and sex. Each person is born at a certain time and every year grows older. At birth the individual is labeled male or female and lives out the rest of life accordingly. It is true that some latitude within the traditional age and sex boundaries was always available to those with special physical characteristics or behavioral traits. But generally speaking, the attributes associated with age and sex have been judged relatively immutable when contrasted with characteristics that presumably everyone could attain if given the requisite educational or social opportunity.

Today, however, the unchangeable and irreversible nature of both age and sex is open to question. Academic research on aging, as well as popular writings on midlife, picture new possibilities for adult development. Revolutionary changes in sex roles open uncharted worlds to women that were formerly reserved for men, and in the near future parallel frontiers will open to males. These transformations in familiar assumptions about age and sex are signs of a symbolic shift in representations of adulthood. Rather than emphasize immutability in fundamental attributes, our culture now envisions crossover in traditionally distinct roles: adults are expected to combine the plasticity of youth with the wisdom of age; to be healthy, they should also express both masculine and feminine sides of the self. This chapter will examine these developments to demonstrate that an underlying dynamic, rather than mere coincidence, is responsible for the simultaneous redefinition of age and sex. Out of the process has emerged a new concept of adulthood.

THE CROSSOVER MOTIF

The sex role revolution of the last decade is instructive because it reveals a process that now seems to be occurring in age roles as well. The change is essentially one that replaces a concept of segregation with a concept of crossover (Giele, 1971; 1978).

In sex roles, crossover increases the domain of shared consciousness between men and women. Not only do they have more common goals in life, but they also behave more flexibly and in less sex-typed fashion. For such change to take place, certain structural changes must occur in the larger society. Segregation between male and female worlds must break down and tasks of both men and women become more interchangeable. The changes result first from differentiation and specialization of tasks within each sex role. A job such as cooking is divided into several different operations, some of which can be done by the woman who originally did the whole job, but other parts of which can as easily be done by a husband or children who can turn on the oven and follow the directions.

The division or differentiation of such tasks then produces two related results. First, some persons who were formerly not thought qualified (males or children) are now seen as perfectly capable of performing the task once thought to be woman's alone. Second, the very fact of this change has an effect on the consciousness of all the people involved: they become aware that certain attributes they formerly believed intrinsically necessary to performance of the job, such as being a woman, are not in fact so, at least not for certain parts of the operation. As a result, the original sex-typed role, which was segmentally related to others around it, is now seen as an integral made up of several parts, some of which can be interchangeably performed by persons of another sex or status. Thus develops a sense of shared capacities and qualities in persons and roles once felt to be quite different from each other. The upshot is that crossover becomes possible in performance of many activities that before were confined to the domain of only one age or sex.

The crossover theme can now be discerned in new writings on adulthood and aging. The differentiation aspect of crossover is evident in numerous theoretical efforts to delineate precise stages of adult development. The integration aspect of crossover appears in competing theories which emphasize the essential similarity of developmental tasks regardless of chronological age or stage of life. From the ensuing dialogue a new shared consciousness about the goals of adulthood is taking shape. Concern for living life to the full and achieving integrity of the self are recognized as central tasks for all age groups, whether young or old or middle-aged.

THE REFINEMENT OF STAGES

The historian John Demos (1978) tells us that people in colonial America hardly spoke of adulthood as such, much less of any stages between youth and old age. Instead the important periods of life were roughly divided between childhood, manhood, and old age, and by far the greatest attention went to the first and last of these, leaving the duties and characteristics of the middle period to be taken almost for granted.

Since 1950 in America there has been a crescendo of research on psychological changes in the individual after age twenty. By now generations of college students have memorized the eight stages of life that Erik Erikson (1950) described in *Childhood and Society.* They have studied the tortuous process of maturation that occurs during "youth" (Keniston, 1965; Cottle, 1972; Friedenberg, 1965). As they enter their own adult years they can read about late adulthood and old age (Neugarten, 1968; Neugarten and Hagestad, 1976). Or they can turn to highly detailed accounts of middle-aged persons in the descriptions of Levinson (1977), Gould (1978), or Vaillant (1977). The enormous success of Gail Sheehy's book, *Passages* (1976), is probably a significant indicator of growing popular interest in a topic expressed in Sheehy's subtitle, *Predictable Crises of Adult Life.* By naming and attempting to codify the abstract characteristics of adult life, Sheehy and her predecessors perhaps have helped to create a new life stage. Like G. Stanley Hall who in 1904 invented the term "adolescence" (Kett, 1977), modern scholars and journalists have shaped a new consciousness of adult development and "the middle years" (Neugarten and Hagestad, 1976; Jordan, 1976).

The question of why adulthood is now so much the focus of popular interest is partly answered by historical demography. At the time of the Renaissance, changing definitions of childhood were principally affected by declining infant mortality (Aries, 1962). In the redefinition of adulthood today the virtual elimination of all major deadly epidemics and plagues is perhaps a key factor. Age-specific death rates show that since the late nineteenth century death has become much more narrowly concentrated in older age groups rather than striking indiscriminately persons of all ages in years of major epidemics (Keyfitz and Plieger, 1968). Thus contemporary Americans frequently do not experience death of close relatives until that of their own parents when they themselves are in middle age. Both Levinson and Sheehy speak of the midlife person's special consciousness of death and their own mortality, but the reason for the phenomenon may be as much demographic as developmental.

Middle age became a salient time of life not only as a result of demographic changes but also as a result of changes in work and family life. Demos (1977) suggests that decrease in physical activity in all jobs probably now contributes to lack of physical fitness in middle-aged persons. Furthermore, concentration of childbearing in the early years of marriage has the inevitable effect of associating the empty nest and sex role transcendence with the middle years. These forces taken together help to identify the middle years as a distinct phase of life that never before stood out as so distinctly from either young adulthood on the one hand or late adulthood on the other.

While this demographic and historical explanation accounts for the appearance of a special midlife stage in our time, there are still other phenomenological questions left unanswered. Why, for example, has the discovery of the middle years been accompanied by a progressive refinement in the tasks and perception of stages in adult life, an event parallel to greater specification of periods in infancy, latency, and adolescence that accompanied the reconceptualization of childhood? Why also are the stages of adulthood paradoxically bound together by an emphasis on independence, identity, integrity, and wholeness that is in some ways similar to the theme of acquiring competence that links the phases of childhood?

Today a number of observers and theorists have distinguished several distinct phases within the adult state. In his formulation of the eight stages of man, Erik Erikson (1950; 1968) assigned the last four stages to the adult period. Youth, a period of transition to young adulthood, is a time of concern for identity versus identity confusion. During the subsequent period young adults grapple with intimacy versus isolation. The middle-aged person is preoccupied with generativity versus stagnation. And finally in old age persons achieve integrity or confront despair.

Other schemes resemble Erikson's model. As a result of his research on males in midlife, Daniel Levinson delineates several "eras" in the individual's evolution of a life structure such as early, middle, and late adulthood (Levinson, 1977). Particularly refined observations on early and middle adulthood come from Roger Gould (1972). In his scheme, persons confront different aspects of their own arbitrary internal beliefs and inhibitions and gradually learn to question them. By age fifty most people will have shed all illusion of absolute safety given by rigid internal beliefs that came from childhood. They will then be freer than before to act as truly autonomous individuals.

Other schemes of individual growth and adult development

exist in the work of Jane Loevinger (1966), Robert Lifton (1976), Carl Jung (1968), Jean Piaget (1972), and Lawrence Kohlberg (1969). All stage models share two distinctive features. First, they imagine the life span as divided into discrete phases associated with specific developmental tasks. Second, they suppose a time order in the sequence of tasks that is roughly associated with age. Because of these assumptions, stage theories have come under criticism by investigators and theorists alike who focus on other aspects of reality.

In contrast with some stage theorists, psychoanalyst Marianne Eckardt (1977), for example, proposes that the fundamental conflicts of life are between being dead or alive and bored or dead. And these issues seem to her "age-independent"; that is, they can occur at any time of life. Moreover, if the person has been stagnating rather than successfully resolving earlier crises, there is no reason why that person cannot, through exposure to stimulating experience, wake up and experience growth and new life. Such a formulation asserts that the developmental issues at any age of life are fundamentally the same. It also implicitly questions both major assumptions of stage theories—that the developmental tasks of each phase are special (differentiated), and that they occur in an orderly, age-related sequence.

Similar challenges to stage theory are raised by observers who have made comparisons between the adult experience of different sociological groups. Leonard Pearlin, for example, finds that developmental issues vary immensely according to a person's socioeconomic location in the society (see Chapter 8). Likewise Marjorie Fiske, in research on "ordinary Americans" of the lower-middle class and middle class, finds no evidence to support stage theory (see Chapter 11; Lowenthal, 1977). Instead, over five-year periods she finds that people's hierarchies of commitment vary widely and in no particular order. The shifts appear to be occasioned by changes in everyday circumstances at home and at work.

Rather than claim that either the stage theorists or their critics better represent the truth, I suggest that both groups describe different aspects of the same phenomenon. Thus stage theory represents a way of symbolizing increasingly complex learning tasks in the socialization process itself. Stages suggest differentiated developmental steps and related learning tasks. On the other hand, the negation of stages is not surprising if the observer's focus is on the unity of the individual or the complexity of social reality. An individual must integrate many discrete experiences in a distinctive style that has continuity over time. Moreover, differences *between* individuals can seem much larger than any similarity based on age that they exhibit.

These two opposite themes — distinct stages of development versus ambiguity and no clear pattern — possibly represent two universal processes that occur in any living system: differentiation and integration. Within the individual, learning may be analogous to processes of differentiation, whereas achievement of identity, integrity, and wholeness may correspond to integration.

This differentiation/integration formula may illuminate current efforts to describe and ritualize the midlife drama. The differentiation process explains efforts to divide developmental tasks into narrow and specific learning tasks. The integrative process accounts for observations that developmental tasks are frequently taken up "out of order" (because crossover between learning tasks can occur at any point in adult life). And observations that the tasks seem no different from one stage to another but always deal with the problem of being alive or dead, unified or fragmented, reflect the shared consciousness that has been found across the ages and stages of adult life.

Among those theorists who discuss differentiation of developmental tasks, there are two recurring themes. One is the complexity of the world to which persons are exposed. The other is the autonomy and freedom that the person can and must achieve to deal with this world. Implicitly in Erikson's scheme the epigenetic unfolding of personality is correlated with exposure to a social environment that is ever more complex, with more role alternatives available, more aspects of the self to cultivate. Such exposure brings about possibility for fragmentation of the self (identity confusion) or individuation without relationship and growth (isolation, stagnation, despair). But the desirable outcome is autonomy of the individual within a context of relatedness.

The autonomy theme also appears in the work of others. In *The Wish to Be Free* Weinstein and Platt (1969) suggest that any exposure to a more complex and differentiated social environment will require of the individual a developed sense of autonomy, self-direction, and freedom. Much of Gould's developmental scheme on the middle years is also concerned with the individual's attempts to free the self from arbitrary internal restraints (see Chapter 10). Analyzing the effects of work on personality, Melvin Kohn shows that those people exposed to a job with high substantive complexity experience an increase in intellectual flexibility and capacity for independent judgment (Kohn and Schooler, 1973). On the other hand, people in dull and boring jobs can actually suffer some decline in intellectual capacity.

Depiction of integration in adult development calls on a somewhat different language. Rather than autonomy in the midst of complexity, it dwells on oneness in the self and unity with others. Identity and integrity imply the wholeness, the undividedness of the self. Interdependence and harmony refer to the integration of self with others. Erikson uses the terms intimacy and generativity. Yet this capacity for interdependence may be under assault in our society. For as Ann Swidler (Chapter 6) notes in her examination of contemporary film and fiction, there appears to be an attempt on the part of many to be all-sufficient unto the self without close and binding ties to others, without the obligations of loyalty and sacrifice.

It is finally, however, in the dialectic between differentiation and integration that the larger organization of life is formed. Klaus Riegel terms the process "dialogical" and conceives of love itself as a dialectic (Riegel, 1973; 1977). According to Eckardt, there are three interacting vital dimensions: "our individual uniqueness," "our social essence," and "the organizing elements of our lives." It is the last that ties together the other two (Eckardt, 1977). Yet how are the organizing structures of our lives attained? By a dialogue between self and other, between individuation and integration. The dialectic is suggested by Erikson's "versus" connecting such polarities as intimacy and isolation.

Stages also describe different structures of cognitive and moral development that result from the dialectic. As Lawrence Kohlberg (1969) puts the matter, "Stage notions are essentially ideal-typological constructs designed to represent different psychological organizations at varying points in development" (p. 372). However, in the popular mind, "stage" is also understood somewhat differently—as an indication of the different *content* of problems that one takes up at different points in life, problems of the empty nest, topping out in a career, facing death, and so on. Part of what the psychological and sociological critics of stage theory are saying is that problems concerning content of life are not necessarily related to age. But they are also saying that even the *form* of psychological organization for dealing with those problems does not seem reliably linked to age. Is their claim valid in light of the double necessity of differentiation and integration to produce more complex psychic and social structures?

THE NEW ADULT IDEAL:
AN EVER-EVOLVING BUT UNIFIED SELF

Skeptics have raised a bewildering array of findings to counter claims that adults attain particular stages of understanding and self-organization in any given sequence (Brim, 1976). Their arguments deserve attention.

Critics of stage theory are probably describing a different part of the differentiation/integration process than the stage theorists. They insist that some developments occur "out of order" and thus point to age crossovers. Critics also make broad statements that all development is a struggle between "being alive" or "being dead" (Eckardt) or "being free" rather than "arbitrarily bound" (Gould). They thus state the developmental ideal at a higher level of generality. Their inclusive terms are associated with the integrative events that surround structural differentiation. Even stage theorists concede that healthy processes can lead the self backward (such as regression in service of ego) or cause it to skip ahead (such as anticipatory socialization). Moreover, stage theorists also imply that the integration of the psyche over time requires continuity in personal goals. Yet, the generality of the integrity ideal can be seen by others as evidence that there are no "stages."

It is logical to expect that there would be crossovers in modern adulthood. Many developmental tasks in adulthood are not age-specific but age-independent. Modern society is so highly differentiated that no coherent synchronized set of role transitions occurs for all people at a given age. Individuals encounter different experiences and negotiate the developmental process in highly individual ways.

The double truth is that modern society both emphasizes age more and at the same time allows more deviation from age-typed categories of behavior. Noting both trends, Bernice Neugarten describes the possibilities for age crossovers (Neugarten and Hagestad, 1976):

> Ours seems to be a society that has become accustomed to 70-year-old students, 30-year-old college presidents, 22-year-old mayors, 35-year-old grandmothers, 50-year-old retirees, 65-year-old fathers of preschoolers, 60-year-olds and 30-year-olds wearing the same clothing styles, and 85-year-old parents caring for 65-year-old offspring. To the extent that the strength of age norms is reflected in the variability around modal patterns, we seem to be moving in the direction of what might be called an age-irrelevant society; and it can be argued that age, like race or sex, is diminishing in importance as a regulator of behavior. (p. 52)

The crossovers are in part an inevitable result of societal complexity. In the words of Peter Blau (1977), "The penetration of differentiation into substructure promotes intergroup relations of all kinds . . . intersecting parameters promote associations among groups and strata" (p. 49). But the matter could as well be put in other terms: that the life course of any generation interacting with history will be unique, or that in a complex society the resources available to each party for exchange will differ. The socialization process, because it is a negotiated outcome, will vary as these resources change (Bengston and Cutler, 1975; Collins, 1975). Expressed in moral and ethical terms, age flexibility becomes the ideal pattern by which persons may strive for wholeness and perfection at the same time that they remain humble and open to learning. Thus Christian precepts have long enjoined persons not only to achieve the "full stature of Christ" but to "be as little children" (Bouwsma, 1976).

The result for the individual adult may be that there is no clear age-connected "season" when certain things are learned. Psychologically, it makes sense to argue that location in the social structure may affect which of the many domains of personal behavior (interpersonal, moral, achievement- or survival-related) are most satisfactorily fulfilled in early adulthood and which will therefore have to be elaborated afterward to maintain equilibrium later on (Lowenthal, 1977). If this is the case, it follows that the time of life for elaborating one or another of these aspects of life will not be the same for everyone.

It is also true that behavior can be modified in a regressive direction as well as in the direction of growth. Thus, for instance, it has been shown that groups treated with arguments from a lower moral stage show significant shifts in the direction of the lower stage just as those exposed to a higher moral stage are likely to move in the more advanced direction (Brown and Herrnstein, 1975). Kohn's research on the effects of work on personality shows that low substantive complexity of a job can cause decline in a person's intellectual flexibility and capacity for independent judgment, just as high substantive complexity can have the opposite effect (see Chapter 9).

Age crossovers must also occur in part because the individual is capable of some self-direction and choice. That is, behavior changes over time not just because of environmental shaping but also because persons interpret their own roles and choose their future locations. Thus there are reciprocal effects between the environment and the person. This dynamic is particularly evident in memories and plans. Yet there seems to be no one formula for shaping either that results in a clear pattern related to age. Similarly, even though a common theme in the study of aging is adaptation to role relinquishment and loss (Riley et al., 1969; Lowenthal, 1977; Rosow, 1976), the opposite theme of growth and development is also familiar.

How can the two themes so easily coexist? Perhaps they mirror the double reality of actual experience. Each individual can reach forward in time, anticipating loss and adjusting to it, while at the same time reaching back to the playful and unformed aspects of the self associated with youth. Daniel Levinson (Chapter 12) conceives the process as a reconciliation between youth and older age that he associates with the healthy resolution of midlife dilemmas. The internalization and interaction of generations occurs within the self so that all of us carry within ourselves aspects of every generation. Thus age crossover occurs not just between older and younger strata of the society but between the age-coded elements of the person's own psyche.

When all is said and done, there are certain general goals and ideals of adulthood that all commentators appear to share. One is growth; another is unification of the self. Together these two threads represent the values or standards against which each person's life can be measured. That even investigators with widely divergent views can share these values is testimony to the fact that within the past two decades the goals of adulthood have been stated in general terms, that is, without insisting on the specific ways by which the standard will be met.

Growth, learning, and the continued evolution of the self have been valued in the Western world for many centuries. William Bouwsma (1976) notes that in the Christian ideal, adulthood requires capacity for indefinite growth and in that sense "is like adolescence, that stage in which the adult seems, however ambiguously, trembling to be born" (p. 81). The ultimate sins are refusal to grow, cessation of growth, arrested development, and that kind of immaturity that puts one's self at the center of the universe. W. D. Jordan in his history of adulthood in America finds that the goal of maturity has been growth and change within each person regardless of age. Henri Bergson's aphorism summarizes the ideal: "To exist is to change; to change is to mature; to mature is to create oneself endlessly" (Jordan, 1976).

Today the social sciences embody the ideal of continued growth in the value they put on cognitive and emotional flexibility. Melvin Kohn's work linking job complexity to intellectual functioning certainly implies that cognitive flexibility and capacity for independent judgment are good and that the person grows in attaining them. In the affective realm, the work of George Pollock on separation and mourning suggests that ability to take up and leave affective attachments in a flexible manner can help the individual cope and at the same time restore his capacity for further development (Pollock, 1975).

Social scientists who study adulthood also celebrate another ideal — the wholeness and integrity of the self. The integrity theme is frequently implicit rather than explicit. For example, in stage theories, when the critical dilemmas of different stages are spelled out, they sound quite similar to each other. The similarity results from the central idea that the individual must constantly, in the face of new experience, attend to the integration of the self. Thus, describing the identity issues for youth, Erikson (1965) defines its essence as "the creation of a sense of sameness, a unity of personality"; Keniston (1965) finds that the task of youth must be to overcome "inner division" and achieve "psychic wholeness." Speaking of middle age, Erikson describes even generativity in terms of the ego. Generativity is a way to cope with "the ability to lose oneself in the meeting of bodies and minds" by expanding "ego interests." Through investment in others the ego grows by accepting an almost parental kind of responsibility. Levinson (1977) speaks of "individuation," beginning at midlife, that "involves a greater freeing of the self from the tyranny of both the tribal demands and the repressed (instinctual) unconscious." In the process the person can deal with and partially overcome "the great polarities which so often produce a splitting in his self and his life" (Erikson, 1950).

In later years the developmental ideal is realized as ego integrity. In Erikson's terms it is a period of emotional integration when the individual, recognizing the relativity and accidental nature of all the various life-styles, "is ready to defend the dignity of his own" against all physical, economic, or cultural threats (1950). Robert Peck (1968) speaks of "ego-differentiation," often experienced in old age or at retirement when persons learn that they have worth beyond their particular role as parents or workers and learn to invest all other activities with a sense of value and involvement.

The two themes of growth and unification thus express the dual nature of adult development. Growth refers to an adaptive process — the differentiation of parts and the new additions that enable the person to respond to changes in the environment and to maturation and aging. Integrity and unity, on the other hand, refer to the pattern-maintaining capacity of the self, the ability to consolidate growth and change to weave the life course together in a continuous piece.

VARIATION BY CLASS AND CULTURE

It seems as though some people experience distinct stages of adult development while others do not. What appears critical is the degree of social complexity that a person encounters on the job or in everyday life. The theory of crossover suggests that persons who confront less change and variety would be less likely to experience development as a refined series of stages. Moreover, their goals for adulthood would remain concrete, specific, and directly tied to competence in familiar roles. However, a person adapting to a greater variety of roles would be likely to experience many small steps of learning and in the process try to evolve an abstract self, conscience, or life structure that would integrate all these discrete events.

Preliminary evidence supports the crossover theory. In other words, persons who are more likely to articulate the need for growth and integration are those who have in fact dealt with a greater degree of specialization and complexity in their daily life. Supporting data come from a variety of studies that examine quality of life in different occupations and social strata.

Aging and adult development appear to be experienced more positively by the advantaged occupational and educational groups, and less so by the materially and educationally deprived. Much of the evidence on class differences in adult feelings of satisfaction and happiness supports this hypothesis. In fact it has often been remarked that stages of adult development have been worked out by psychoanalysts such as Gould and Erikson whose observations were largely derived from a privileged upper-middle class and professional elite. An investigator such as Marjorie Fiske, observing a wider range of lower-middle class or blue-collar people, simply does not see a clear pattern of stages emerging among them (Chapter 11). Some of the reasons for this are clear from Tamara Hareven's (1976) portrayal of working-class adults in the nineteenth century. The nature of work in textile factories eventually consigned middle-aged and older workers to the industrial scrap heap. They began as sweepers and mechanical helpers, then in the peak of their vigor took up the heavy and physically demanding job of tending machines. But when their vitality declined, sweepers they again became.

It is not surprising that if one's job is fairly simple, limited by meager education and narrow contacts, growing old will less likely result in elaboration of mental powers than for a person working in a more complex and intellectually demanding environment. But will it result in any less happiness? Campbell, Converse, and Rodgers, in their recent study, *The Quality of American Life* (1976), found that there were noticeable differences in "happiness" as indicated by answers to the question, "Taking all things together, how would you say things are these days—would you say you are very happy, pretty happy, or not too happy?" For college-educated people, they found that happiness increased with age as did overall life satisfaction with such specifics as housing or income. But there was a marked tendency for happiness to decline with age among the most poorly educated. This was true for the national survey findings collected both in 1957 and in 1971-72. Even though the general trend was for "satisfaction" to increase with age, the reports of happiness were opposite for the poorly educated.

Why would older people's reports of happiness differ so much according to the amount of education they had? Perhaps happiness is an overall summary measure of the personal meaning of life and one's place within it. Such integration may exist largely in the symbolic realm rather than the material realm (especially since older people's reports of satisfaction do not differ so greatly by socioeconomic level). In the symbolic realm, the well-educated would perhaps have greater cognitive resources and perhaps also greater affective flexibility to work out a framework of internal meaning and social networks that would facilitate integration. Such an interpretation would make sense out of what at first seems a counterintuitive finding by the authors of *The Quality of American Life*. They found that many persons with lower education and lower happiness reported high satisfaction in such specific concrete domains as residence, work, or family. The relatively high indices of satisfaction (that on the whole tended to increase with age) were interpreted as a sign of habituation or accommodation to one's actual circumstances. Thus while these persons might accommodate to real circumstances, their hopes might still be unfulfilled and, not having the personal resources and material circumstances to realize them, they might be less successful in achieving that symbolic integration of self-in-the-world that the more educated and "happy" person could attain.

This concreteness of life's goals in the lower socioeconomic groups and the failure to attain a higher, more abstract sense of meaning and of self is a theme running through the work of a number of other observers who have compared middle-class and working-class life patterns. Lillian Rubin (1976) quotes the standard thanksgiving of the working-class wife, "He's a steady worker; he doesn't drink; he doesn't hit me." Rubin comments that:

These are the three attributes working-class women tick off most readily when asked what they value most in their husbands. Not a surprising response when one recalls their familiarity with unemployment, alcoholism, and violence, whether in their own families or in those around them. That this response is class-related is evident from the fact that not one woman in the professional middle-class families mentioned any of these qualities when answering the same question. Although there was no response that was consistently heard from the middle-class wives, they tended to focus on such issues as intimacy, caring, and communication and, while expressed in subtle ways, on the comforts, status, and prestige that their husband's occupation affords.

Commenting on findings from a study of 2,300 working-class and other people in Chicago, Leonard Pearlin (Chapter 8) remarks on the specific life transitions and unexpected crises that confront people. These concrete events dominate their lives more than any abstract life purpose or major life-stage dilemmas. However, the process by which they handle crises is illuminating. The more intense the strains they confront, the more likely they are to be anxious or depressed, regardless of age. But their ability to cope depends on the abstract meaning that they assign to the event. This capacity to cope by interpretation and reintegration may well vary by such characteristics as education.

In a review of major studies of aging in different social classes, Bengston, Kasshau, and Ragan (1977) show that the major decrements normally associated with aging are uniformly experienced later or in much more attenuated fashion by higher than by lower socioeconomic groups. Poor people have poorer health, shorter lives, poorer living arrangements and housing. Their life cycle is quickened: they leave the parental home earlier, marry, have children, empty the nest, and retire at younger ages. Their lives are more locally focused than the middle class, who have more contacts and more involvement in community and volunteer associations. Only in amount of contact with their children are the lower socioeconomic groups somewhat at an advantage.

What do these findings suggest about the nature of adult development as it will be experienced by more and less privileged groups in any modern society? In sum, it appears that those more adept at symbol manipulation (the better-educated) will experience aging as a somewhat happier development than will the less adept. Moreover, the better material circumstances of the higher socioeconomic groups will probably help them come closer to achieving the life goals that they hoped for. Thus a theory of positive developmental stages will probably apply better to the people who both symbolically and materially are able to experience aging as a process of learning and self-integration. These stages will seem less applicable to those who, because of lack of education and material resources, will experience aging as specific decrements and disengagements.

Viewed on a cross-cultural canvas, the same principles appear to explain differences in aging in a simple Polynesian island, an ancient city, traditional and modern Japan, contemporary Kenya, or the United States. In general, the simpler the society, the less differentiated the stages of adult development and the less abstract the developmental goal toward which life is directed. Robert Levy (1977) has drawn this conclusion from his comparison of growing up in a simple Tahitian village and in a complex archaic city, Bhaktapur in Northwest India. Levy finds that adulthood is differently conceived by the two societies. The Tahitians have no memory of having been taught how to walk, talk, eat, urinate; they just learned by beginning to do it themselves one day. The Newars of Bhaktapur, however, remember refined stages of learning, in which some adult made an effort to teach them. The Tahitians have a much less differentiated concept of the learning process reflected in their notions of adulthood — they hardly have a word for it. By contrast, the Newars have a clear set of successive stages that correspond with those of the larger Hindu culture — young manhood, the householder period, the "forest" period, and finally the priestly role. At the same time that the Newars' conception of adulthood is more differentiated, it is also more unified and abstract in its perception of the ultimate developmental goals of adulthood. The Newars speak of conscience and the self, but the Tahitians find it almost impossible to speak of the self other than as a description of a set of concrete activities.

In several societies changing from traditional to modern there seems to be a shift from a traditional set of clearly demarcated age grades to an even more differentiated system of life transitions, and with it, an increasingly abstract idea of life goals. Hiroshi Wagatsuma (1977) has shown that, in Japan since the Second World War, a new concept has appeared — "that for which life is worth living" (*ikagai*). Where before persons passed through a complicated set of age grades and rituals to complete the prescribed life cycle, today these age grades are implicitly called into question. More roles are possible for both women and men and with the new complexity emerges a new question: What is it all good for? Several answers are possible — happy home, healthy body, money, longevity, and house and property. What has gradually emerged in the postwar era is a new emphasis on the happy home, "my-home-ism" (*mai homu shugi*). But this may be an intermediate result that will eventually shift toward an even more ineffable and general search for quality of life and personal well-being much as is found in the United States today.

TRANSCENDENCE WITH AGING

In America recent discussion of the middle years has given rise to a new concept of adulthood. The mature person today is one who keeps alive the energy and adaptability of youth while cultivating the wisdom of age. In similar fashion, the ideal adult also combines and blends both masculine and feminine traits — women becoming more assertive and independent, men tending toward greater nurturance, passivity, dependence, or contemplativeness. Orville Brim (1976) summarizes these themes of adulthood as follows: "The older men are more diffusely sensual, more sensitive to the incidental pleasures and pains, less aggressive, more affiliative, more interested in love than conquest or power, more present- than future-oriented. At the same time, women are aging in the reverse direction, becoming more aggressive, less sentimental, and more domineering. While in the earlier years the husband tends to be dominant, during the aging process he becomes more dependent" (p. 6).

David Gutmann (1977) has made the boldest and most far-reaching attempt to interpret the links between age and sex crossovers in midlife. In a series of anthropological and psychological studies undertaken in the Mayan highlands, among the Navaho, and in the Levant, Gutmann demonstrated a common tendency on the part of older males to abandon the vigorous assertive manner of their young adulthood and gradually take up more passive and contemplative roles. Women, on the other hand, are more likely to become increasingly powerful in domestic affairs as they grow older, abandoning the more dependent and passive ways of their youth. To Gutmann, these patterns seem the result of universal exigencies of human parenthood: Males must provide for and defend the domestic group during the early years of childbearing when women are more vulnerable and specialized in the nurture of the young. Later, as the parental generation ages and gradually gives over property and control to its successors, older males serve the interests of the group by relinquishing their grip on material things and concentrating on the spiritual order. Meanwhile women become the major managers of domestic affairs, often wielding power through their influence over younger men.

Gutmann's theory looks for a universal tendency to sex crossover in later adulthood and therefore emphasizes biological and cultural imperatives associated with human parenting. However, his scheme does not directly explain the current American experience with sex crossovers in adulthood. Its roots appear to lie in the social and demographic changes that accompanied the Industrial Revolution. In the life of the individual, the decline in mortality and the discovery of more efficient contraception resulted in a separation of the biological life cycle from the social life cycle. In social life, the rationalization of production split apart the spheres of work and family life and associated each with certain age grades and sex roles. The consequence has been a division in our consciousness between the themes of work and love, autonomy and caring, that are only now being rejoined within the individual and the larger social fabric.

At the individual level, the separation of the biological and social life cycles has had consequences for sex roles. The socially accepted time for childbearing corresponds ever less closely to the onset of puberty, and menopause at the other end of the fertile period occurs long after the last child has been born. Delay or abstention from parenting and the long empty nest period create transitional periods that traditional age-sex roles no longer easily "handle." New forms of self-integration and new social guidelines are needed that will symbolize these transitions and help the individual to negotiate them in a way that is not just idosyncratic but has some socially shared meaning. Rather than rites of passage that move the person in lockstep fashion from one age-sex grade to the next, what is needed in modern society is a new symbolic statement of the transformations that a person will experience throughout the life course. The new image would depict movement *back and forth* across different functional and hierarchical domains.

The possibility of a different order for men and women in the life course has just begun to surface in scholarly descriptions of adult development. Carol Gilligan (1977) discovered when she studied women and abortion that Kohlberg's autonomy-oriented stages of moral development did not apply. The women were concerned about caring and responsibility for others. They were dealing with multiple, sometimes conflicting obligations and were concerned not to hurt others in the process. By Kohlberg's scoring scheme, such concerns on the part of women had always been judged as being at a "lower" moral stage than the more "autonomous" focus of males. But Gilligan suggests that the implicit values behind the scoring scheme should be called into question rather than the maturity of the women's response. Rather than be judged as merely "conventional," the women's orientation to the needs of others deserves to be considered as fully adult, perhaps even as more advanced than the "autonomous" behavior of the males. For in their awareness of the dilemmas inherent in meeting potentially conflicting needs, the women exhibit a high level of moral development. Recently Erikson (1977) also has put new emphasis on "caring" as the primary task of adulthood. In his discussion of the letters between Freud, Fliess, and Jung, he notes that learning how "to care" and "to take care" are central themes.

In popular consciousness one also sees a new appreciation for the dual capacity to be autonomous and interdependent. In the past men were stereotypically associated with being autonomous and women with being interdependent. Now these are considered to be qualities that the healthy personality of both sexes should have (Barnett and Baruch, 1978). The women's movement encourages women who have traditionally been trained to care for others also to be independent and assertive. And indeed, studies of popular opinion show that women now place greater emphasis on individual achievement and equal rights than was true a decade ago (Mason, Czajka, and Arber, 1976). For males the trend is in the opposite direction. A nascent "men's liberation" movement has developed its own critique of machismo which teaches that males with the best balanced personalities have learned to be sensitive to others, tender, and caring as well as autonomous and assertive (Pleck and Brannon, 1978; Pleck and Sawyer, 1974; J. Pleck, 1977; Bem, 1976).

However, the task of integrating autonomous action with interdependence and caring cannot be accomplished solely at the individual level. Social institutions and cultural assumptions are also involved. The separation of work and family life and sex-role spheres was not simply a result of demographic change in the life cycle. It was also the result of social transformations related to the industrial era. Therefore to reduce the separation of work and love in adult life requires not merely individual but social adjustments. Policy changes that affect the way that economic institutions and the family interact are called for.

Recently economists, historians, and sociologists have been concerned with time allocations among various spheres of human activity. Significantly, their suggestions for policy all point in the same direction — greater opportunity for overlap, interchange, linkages, flexibility, and alliances between the worlds of family and work. Rhona Rapoport, Robert Rapoport, and Ziona Strelitz (1977) summarize the trend: "We can state that the key element in the new directions is that of new alliances: alliances between fathers and mothers; between parents and children; between families and experts; and between families and society" (p. 348; see also E. Pleck, 1976; Kanter, 1977; Kahne, 1978; J. Pleck, 1975; Smelser, 1976).

Flexible hours, maternity leaves, child-care centers, social security for homemakers — all are signs of the effort to rejoin the instrumental and expressive components of life.

Ultimately, as a result of the new metaphors of linkage and crossover, on both the individual and social planes, a new cultural formula for aging is being devised. Along with the increase in differentiation and separation and the resultant emphasis on autonomy, a new motif is emerging based on intermingling, interdependence, and exchange. Crossover is its emblem.

That it is possible to be young and old at the same time, to be both masculine and feminine, is a significant discovery, for it suggests that relatedness between different elements of the personality is possible without regression to an earlier undifferentiated state. Crossover presupposes differentiation and builds on it; it does not presume that the single individual, though autonomous, can be self-sufficient. Instead the very task of learning special skills requires that the individual enter other spheres to achieve wholeness. And the very fact that society is made up of many small, specialized units requires that individuals learn to move back and forth across boundaries between settings. True, this development can be perceived, felt, and interpreted not as a search for completion associated with traditional metaphors of love and integration but, as Swidler (Chapter 6) finds in contemporary novels, a narcissistic attempt at complete self-sufficiency. However, I believe the narcissistic manifestation is merely an intermediate step. It is an extreme expression of the industrial focus on autonomy. Alongside it is found a fuller awareness of what a major newspaper recently termed "the ethic of interdependence and care" (Saikowski, 1976). Witness the recent interest of social scientists in "networks," in "quality of life" and "well-being," the resurgence of popular and political interest in the family, and the renaissance of religion — the contemplative life focused on ultimate values as distinct from the active life focused on the here and now (Bellah, 1976).

Modern society is forced to confront the limits of technology and mastery over nature as a solution to physical shortages. It must accept also the limits of autonomous action as a way of achieving equality and justice. Only by enlarging the terms of social and psychological discourse to include values beyond the self is it likely that modern culture can select those behaviors that will allow it to survive (LeVine, 1973).

The current interest in adulthood is probably adaptive for

modern society. The ideal adult today is capable of autonomous and assertive action as well as contemplative and caring behavior. Both age and sex crossovers have contributed to an articulation of this ideal. The new concern with adulthood combines an interest in growth and individuation with wholeness and integrity. The sex role revolution has developed an image of the well-rounded adult as both masculine and feminine. Both revolutions thus make possible a new degree of transcendence over traditional limitations imposed by age and sex.

Notes

For stimulating many of the questions raised in this paper, I wish to express gratitude to the Social Science Research Council and its Committee on Work and Personality in the Middle Years, of which I was a member from 1975 to 1979. In addition, members and guests of the SSRC Study Group on Women in the Middle Years, which I chaired at Brandeis University during 1977 and 1978, illuminated many of the issues discussed here.

References

ARIES, PHILIPPE. 1962. *Centuries of childhood: a social history of family life.* New York: Knopf.

BARNETT, ROSALIND C., AND GRACE K. BARUCH. 1978. Women in the middle years: a critique of research and theory. *Psychology of Women,* 3:187-197.

BELLAH, ROBERT N. 1976. To kill and survive or to die and become: the active life and the contemplative life as ways of being adult. *Daedalus,* 105:57-76.

BEM, SANDRA L. 1976. Probing the promise of androgyny. In *Beyond sex-role stereotypes: readings toward a psychology of androgyny,* ed. A. G. Kaplan and J. P. Bean. Boston: Little, Brown.

BENGSTON, VERN L., AND NEAL E.CUTLER. 1976. Generations and intergenerational relations: perspectives on age groups and social change. In *Handbook of aging and the social sciences,* ed. R. H. Binstock and E. Shanas. New York:Van Nostrand Reinhold.

BENGSTON, VERN L., PATRICIA L.KASSCHAU, AND PAULINE K.RAGAN. 1977. The impact of social structure on aging individuals. In *Handbook of the psychology of aging,* ed. J. E. Birren and K. W. Schaie. New York: Van Nostrand Reinhold.

BLAU, PETER M. 1977. A macrosociological theory of social structure. *American Journal of Sociology,* 83:26-54.

BOUWSMA, WILLIAM J. 1976. Christian adulthood. *Daedalus,* 105:77-92.

BRIM, ORVILLE G., JR. 1976. Theories of the male mid-life crisis. *The Counseling Psychologist,* 6:2-9.

BROWN, ROGER, AND RICHARD J.HERRNSTEIN. 1975. *Psychology.* Boston: Little, Brown.

CAMPBELL, ANGUS, PHILIP E. CONVERSE, AND WILLARD L. RODGERS. 1976. *The quality of American life.* New York: Russell Sage.

COLLINS, RANDALL. 1975. *Conflict sociology.* New York: Academic Press.

COTTLE, THOMAS J. 1972. *The prospect of youth.* Boston: Little, Brown.

DEMOS, JOHN. 1977. Changing life cycles in American history. Paper presented at the Smithsonian Institution's Sixth International Symposium, June 14-17.

————. 1978. Old age in early New England. In *Turning points: historical and sociological essays on the family,* ed. J. Demos and S. S. Boocock. Chicago: University of Chicago Press.

ECKARDT, MARIANNE. 1977. New challenges for adulthood in our times. Paper presented at the American Academy Conference on Love and Work in Adulthood, Palo Alto, May 6-7.

ERIKSON, ERIK H. 1977. Adulthood and world views. Paper presented at the American Academy Conference on Love and Work in Adulthood, Palo Alto, May 6-7.

————. 1968. Life cycle. In *International encyclopedia of the social sciences,* ed. D. L. Sills. New York: Free Press.

————, 1965. Youth: fidelity and diversity. In *The challenge of youth,* ed. E. H. Erikson. New York: Doubleday Anchor.

————. 1950. *Childhood and society.* New York: Norton.

FRIEDENBERG, EDGAR Z. 1965. *Coming of age in America.* New York: Random House.

GIELE, JANET ZOLLINGER. 1978. *Women and the future: changing sex roles in modern America.* New York: Free Press.

————. 1971. Changes in the modern family: their impact on sex roles. *American Journal of Orthopsychiatry,* 41:757-766.

GILLIGAN, CAROL. 1977. In a different voice: women's conception of self and of morality. *Harvard Educational Review,* 47:481-517.

GOULD, ROGER L. 1978. *Transformations: growth and change in adult life.* New York: Simon and Schuster.

————. 1972. The phases of adult life: a study in developmental psychology. *American Journal of Psychiatry,* 129:521-531.

GUTMANN, DAVID. 1977. The cross cultural perspective: notes toward a comparative psychology of aging. In *Handbook of the psychology of aging,* ed. J. E. Birren and K. W. Schaie. New York: Van Nostrand Reinhold.

HAREVEN, TAMARA K. 1976. The last stage: historical adulthood and old age. *Daedalus,* 105:13-27.

JORDAN, WILLIAM D. 1976. Searching for adulthood in America. *Daedalus,* 105:7-8.

JUNG, CARL G. 1968. *The archetypes and the collective unconscious.* Princeton: Princeton University Press.

KAHNE, HILDA. 1978. Economic research on women and families. *Signs,* 3:652-665.

KANTER, ROSABETH MOSS. 1977. *Work and family in the United States: a critical review and agenda for research and policy.* New York: Russell Sage.

KENISTON, KENNETH. 1965. *The uncommitted: alienated youth in American society.* New York: Harcourt, Brace.

KETT, JOSEPH F. 1977. *Rites of passage: adolescence in America, 1790 to the present.* New York: Basic Books.

KEYFITZ, NATHAN, AND WILHELM PLIEGER. 1968. *World population: an analysis of vital data.* Chicago: University of Chicago Press.

KOHLBERG, LAWRENCE. 1969. Stage and sequence: the cognitive-developmental approach to socialization. In *Handbook of socialization theory and research*, ed. D. A. Goslin. Chicago: Rand McNally.

KOHN, MELVIN L., AND CARMI SCHOOLER. 1973. Occupational experience and psychological functioning: an assessment of reciprocal effects. *American Sociological Review*, 38:97-118.

LEVINE, ROBERT A. 1973. *Culture, behavior, and personality.* Chicago: Aldine.

———. 1969. Culture, personality, and socialization: an evolutionary view. In *Handbook of socialization theory and research*, ed. D. A. Goslin. Chicago: Rand McNally.

LEVINSON, DANIEL J. 1977. Middle adulthood in modern society: a socio-psychological view. In *Social character and social change*, ed. F. DiPenso. Westport, Conn.: Greenwood Press.

LEVY, ROBERT I. 1977. Notes on being adult in different places. Paper presented at the Social Science Research Council Conference on Cultural Phenomenology of Adulthood and Aging, Harvard University, October 13-16.

LIFTON, ROBERT J. 1976. *The life of the self.* New York: Simon and Schuster.

LOEVINGER, JANE. 1966. The meaning and measurement of ego development. *American Psychologist*, 21:195-217.

LOWENTHAL, MARJORIE FISKE. 1977. Toward a socio-psychological theory of change in adulthood and old age. In *Handbook of the psychology of aging*, ed. J. E. Birren and K. W. Schaie. New York: Van Nostrand Reinhold.

MASON, KAREN OPPENHEIM, JOHN L. CZAJKA, AND SARA ARBER. 1976. Change in U. S. women's sex-role attitudes, 1964-1974. *American Sociological Review*, 41:573-596.

NEUGARTEN, BERNICE L. 1977. Personality and aging. In *Handbook of the psychology of aging*, ed. J. E. Birren and K. W. Schaie. New York: Van Nostrand Reinhold.

NEUGARTEN, BERNICE L., ED. 1968. *Middle age and aging.* Chicago: University of Chicago Press.

NEUGARTEN, BERNICE L., AND GUNHILD O. HAGESTAD. 1976. Age and the life course. In *Handbook of aging and the social sciences*, ed. R. H. Binstock and E. Shanas. New York: Van Nostrand Reinhold.

PECK, ROBERT C. 1968. Psychological developments in the second half of life. In *Middle age and aging*, ed. B. L. Neugarten. Chicago: University of Chicago Press.

PIAGET, JEAN. 1972. Intellectual evolution from adolescence to adulthood. *Human Development*, 15:1-12.

PLECK, ELIZABETH. 1976. Two worlds in one: work and family, *Journal of social history*, 10:178-195.

PLECK, JOSEPH H. 1977. Developmental stages in men's lives: how do they differ from women's? Unpub. paper, University of Massachusetts, Center for the Family, Amherst.

———. 1977. The psychology of sex roles: traditional and new views. In *Women and men: changing roles, relationships, and perceptions*, ed. L. A. Cater and A. F. Scott. New York: Praeger.

———. 1975. Work and family roles: from sex-patterned segregation to integration. Paper presented at the annual meetings of the American Sociological Association, San Francisco, August.

PLECK, JOSEPH H., AND ROBERT BRANNON, EDS. 1978. Male roles and the male experience. *Journal of Social Issues, 34, no. 1.*

PLECK, JOSEPH H., AND JACK SAWYER, EDS. 1974. *Men and masculinity.* Englewood Cliffs, N.J.: Prentice Hall.

POLLOCK, GEORGE H. 1975. The mourning process and creative organizational change. Paper presented at the Mid-Winter Meetings of the American Psychoanalytic Association, New York, December 20.

RAPOPORT, RHONA, ROBERT N.RAPOPORT, AND ZIONA STRELITZ. 1977. *Fathers, mothers, and society: towards new alliances.* New York: Basic Books.

RIEGEL, K. F. 1977. Labor and love: some dialectical commentaries. Paper presented at the American Academy Conference on Love and Work in Adulthood, Palo Alto, May 6-7.

———. 1973. Dialectic operations: the final period of cognitive development. *Human Development*, 16:347-370.

RILEY, MATILDA W., ANNE FONER, BETH HESS, AND MARCIA L. TOBY. 1969. Socialization for middle age and old age. In *Handbook of socialization theory and research*, ed. D. A. Goslin. Chicago: Rand McNally.

ROSOW, IRVING. 1976. Status and role change through the life span. In *Handbook of aging and the social sciences*, ed. R. H. Binstock and E. Shanas. New York: Van Nostrand Reinhold.

RUBIN, LILIAN.1976. *Worlds of pain: life in the working-class family.* New York: Basic Books.

SAIKOWSKI, CHARLOTTE. 1976. Regaining America's unity of purpose. *Christian Science Monitor*, April 22, 1976, pp. 16-17.

SHEEHY, GAIL. 1976. *Passages: predictable crises of adult life.* New York: Dutton.

SMELSER, NEIL J. 1976. "Communication" to the participants in the American Academy Conference of Love and Work in Adulthood, Palo Alto, May 6-7, 1977.

VAILLANT, GEORGE E. 1977. *Adaptation to Life.* Boston: Little, Brown.

WAGATSUMA, HIROSHI. 1977. Aspects of life cycle in Japan: past and present. Paper presented at the Social Science Research Council Conference on Cultural Phenomenology of Adulthood and Aging, Harvard University, October 13-16.

WEINSTEIN, FRED, AND GERALD M.PLATT. 1969. *The wish to be free.* Berkeley: University of California Press.

—————————— EIGHT ——————————
Life Strains and Psychological Distress among Adults
—————————— LEONARD I. PEARLIN ——————————

IN RECENT YEARS my colleagues and I have sought to draw out the complex linkages between the social circumstances of adults and the emotional distresses they experience. Although this work is far from being either definitive or complete, it has brought into view a number of general features of the adult portion of life. For example, we see adulthood as a period in which newness is more commonplace than stability. Adulthood is not a quiescent stretch interspersed with occasional change; it is a time in which change is continuous, interspersed with occasional quiescent interludes.

It has become similarly apparent from our work that adults are responsive to life circumstances and to fluctuations in these circumstances. This means, as Bernice Neugarten (1969) has observed, that adulthood is much more than that part of life in which people simply act out feelings and dispositions acquired from childhood experience. Thus, a satisfactory explanation of levels of emotional distress among adults cannot rely only on personality characteristics formed early in life, but must also take into account current experience and on-going change. Furthermore, the results of our work indicate that no single phase of adulthood seems to have a monopoly on change. There may be distinctive constellations of problems that are especially likely to converge at particular periods, such as the transitions of middle age (Levinson, 1977), but people have to confront severe challenges at other times of their lives as well.

Although much of our analysis has emphasized variations in psychological distress, we recognize that there are many ways in which lives can take on new directions. Values, beliefs, ideologies, interactional patterns, interests, and activities—indeed, the entire range of dispositions and behaviors—are subject to modification as one moves across the life span. However, these kinds of changes, which may give the appearance of being removed from and unrelated to distress, often find expression in anxiety and depression, for such feelings represent the emotional summation of important circumstances in the lives of people. In addition, of course, distress is important in its own right. It is an unpleasant condition that can come to dominate our awareness and from which we actively seek relief. Thus emotional distress both signals important life changes that are under way and, at the same time, constitutes a state against which people are likely to launch a barrage of coping responses. In either case, psychological distress is a central element in life changes, though certainly not the sole element.

The search for conditions affecting the emotional states of people necessarily leads to the larger society and its organization. Inevitably, the study of adult development entails more than the study of adults: it must also seek to identify those elements of social structure that are intertwined with and give direction to the lives of people. There are at least three ways in which societies and their organization are implicated in the emotional development of their members. First, they may be the source of the forces that have the capacity to adversely (and beneficially, too) affect the well-being of people. Even stressful situations that appear to stem from the confluence of chance conditions, as in marital conflict, are often traceable to fundamental social arrangements (Pearlin, 1975b). But the most convincing indication of the contributory role of basic social organization is that many stress-provoking circumstances are unequally distributed among people having different social positions and statuses (Pearlin and Lieberman, 1979). The different life strains among the rich and the poor, for example, or among men and women, or among the married and unmarried provide a clue that strains do not result from the chance experience of individuals but that they derive from the locations of people within the broader societal organization. Thus, in studying adult development in general and psychological distress in particular, a foremost task is to determine the difference in vulnerability to stressful circumstances of different groups within the society.

Second, while exposure to stressful circumstances varies with the social characteristics of people, it is also true that identical circumstances may have very different effects on individuals within a group if they occur in different social contexts. For example, retirement may result in chronic depression for the person who is separated from the sole source of activities he loved, but may be the source of elation for another to whom retirement is an escape from dreaded labor. Giving birth can be a blessed event for the mother having her first child, or an event leading to depression for the mother who already has several young children (Pearlin, 1975a). There are many events and circumstances, then, that do not by themselves move people along a particular course of emotional change or development; instead, the consequences of these circumstances are given meaning by the context or situation in which people are embedded at the time.

A third general mode of social influence on adult development is represented in the coping resources people possess. Some of these resources are represented by the informal and formal helping agents to whom one can look for aid. Because the availability of these resources varies for different social groups, people do not necessarily have equal access to important social supports. There are also psychological resources that one draws upon from within oneself, and the distribution of these, too, may follow lines of social demarcation. For example, among the psychological coping resources of adults, self-esteem and mastery are most effective (Pearlin and Schooler, 1978), and the likelihood of having these important elements of personality increases with one's position in the socioeconomic system (Rosenberg and Pearlin, 1978). Status within the broader society, therefore, helps to determine access to crucial coping resources. And these are indeed resources to be prized, for they are instrumental in helping people withstand some of the deleterious effects of severe social and economic hardships.

Thus, societies have a dominant part in influencing individual change and adaptation by being the source of challenges and hardships, by providing the contexts that give meaning to and determine the consequences of these hardships, and by allocating resources — both social and psychological — that help people fend off the harmful emotional distress that may otherwise result. Social organization is both a wellspring of many life strains and, paradoxically, of the resources capable of moderating the negative effects of the strains. I point out these different contributions for two reasons. First, I wish to underscore that adult development does not go on apart from surrounding social circumstances, as though it simply involves the acting out of a preexisting scenario. Second, in calling attention to the different modes of social contributions to adult development, I seek to emphasize that development should not be construed as a single course universally followed by all people. It would perhaps fit reality better if we were to assume that there are many developmental patterns, each shaped and channeled by the confluence of the social characteristics of adults, their standing in the social order, the problematic experiences to which they must adapt, the social contexts and situations in which they are embedded, and the coping resources with which they are equipped. Simply knowing that most adults get married, have children, enter occupational life, and retire does not come close to providing us the information we need to examine properly the processes of adult development.

In our own work we are far from having evaluated all of these considerations as they relate to psychological distress, but we do have information that cuts across some of the issues. For much of this information I shall rely largely on research in which I and several collaborators have been engaged in recent years. For this reason, it would be useful to provide some of the background and perspectives of our work.

The aim of this research, which began several years ago, was to explore the relationships between persistent hardships threaded through daily life and psychological distress. We first conducted unstructured exploratory interviews with about 100 people, asking them to discuss the problems they faced as workers, breadwinners, wives and husbands, fathers and mothers. From these discussions several recurring themes concerning the problems people face in their occupational and family life were identified. Through a series of pre-tests these themes were gradually transformed into standardized questions that, in 1972, were asked in scheduled interviews with a sample of 2,300 people between the ages of eighteen and sixty-five representative of the adult population of the Chicago urban area. The detailed and lengthy enumeration of the problems about which people were queried and the batteries of questions used to measure them are partially reproduced in Pearlin and Schooler (1978). Here I shall provide only a general description.

With regard to the occupational arena, first of all, we assessed the presence and intensity of a range of problems, such as the noxiousness of the work setting (the existence of dirt, dust, noise, or danger); estrangement from and conflicts with both fellow workers and authorities; and various work pressures and overloads. Next, information was gathered indicative of three types of marital problems and conflicts: the lack of reciprocity, or inequalities in give and take between husbands and wives; the failure of one's spouse to fulfill a variety of role expectations, such as affection, sexual partnership, and provider-homemaker duties; and, third, the lack of recognition and acceptance by one's spouse of one's own "real," quintessential self. Finally, in the parental area, the problems about which we inquired concerned children's violations of parents' standards of general conduct; deviations from long-range parental aspirations and goals; failure to accept parental definitions of morality; and lack of consideration or respect for parents. Much of the inquiry, then, sought to evaluate the extent to which the lives of individuals are invaded by a host of conflicts and hardships arising from work and economic life, marriage and child rearing—indeed, from labor and love.

In addition to measures of these relatively persistent role problems, information was gathered regarding a large array of devices people employ to cope with the problems. As in the case of the role problems, coping behavior was first identified in the early, unstructured interviews; questions were then systematically developed and standardized for use in the sample survey. Still another body of questions was intended to provide measures of various manifestations of psychological distress. For this purpose we employed scales that had been developed from presenting symptoms of patients diagnosed as suffering from such emotional ailments as anxiety and depression (Derogatis et al., 1971; Lipman et al., 1969).

Overall, then, the range of information gathered by the research conducted in 1972 has made it possible to examine a network of connections between the social characteristics of people, the persistent problems that pervade their daily experiences in major social roles, their patterns of coping with such experiences, and the psychological outcomes that emerge from the confluence of these factors.

During 1976 we returned to Chicago and reinterviewed a sub-sample of our respondents.[1] We repeated virtually all of the questions about role problems, coping responses, and symptomatologies of emotional distress, thus providing the opportunity to assess changes that may have occurred in these domains between 1972 and 1976. However, in concentrating on persistent role problems, the initial survey omitted from consideration other key sources of psychological distress. In particular, it did not include the many crucial life events that have the potentiality for arousing psychological disturbance. While the persistent role problems are likely to surface so insidiously that their onset may be difficult to recognize, life is liberally sprinkled, too, with events that have discrete temporal origins, are difficult to ignore, and require accelerated adjustments. The follow-up survey was designed to capture these events.

A good deal of attention has been given in recent years to life events and their effects (Myers et al., 1972; Paykel et al., 1971), much of it based on the Social Readjustment Rating Scale developed by Holmes and Rahe (1967). Considerable criticism has been leveled at this scale on methodological grounds (Brown, 1974; Rabkin and Struening, 1976), but the conceptual deficiencies of the instrument are equally outstanding. On the positive side, the scale does succeed in identifying a number of apparently potent events. Unfortunately, it does not differentiate among events in ways that permit the reconstruction of an individual's experience as he traverses time and space. Instead, it treats important life events as haphazard and interchangeable occurrences, thus obscuring the variations in patterns of events among people with different social status, the anchoring of these patterns in different social roles, and the emergence of events at different stages of adult life. It was our goal to distinguish among events in a manner that goes beyond the simple compilation of undifferentiated occurrences.

Pivotal to our efforts in this direction is the distinction between scheduled and nonscheduled events.[2] Scheduled events involve those transitions into and out of roles and statuses that are normally experienced in the course of the life cycle. Because they are so closely tied to the life cycle, they usually have a high predictability. We refer to them as scheduled events in order to underscore the regularity of their unfolding in the lives of people. Thus, whereas the enduring role problems entail the chronic frustrations, conflicts, and hardships people encounter within existing roles and statuses, transitional events focus on the scheduled yielding and acquiring of those roles and statuses attendant upon life-cycle changes.

Our follow-up interview inquired into a number of such events within each role area. In occupation we considered the following to represent events of this type: entry into the labor market; withdrawal from occupation in order to have and care for a family; and retirement because of age. Being newly married and experiencing "timely" widowhood are the two transitional events in the marital area. The parental role is somewhat unique because, strictly speaking, one can only acquire the role of parent but not lose it. However, we do treat as scheduled events a number of critical junctures which serve as benchmarks in the child's progress toward eventual independence. These include such transitions as the child's entry into school, completion of school, departure from the parental household, and marriage of the adult child. At each of these steps the parental role, although it is retained, undergoes some transformation.

The second type of event about which we inquired in our follow-up survey involves crises, eruptive circumstances, and other unexpected occurrences that are not the consequence of life-cycle transitions — the nonscheduled events. Although events of this order may be widespread, people typically do not count on them occurring within their own lives. Such exigencies may be no less common than problems woven into the fabric of day-to-day roles or those that emerge in the course of scheduled transitions, but they are ordinarily not among the occurrences that people expect to experience personally. Events of this type in the occupational arena are being fired, laid-off, or demoted, having to give up work because of illness, and — more desirable — being promoted and leaving one job for a better one. Divorce, separation, and the illness or premature death of a spouse are events within marriage that, while widespread, do no. have the scheduled regularity of transitional events. And finally, the illness or death of a child represents such events in the parental arena.

Underlying our research, then, are a few simply perspectives. We hold, first, that adult emotional development does not represent the gradual surfacing of conditions that happen to reside within individuals. Instead, we see it as a continuing process of adjustment to external circumstances, many of them rooted in the organization of the larger society and therefore distributed unequally across the population. We have identified three types of circumstances that have the capacity to arouse emotional distress; we refer to these collectively as life strains. This category includes the dogged, slow-to-change problems of daily life; the highly predictable, scheduled regular events that are attached to the life cycle; and the less expected and often (though not always) undesirable eruptive events. Because many of these vicissitudes are anchored to major social roles, they vary in space as people move among their multiple roles, as well as through time as the roles they occupy undergo change. The configuration of life strains may differ from one stage of adulthood to another, but the process of adjustment and change goes on through the entirety of life.

Although these are the guiding considerations and perspectives of our research into psychological distress among adults, we have only begun to discern the outlines of the vast web of interrelationships among the issues. In the following pages I shall describe some of our empirical findings, looking first at the periods of life when different life strains are likely to surface, the effects of the strains on psychological distress, and then how people cope with them.

AGE DISTRIBUTION AND THE EMOTIONAL
IMPACT OF LIFE STRAINS

Many of the life strains we have delineated for study have previously been shown to occur unequally across important groups in the society (Pearlin and Lieberman, 1979). The distribution of the strains among people of different age levels is especially germane to developmental concerns. There is no simple way to summarize this distribution, for the persistent problems, the scheduled transitional events, and the nonscheduled events each have somewhat distinctive associations with age. Furthermore, the strains rooted in the world of work are related to age in a different fashion than are the strains involving the more expressive worlds of marriage and parenthood. Thus, the relationships of life strains to age vary both with the type of strain and with the role from which the strains arise. The data are somewhat complex, therefore, but it is this very complexity and richness, so often overlooked in research into psychological well-being, that we seek to capture in conceptually distinguishing different types of circumstances and events as they present themselves within major social roles.

Within the occupational arena we find that the younger the worker is, the more likely it is that he will be exposed to most of the strains included in our study. With regard to the relatively persistent problems, for example, younger workers are somewhat more apt than older workers to feel job pressures and overloads and to have depersonalizing and separating experiences with fellow workers and authorities. Even more powerful associations with age are found for those strains represented by scheduled life events. Thus, people leaving the work force to have or to care for families are usually young (and almost always women). It is typically the younger, too, who are either entering or re-entering the job market. The only predictable transition more commonly found among older than younger workers is, of course, retirement from work for reasons of age. Finally, the nonscheduled events, such as being fired, laid-off, or demoted are almost exclusively the experiences of younger workers, as are promotion and movement between jobs. The only nonscheduled event occurring with disproportionate frequency among older people is retirement from work because of ill health. Overall, there is a very clear picture of younger workers more often having to confront the changes associated with the establishment, interruption, or advancement of career, of being vulnerable to occupational insecurities and disruptions, and of facing the more continuing and persistent problems of work. These findings suggest that the world of labor may become gentler with age.

Some of this picture changes when we examine marital strains, for these are somewhat more evenly distributed across the age span. As in occupation, the relatively persistent problems of marriage tend to be found among the younger wives and husbands. Thus, it is the younger married men and women who are particularly likely to see their spouses as failing to fulfill ordinary role expectations; they are also less likely to feel accepted by their spouses in a fashion that supports the valued elements of their self-image. The two scheduled transitions, being newly married and being widowed, are divided between extreme age groups, the first being predominantly an experience of the younger and the latter, of course, of the older. There is a similar age split involving, on the one hand, divorce and separation and, on the other, illness and disability, the former, expectedly, being mainly an experience of younger people and the latter of older people. In the parental area, we find that the persistent problems of child rearing are primarily confronted by younger parents. However, the transitional events occur across a wide age range, for they closely follow life-cycle developments. Thus, it is younger people who are becoming parents and seeing their children off to school and then through adolescence. But it is the older parents who see the departure of children from the household and into marriage.

An overview of the age distribution of the life strains described above reveals several patterns. Young adults simultaneously face the formidable tasks of having to establish themselves in their occupations, having to accommodate to marital relations that probably are not yet crystallized, and having to take responsibility for young children who of necessity are heavily dependent on them. Thus, chronic hardships and conflicts that can be found within these major social roles are much more likely to invade the lives of young adults, and to have been reconciled or left behind by the older adults. Some of the more undesirable nonscheduled events are also more common at younger ages, particularly those involving the loss of jobs and the termination of marriage by divorce and separation. By contrast, a number of the scheduled transitions are events experienced later in life, especially such life-cycle transitions as retirement, the loss of a spouse because of death, or the departure from the household of the last child.

Younger people, then, have more life strains to contend with, but they are frequently of a sort that dissipate with time. The strains faced by older people, although perhaps fewer in number, are more irreversible in their character. These differences make it difficult to judge on which group the greatest demands for adjustment fall. There is one matter of which we can be quite certain, however: as the adult part of the life span unfolds, people are exposed to a continuous, although shifting, flow of circumstances that challenge their adjustive capacities and have the potential for creating intense psychological distress. The study of adults, therefore, is to a large extent the study of conditions of work and of expressive relations as these engage people at different segments of the adult period of life, setting the stage for further psychological development.

Let us turn from the age distribution of the various life strains to a consideration of their emotional impact. The problems and vicissitudes that people encounter are not equal in their potential to arouse distress. On the contrary, we have observed considerable difference among them in this regard (Pearlin and Lieberman, 1978). In the world of work, for example, it is the nonscheduled loss of job or job status that is most likely to result in anxiety and depression, emotional states that we have combined into a composite measure of distress. Thus those who have been fired or laid off in the four-year period between 1972 and 1976 are considerably more apt than those whose occupational life has been stable to experience distress. The coefficient of association for this relationship (gamma) is .31. Being demoted produces an even closer relationship (gamma = .41), and having to give up work because of poor physical health is most closely associated of all (gamma = .74). Somewhat surprising, retirement from work because of age has no appreciable consequence for emotional distress, but giving up work in order to have or care for a family does have fairly substantial consequences for distress (gamma = .30). Promotion and changes in place of employment, despite their being apparently desired events, still have significant positive (although quite modest) relationships (.14 and .22, respectively). Finally, each of the more persistent problems of work (with the exception of working in noise, dirt, or other noxious environmental conditions) has distressful effects, the most notable among them being problems with fellow workers and authorities (gamma = .32). It is noteworthy that those circumstances and events in the work world that are most emotionally painful are also those most likely to impinge on younger people.

Marital strains are somewhat different from those in occupation, for in this domain it is the more durable strains encountered in everyday marital relations that exert the greatest impact, not the scheduled or nonscheduled events. Thus the coefficient of association for the relationship of distress to divorce and separation is .23, and that of distress to widowhood, .31. By contrast, perceived failure of spouses to fulfill role expectations, to exercise reciprocities in the relationship, and to recognize and accept their partners as they want to be seen have coefficients of association with distress of .40, .34, and .40, respectively. Where marriage is concerned, therefore, it is evi-

dently psychologically less disturbing to have the relationship termi-
nated than to live out the relationship under conditions of frustration
and conflict. New marriages have some special interest in this context. From one perspective they represent a transition to a new role
whose importance presumably makes it capable of producing distress. Yet, from another perspective, being newly married means that
the more chronic strains may not have had the opportunity to appear
or become crystallized, thus minimizing psychological distress. The
latter effect apparently prevails, for being newly wed has no statistically discernible deleterious psychological effects.

From the very few cases in our sample where the death of a child
has occurred, it is evident that for parents to outlive a child is probably the most severe hardship that people can endure. On the other
hand, there are a number of more common events of parenthood
linked to the life cycle which, although often viewed as emotionally
difficult, are not at all inimical to well-being. I refer to such events as
the last child's entrance into school, or completion of school, or of his
departure from the parental home. Indeed, the marriage of a last
child is to a notable extent negatively associated with emotional distress (gamma $= -.21$). The surge of well-being associated with seeing one's children married and out of the house may result not only
from contemplating the delights of the empty nest but also from
knowing that a succeeding generation is in the process of creating its
own nests. Perhaps the caring for and commitment to succeeding
generations, what Erik Erikson refers to as generativity (1950), extends beyond one's children to embrace one's grandchildren as well.
Whatever the reason, the confrontation by parents of the daily problems of child care and training is considerably more distressful than
those transitional events signaling the growing independence of children and their final departure from the household.

These, then, are some of the principal relationships between life
strains and psychological distress. But regardless of how well we succeed in identifying pivotal events and persistent problems in the
various role sectors of adulthood, our ability to predict their emotional consequences will be limited if we do not also take into consideration how people cope with them.

COPING

It is fair to state that interest in coping far exceeds our knowledge about it. Because it has been approached from a variety of perspectives by scholars representing a variety of disciplines, the growth
of our understanding of coping has not been cumulative. Our work
differs from that of most others in that it emphasizes those elements

of coping that are learned from and shared with the groups to which one belongs, ignoring the more idiosyncratic individual coping styles. But despite differences in their perspectives, all students of coping are in agreement, at least implicitly, that people are not merely passive targets of problems that arise in their lives, but that they actively respond to them in an effort to avoid being harmed by them. Largely because of these responses, emotional distress cannot be explained solely in terms of impinging life strains, for the manner in which people cope mediates the psychological consequences of the strains.

Although much remains to be discovered, a great deal has already been learned about coping from the 1972 data (Pearlin and Schooler, 1978), more than can be presented in detail here. I shall confine myself to discussing the connections between the coping dispositions of individuals and the value system of the surrounding society. To understand these connections, it must be recognized that the most common mode of response to life strains is the employment of a large inventory of perceptual and cognitive devices enabling one to view one's problems as relatively innocuous. Essentially this entails defining a situation or problem in a manner that reduces its threat and consequently minimizes its stressful impact. This type of coping does not eradicate the problem itself; it controls and shapes the meaning that the problem has for the individual so that its stressful effects are buffered.

The control of meaning typically relies heavily on the selective use of socially valued goals and activities. Many illustrations can serve to explicate this statement. If a man is exposed to intense strain in his work, he may avoid distress by relegating work to a marginal place in his life, committing himself instead, for example, to being a good husband or father. Thus, adults not infrequently will move those roles in which there is painful experience to the periphery of importance, making more central those that are comparatively free of hardship. In rearranging their priorities, people temper stress by demeaning the importance of areas in which failure and conflict are occurring. This selective commitment to different areas of life is possible, first, because there is a temporal and spatial segregation of important roles, and, second, because societies offer a veritable smorgasbord of values to their members. It is the plethora of equally acceptable desiderata, each congenial to society's ideals, that makes it a simple matter to substitute one commitment for another. One doesn't *have* to be a dedicated worker; he will still be conforming to the cherished values of the society if he chooses instead to be a devoted father. And this option may save him a great deal of pain.

The rearrangement of priorities may take place within roles as well as between roles. A woman reports, for example, that when her husband drinks to excess, which is frequently, he becomes abusive toward her. When asked how she deals with this problem, she replies that she pays no attention to it, for in the things that really matter — being a steady worker and a good earner — he is a prince. One can predict what she would prize if he were an inadequate breadwinner but a considerate husband. And if the situation were reversed so that she did esteem her husband for his kindness and ignored his failure as a breadwinner, she would be no less adhering to social values.

The selective use of valued goals and activities to mold the meaning of circumstances is an easily available coping tool, commonly used and quite efficacious. But whereas this strategy functions to limit the intensity of emotional distress, other devices function more as strategies for enduring distress. The coping strategies of this type help people live with and manage distress without being overwhelmed by it. There are many devices that potentially serve this function, such as immersing oneself in television viewing (Pearlin, 1959) or drinking for the relief of anxiety (Pearlin and Radabaugh, 1976). Here, however, I shall focus on those distress management techniques that make use of widespread beliefs and precepts. Many of these find expression in commonly used and easily recognized adages that represent prescriptions for surviving stress. Some, for example, seem to promote a passive forebearance in the face of adversity with a promise of better things to come: "things always work out for the best," "time heals all wounds," and so on. Others urge that we "look on the positive side," or that we "count our blessings." Sometimes it is the problems of others that make us aware of our blessings. This is powerfully illustrated in Betty Rollin's account (1976) of her intense effort to adjust to her mastectomy. She relates that some weeks after her surgery a friend called and recited a litany of domestic problems. Rollin became involved in her friend's travails and describes how, following the telephone conversation, "it occurred to me that I was doing something I hadn't done for a long time. I was worrying about someone else. At last, I thought" (p. 188). Other people's miseries can lighten our own.

Other beliefs indicate that our suffering is an inherent part of the design of life, perhaps even a manifestation of higher purpose. Commonly used exhortations to "take the bad with the good," or that "it is meant to be" suggest that people attempt to cope with hardships by seeing them as preordained, part of a divine plan. This theme is poignantly expressed by miners' wives in interviews that are being conducted as part of an investigation into the ways people cope with this perilous occupation.³ One woman whose husband was killed in a mine accident, for example, tells us that when she is depressed and asking herself why her husband died, she tells herself: "You know God doesn't make mistakes, you know that, so why are you acting like an idiot." She states: "Talking out loud to myself . . . does help." Societies, then, offer a potpourri of beliefs, and their selective use enables people not only to survive distress but to make a moral virtue of it. As might be guessed, coping at this level is more commonly found among older than younger adults.

There is a possibility that changes in adults' lives resulting from scheduled role transitions and those stemming from nonscheduled crises bring forth different coping modes. We have little empirical information to go on at this time, but there is reason to believe that the different types of life strains evoke coping efforts particularly suited to their nature. Thus the salient feature of role transitions is the predictability of their emergence; scheduled changes can be anticipated far in advance of their actual occurrence. We know about retirement before we receive our gold watches; we know something about marriage before the wedding ceremony. Because such role transitions are built into the life cycle, we begin learning about some of the changes they entail far ahead of the events themselves. Our adjustments to the conditions imposed by the loss and gain of roles thus depend to some extent on how accurately or with what distortions we foresee what we will later encounter. Effective coping with role transitions, therefore, would seem to depend on the role rehearsals that we conduct in our imaginations, the selection and use of role models, and other techniques that enable us to estimate how well present dispositions will fit with future demands. Where there is a perceived lack of congeniality between the present and the future, we engage in anticipatory adjustments. The success or failure of coping with transitions is very likely predetermined by the authenticity of the preparatory learning and the anticipatory adjustments people begin to make prior to the actual change.

Neither the selective use of values and beliefs to control meaning or to control distress itself—the responses I described earlier—nor the anticipatory role rehearsals used to contend with scheduled transitions would appear to be well-suited to coping with more sudden and eruptive life changes. Events of this sort lack the persistence needed for the crystallization of perceptual and cognitive adjustments; and because they also lack the predictability of the scheduled transitions, anticipatory preparation for the event is more difficult. How, then, do adults cope with eruptive conditions? It is in dealing with events having a crisis quality, perhaps, that people are most likely to engage in help-seeking behavior. The nature of the particular crisis, of course, has a great deal to do with what help people want and from whom they may seek it. To deal with some kinds of nonscheduled events, people, without necessarily being aware of it, may seek only subtle emotional support within an informal network of friends or family; for other problems they may turn to experts in the hope of receiving from them information or prescriptions for ameliorative actions. In any event, it is likely that seeking help, as in the case of other coping modes, is selectively invoked by adults in dealing with different kinds of exigencies and crises.

The adult portion of the life span, then, is peppered with socially generated life strains that differ with regard to their persistence and predictability. Many life strains may have their roots in the fundamental arrangements of society; but societies are at the same time also the source of many efficacious devices people use to withstand the full impact of the strains. Indeed, as varied as the life strains are, the ways of responding to them are richer yet. One learns from his experiences, from his membership groups, and from his culture a vast array of acceptable modes of anticipating, appraising, and meeting challenge. If these modes fail him, either because of their inherent lack of coping efficacy or because the challenging circumstances are not amenable to individual coping efforts, then he becomes vulnerable to psychic distress. But if one copes effectively, as people typically appear to do, then life strains may even have a positive contribution to one's development through the adult portion of the life span. Although much is still conjectural, we can be quite certain that to understand the well-being of adults, we need to observe the unfolding of the circumstances and events they experience, the meaning of the experience for them, and their attempts to avoid being harmed by it.

I have to this point deliberately omitted certain complexities so as to delineate more clearly the main currents of our work. One of these omissions concerns the reciprocity between the circumstances and events of life and psychological distress. Although I have talked of distress solely as following from life strains, there is a distinct possibility that distress, in addition to being an effect of life strains, is also an antecedent of strains. Even with the availability of longitudinal data such as ours, a great deal of care and rigor is required before the casual ordering of important social and psychological phenomena can be established. However, certain of our data, especially the discrete events that occurred in the lives of respondents in the four-year period between interviews, give some ready indication of what is causing what. By their very nature particular events can be considered as relatively impervious to influence by preexisting psychological dispositions. Being widowed may be taken as a suitable case in point. The coefficient of association (gamma) between the 1972 psychological distress level and subsequent widowhood is .19, but the coefficient between widowhood and the later, 1976 identical measure of distress is .32. It is remotely possible that preexisting distress could contribute to the demise of a spouse, but it is clearer, both because of the nature of the event and the magnitude of the associations, that the spouse's death is an antecedent condition for distress. Virtually all of the preliminary examinations made along these lines, including those of events that are less clearly susceptible to influence from prior distress, indicate a similar asymmetry of influence. Psychological distress, although it may very well contribute to future events, is more likely to result from conditions of life than to give shape to these conditions. However, it is clear that new methodologies are needed in order to reconstruct with confidence the processes by which social forces and events affect people, and by which people may come to affect the forces and events that play upon their lives.

Under special conditions, some events may lose their scheduled or nonscheduled distinctiveness; that is, many of the events that are ordinarily highly predictable may, in a given set of circumstances, lose their predictability. Consider a woman who, after years of trying to have children, becomes pregnant at the age of forty. Not only is she outside the remarkably clear timing norms for this kind of event (Neugarten et al., 1965), but she may also feel that she is at some special risk. Consequently, an event easily anticipated and prepared for under usual circumstances can, under unusual circumstances of timing and meaning, become cloaked in uncertainty and doubt. Correspondingly, other events that are usually considered as eruptive crises may acquire the features of highly regular occurrences. Thus, a miner's wife relates that she anticipates that after ten years of work her husband will become ill with black lung disease. She is not merely engaging in gloomy guesswork in making this prediction, for this is what happened to her father and two uncles. A limiting illness at the age of about forty is, in these circumstances, a predictive event tied to a patterned occupational career. Where the meaning and nature of events is altered by special conditions, the effects of these events and the coping responses they evoke will probably also be altered.

Underlying many of the relationships that I have talked about is a question that merits consideration if we are better to understand adult development and change: what is it about events that creates anxiety and depression? One possible answer might hold that it is the undesirability of many events that explains their exacerbation of psychological distress. This does not stand up, however, for even events that are patently desirable, such as being promoted, are nonetheless still associated with distress. Another explanation might emphasize the loss entailed by certain events, that being separated from something that was once part of ourselves leads to emotional disturbances. This argument may have some merit, for several of the events most powerfully related to distress do involve the loss of role or status. Nevertheless, there are some losses — for example, those represented in the departure of children from the home or in retirement — that do not have deleterious effects. And if loss is painful, it could be reasoned that gain should be beneficial. But this is not the case, for there are some acquisitions, such as entering into a new occupation, that are capable of generating distress. A third explanation would assert that events impose an alteration in a delicate balance within us. Disequilibrium among our inner psychic forces, in turn, is an inherently intolerable condition that produces tension and other symptoms of distress that are likely to persist until a new equilibrium is established. This explanation, however, fails to explain the low level of distress following some quite dramatic changes, such as retirement or the emptying of the nest.

There is yet another possible explanation, one that we tested empirically. Events may not affect adults because they are unwanted, or invoke loss, or because they throw the organism out of delicate psychic balance. Instead, events promote emotional distress when they adversely alter the more durable conditions of life with which people have to contend. The effects of events, we suggest, are channeled through the structured circumstances that people have to grapple with over time. Considerable support for this interpretation emerged from the analysis of our data. Thus, in looking at certain events involving role loss, such as retirement, divorce, or widowhood, the loss itself matters far less to psychological well-being than the quality of experience one has in being newly retired, divorced, or widowed. For example, if retirees who are free of economic hardships and who enjoy ties to social networks are compared with those who have limited economic resources and are relatively isolated, it is only the latter who are found to possess the symptoms of distress. The same is true for those who are newly single, whether because of the death of a spouse or divorce: when the durable conditions of singlehood are benign, the yielding of the marital role does not arouse distress. Where newly single persons experience hardships, on the other hand, they are very likely to suffer intense distress. The injurious psychological effects of events entailing the movement from one role to another, therefore, appear to depend not on the loss or transition per se but almost entirely on conditions people live with at the end of their role passage. Change by itself does not affect emotional well-being; change that leads to hardships in basic, enduring economic and social conditions of life, on the other hand, does. Even those transitions brought about voluntarily may result in pain when they lead to negative conditions that are beyond one's ameliorative control.

In mulling over what we have learned from observing the distressful effects of life strains, we have addressed a question that is a fundamental concern of this book: Do problems in labor and in love intrude upon each other? More concretely, can one confront hardships in one's occupation without these eventually leading to strife in one's family relations; can one suffer frustration and conflict as a husband or wife, father or mother, without experiencing increased strains as a worker? On the one hand, people are whole, and it is difficult to think of important experiences occurring in one part of life without influencing the other parts. But on the other hand, there is a structural separation of social roles that enables people to segregate painful experiences arising in one role from the experiences arising within other roles. Our efforts to find the answers to this question are hardly final, but from evidence at hand it appears that disruptions of labor and love are indeed somewhat independent. Thus the intensity of strain a person experiences in his occupation bears relatively little relationship to those he experiences as a spouse or parent. To an appreciable extent adults apparently do contain strains and stresses in time and space; and this, in turn, says a great deal about the organization of coping behavior.

Notes

1. This time in collaboration with Morton A. Lieberman of the Committee on Human Development at the University of Chicago.
2. I am grateful to Neil Smelser for suggesting these conceptual labels.
3. These are currently being conducted in collaboration with Nancy Datan and Carol Giesen of the Department of Psychology at West Virginia University.

References

BROWN, GEORGE W. 1974. Meaning, measurement and stress of life events. In *Stressful life events,* ed. Barbara S. Dohrenwend and Bruce P. Dohrenwend. New York: Wiley.

DEROGATIŚ, L. R., R. S. LIPMAN, L. COVI, AND K. RICKLES. 1971. Neurotic symptom dimensions. *Archives of General Psychiatry,* 24:454-464.

ERIKSON, ERIK H. 1950. *Childhood and society.* New York: Norton. (2nd ed., 1963).

HOLMES, THOMAS H., AND RICHARD H. RAHE. 1967. The social readjustment rating scale. *Journal of Psychosomatic Research,* 22:324-331.

LEVINSON, DANIEL J. 1977. The mid-life transition: a period in adult psychological development. *Psychiatry,* 40:99-112.

LIPMAN, R.S., K. RICKLES, L. COVI, L.R. DEROGATIS, AND E.H. UHLENHUTH. 1969. Factors of symptom distress. *Archives of General Psychiatry* 21:328-338.

MYERS, J. K., J. J. LINDENTHAL, M. P. PEPPER, AND D. R. OSTRANDER. 1972. Life events and mental status: a longitudinal study. *Journal of Health and Social Behavior,* 13:398-406.

NEUGARTEN, BERNICE L., JOAN W. MOORE, AND JOHN C. LOWE. 1965. Age norms, age constraints, and adult socialization. *American Journal of Sociology,* 70:710-717.

NEUGARTEN, BERNICE. 1969. Continuities and discontinuities of psychological issues into adult life. *Human Development,* 12:121-130.

PAYKEL, E.S., B. A. PRUSOFF, E.H. UHLENHUTH. 1971. Scaling of life events. *Archives of General Psychiatry,* 25:340-347.

PEARLIN, LEONARD I. 1959. Social and personal stress and escape television viewing. *Public Opinion Quarterly,* 23:255-259.

———. 1975a. Sex roles and depression. In Nancy Datan and Leon Ginsberg (eds.), Life-span developmental psychology conference: normative life crises, ed. New York: Academic Press, pp. 191-207.

———. 1975b. "Status inequality and stress in marriage." *American Sociological Review,* 40:344-357.

PEARLIN, LEONARD I., AND MORTON A. LIEBERMAN. 1979. Social sources of emotional distress. In *Research in community and mental health,* ed. Roberta Simmons. Greenwich, Conn.: JAI Press.

PEARLIN, LEONARD, AND CLARICE RADABAUGH. 1976. Economic strains and the coping functions of alcohol. *American Journal of Sociology,* 82:652-663.

PEARLIN, LEONARD I., AND CARMI SCHOOLER. 1978. The structure of coping. *Journal of Health and Social Behavior,* 19:2-21.

RABKIN, JUDITH G., AND ELMER L. STRUENING. 1976. Life events, stress and illness. *Science,* 194:1013-1020.

ROLLIN, BETTY. 1976. *First you cry.* New York: New American Library.

ROSENBERG, MORRIS, AND LEONARD I. PEARLIN. 1978. Social class and self-esteem among children and adults. *American Journal of Sociology,* 84:53-77.

NINE

Job Complexity and
Adult Personality

————— MELVIN L. KOHN —————

THERE HAVE BEEN several distinct approaches to the study of
work, each of them emphasizing some aspect that bears on a particular theoretical concern of the investigator. Rarely, though, has that
concern been the effect of work on personality. Sociologists have
learned much about social stratification and mobility, for example,
by focusing on the dimension of work most pertinent to the strat-
ificational system, the status of the job (Blau and Duncan, 1967;
Duncan, Featherman, and Duncan, 1972; Sewell, Hauser, and
Featherman, 1976). But however important status may be for studies
of mobility, it would be unwise to assume — as is often done — that the
status of a job is equally pertinent for personality. In terms of impact
on personality, job status serves mainly as a gross indicator of the
job's location in the hierarchical organization of the economic and
social system. The status of the job is closely linked to such structural
conditions of work as how complex it is, how closely it is supervised,
and what sorts of pressures it entails. It is these structural realities,
not status as such, that affect personality (Kohn and Schooler, 1973).

It is also indisputable that economists have learned much about
the functioning of the economic system by focusing on the extrinsic
rewards the job confers — in particular, income. Just as with occupational status, though, it would be incorrect to assume that because
income is important for an understanding of the economic system
qua system, income is also the most significant aspect of the job
in terms of the meaning of work to the worker or the impact of work
on his sense of self and orientation to the rest of the world (Whyte,
1955; Kohn and Schooler, 1973).

Organizational theorists, both the Weberian sociologists and those more applied scholars who call themselves administrative scientists, have, by studying formal organizational structure, undoubtedly contributed much to our understanding of how organizations function (Blau and Schoenherr, 1971). But the very strength of their approach — its systematic attention to how formal organizations function as systems, regardless of the personalities of those who play the various organizational roles — means that they largely ignore the effect of organizational structure on the individual worker and his work. When they do pay attention to the individual worker, their interest rarely goes beyond his role as worker.

The human-relations-in-industry approach, in deliberate juxtaposition to the formal organizational approach, focuses on informal, interpersonal relationships and the symbolic systems that emerge out of such relationships (Whyte, 1961; 1969). Scholars using this approach supply a needed corrective to the formal organizational perspective. But they sometimes seem unaware that people not only relate to one another on the job; they also work. Moreover, this perspective has been concerned almost exclusively with the implications of work for on-the-job behavior, paying little attention to the effects of the job on other realms of life.

Occupational psychologists come close to understanding the relationship between work and personality, but there are two major limitations to their studies. First, many of them misinterpret Kurt Lewin (and, I would add, W. I. Thomas) by dealing exclusively with how people perceive their work while neglecting the actual conditions under which that work is performed. (This criticism applies as well to most sociological studies of alienation in work.) Thus, they measure boredom rather than routinization, interest in the work rather than its substantive complexity, and "alienation in work" rather than actual working conditions. Such an approach ignores the possibilities that there can be a gap between the conditions to which a person is subjected and his awareness of those conditions; that the existence or nonexistence of such a gap is itself problematic and may be structurally determined; and that conditions felt by the worker to be benign can have deleterious consequences, while conditions felt to be onerous can have beneficial consequences. The second limitation is the preoccupation of most occupational psychologists with job satisfaction, as if this were the only psychological consequence of work. I am less disturbed by the technical difficulties in measuring job satisfaction — a notoriously slippery concept — than I am by the assumption that work has no psychological ramifications beyond the time and place during and within which it occurs. Work affects people's values, self-conceptions, orientation to social reality, even their intellectual functioning. Job satisfaction is only one, and far from the most important, psychological consequence of work.

.The research that comes closest of all to dealing straightforwardly with work and its consequences for personality employs an old tradition of sociological study—case studies of occupations. Practitioners of this art have sometimes done a magnificent job of depicting the reality of work as it impinges on the worker. Unfortunately, though, their studies cannot determine which aspects of work are most pertinent for which aspects of psychological functioning. W. Fred Cottrell's (1940) classic study of railroaders, for example, pointed out a multitude of ways that the job conditions of men who operate trains differ from those of men in many other occupations —including the unpredictability of working hours, geographical mobility, precision of timing, outsider status in the home community, and unusual recruitment and promotion practices. Since all these conditions are tied together in one occupational package, it is not possible to disentangle the psychological concomitants of each. More recent comparative studies face similar interpretative problems. For example, Robert Blauner's (1964) study of alienation among blue-collar workers in four industries, chosen to represent four technological levels, showed that differences in working conditions are systematically associated with the stage of technological development of the industry. But these differences, too, come in packages: Printing differs from automobile manufacture not only in technology and in the skill levels of workers but also in pace of the work, closeness of supervision, freedom of physical movement, and a multitude of other conditions. One cannot tell which, if any, of these interlocked occupational conditions are conducive to alienation.

DISENTANGLING OCCUPATIONAL CONDITIONS

Disentangling occupational conditions to assess their psychological impact requires a mode of research different from that employed in studies of particular occupations and particular industries. Carmi Schooler and I have dealt with the problem by shifting the focus from named occupations—carpenter, surgeon, or flight engineer—to dimensions of occupation (Kohn, 1969; Kohn and Schooler, 1969; 1973). Our strategy has been to secure a large and representative sample of employed men, who necessarily work in many occupations and many industries.[1] We have inventoried the men's job conditions and then differentiated the psychological concomitants of each facet of occupation by statistical analysis. In our most recent research, my colleagues and I have done comparable analyses for employed women (Miller et al., 1979).

Even though occupational conditions are intercorrelated, they are not perfectly intercorrelated. Thus, substantively complex jobs are likely also to be time-pressured; but there are enough jobs that are substantively complex yet not time-pressured, and enough that are substantively simple yet time-pressured, for us to examine the relationship between substantive complexity and, say, receptiveness or resistance to change, while statistically controlling time pressure. We can also look for statistical interaction between the two, asking whether the impact of substantive complexity on, let us say, stance toward change is different for men who are more time-pressured and for men who are less time-pressured. And, at the same time, we can statistically control many other occupational conditions, as well as important nonoccupational variables, for example, education, which usually precedes and is often a prerequisite for the job.

In all, we have indexed more than fifty separable dimensions of occupation, including such diverse aspects of work experience as the substantive complexity of work, the routinization or diversity of the flow of work, relationships with co-workers and with supervisors, pace of work and control thereof, physical and environmental conditions, job pressures and uncertainties, union membership and participation, bureaucratization, job protections, and fringe benefits. (For complete information, see Kohn, 1969, pp. 236, 244-253.) These indices provide the basis for a broad descriptive picture of the principal facets of occupations, as experienced by men in all types of industries and at all levels of the civilian economy.

I must admit that this approach—based as it is on a sample survey of all men employed in civilian occupations—is not optimum for securing some kinds of job information. Men may have only limited information about certain aspects of their jobs, such as the overall structure of the organization in which they work. Moreover, a sample of men scattered across many occupations and many work places does not contain enough people in any occupation or any workplace to trace out interpersonal networks and belief systems. Similarly, the method is not well adapted for studying the industrial and technological context in which the job is embedded. The method is most useful for studying the immediate conditions of a man's own job—what he does, who determines how he does it, in what physical and social circumstances he works, to what risks and rewards he is subject.

We found that nearly all of the more than fifty occupational conditions that we had inventoried are correlated with at least some of the several aspects of values, self-conception, social orientation, and intellectual functioning that we had measured (Kohn and Schooler, 1973).[2] But most of these statistical relationships reflect the interrelatedness of occupational conditions with one another and with education. Only twelve of the occupational conditions we studied appear to have any substantial relationship to men's psychological functioning when education and all other pertinent occupational conditions are statistically controlled. Few though they are, these twelve occupational conditions are sufficient to define the "structural imperatives of the job," in that they identify a man's position in the organizational structure, his opportunities for occupational self-direction, the principal job pressures to which he is subject, and the principal uncertainties built into his job.[3] These job conditions are "structural" in two senses: they are built into the structure of the job and they are largely determined by the job's location in the structures of the economy and the society.

SUBSTANTIVE COMPLEXITY

Because of its theoretical and empirical importance, I devote the remainder of this essay to one of the twelve structural imperatives of the job, the substantive complexity of work.[4] By the substantive complexity of work, I mean the degree to which the work, in its very substance, requires thought and independent judgment. Substantively complex work by its very nature requires making many decisions that must take into account ill-defined or apparently conflicting contingencies. Although, in general, work with data or with people is likely to be more complex than work with things, this is not always the case, and an index of the overall complexity of work should reflect its degree of complexity in each of these three types of activity. Work with things can vary in complexity from ditch digging to sculpting; similarly, work with people can vary in complexity from receiving simple directions or orders to giving legal advice; and work with data can vary from reading instructions to synthesizing abstract conceptual systems. Thus, the index of substantive complexity that we have generally employed is based on the degree of complexity of the person's work with things, with data, and with people; our appraisal of the overall complexity of his work, regardless of whether he works primarily with things, with data, or with people; and estimates of the amount of time he spends working at each type of activity (Kohn and Schooler, 1973; Kohn, 1976). The several components receive weightings based on a factor analysis.[5]

I focus on substantive complexity for two reasons. The first is that I conceive substantive complexity to be central to the experience of work. The other structural imperatives of the job—even closeness of supervision and routinization—set the conditions under which work is done but they do not characterize the work itself. The substantive complexity of work, by contrast, is at the heart of the experience of work. More than any other occupational condition, it gives meaning to this experience.

The second reason for my preoccupation with substantive complexity is empirical. Our analyses show that substantive complexity of work is strongly related to a wide range of psychological variables. The substantive complexity of work is of course correlated with job satisfaction and with occupational commitment. It also bears on many facets of off-the-job psychological functioning, ranging from valuation of self-direction to self-esteem to authoritarian conservatism to intellectual flexibility. It is even related to the intellectual demands of men's leisure-time pursuits. Moreover, these correlations remain statistically significant and large enough to be meaningful even when education and all other pertinent dimensions of occupation are statistically controlled. Thus, the substantive complexity of work has a strong, independent relationship to many facets of psychological functioning, a relationship stronger than that of any other dimension of occupation we have studied. This is true for men, and our most recent analyses show it to be equally true for employed women (Miller et al., 1979).

THE DIRECTION OF CAUSAL EFFECTS

There is evidence that the substantive complexity of work is not only correlated with, but has a causal impact on, psychological functioning. The evidence of causal directionality is of two types. The more extensive but less definitive evidence comes from our analyses of cross-sectional data, derived from a large sample of men employed in civilian occupations. Social scientists have long recognized that one cannot make inferences about the direction of causal effects from cross-sectional data unless some of the described phenomena clearly preceded others in their time of occurrence. But where one can realistically assume reciprocity—that a affects b and b also affects a—it is possible to assess the magnitude of these reciprocal effects, using econometric techniques for solving simultaneous equations. The simplest of these, which we used, is called two-stage least squares.[6] With this technique, we have assessed the relationships between the substantive complexity of work and many facets of psychological functioning: occupational commitment, job satisfaction, valuation of self-direction or of conformity to external authority, anxiety, self-esteem, receptiveness or resistance to change, standards of morality, authoritarian conservatism, intellectual flexibility, the intellectuality of leisure-time activities, and three types of alienation — powerlessness, self-estrangement, and normlessness.

Our findings indicate that the substantive complexity of men's work affects all these facets of psychological functioning, independent of the selection processes that draw men into particular fields of work and independent of their efforts to mold their jobs to fit their needs, values, and capacities. Moreover, the substantive complexity of work in every instance affects psychological functioning more — often, much more — than the particular facet of psychological functioning affects the substantive complexity of work. This evidence is not definitive — only longitudinal studies can provide definitive evidence — but it does establish a strong prima facie case that the substantive complexity of work has a real and meaningful effect on a wide range of psychological phenomena.

More definitive, albeit less extensive, evidence comes from a follow-up study we conducted with a representative subsample of men in the original study ten years after the initial survey (Kohn and Schooler, 1978). Analyses of longitudinal data require the development of "measurement models" that separate unreliability of measurement from change in the phenomena studied. The essence of the method employed in constructing these models is the use of multiple indicators for each principal concept, inferring from the covariation of the indicators the degree to which each reflects the underlying concept that they are all hypothesized to reflect and the degree to which each reflects anything else, which for measurement purposes is considered to be error (see Jöreskog, 1969, and other papers cited in Kohn and Schooler, 1978). These models permit us to take into account that errors in the measurement of any indicator at the time of the initial survey may well be correlated with errors in the measurement of that same indicator at the time of the follow-up survey. Disregarding such correlated errors in the indicators might make the underlying concept seem more stable or less stable than it really is — thereby distorting any causal analysis in which that index is employed.

We have thus far constructed measurement models for the substantive complexity of work and for one facet of psychological functioning — intellectual flexibility. We chose intellectual flexibility as the first aspect of psychological functioning to be assessed because it offers us the greatest challenge — intellectual flexibility obviously affects recruitment into substantively complex jobs, and there is every reason to expect it to be resistant to change. Still, intellectual flexibility — though not much studied by sociologists — is so important a part of psychological functioning that we must not unthinkingly assume it to be entirely the product of genetics and early life experience. Rather, we should empirically test the possibility that intellectual flexibility may be responsive to adult occupational experience.

Our index of intellectual flexibility is meant to reflect men's actual intellectual performance in the interview situation. We used a variety of indicators — including the men's answers to seemingly simple but highly revealing cognitive problems, their handling of perceptual and projective tests, their propensity to agree when asked "agree-disagree" questions, and the impression they made on the interviewer during a long session that required a great deal of thought and reflection. None of these indicators is believed to be completely valid; but we do believe that all the indicators reflect, to some substantial degree, men's flexibility in coping with an intellectually demanding situation.

The stability of intellectual flexibility, thus measured, is remarkably high over time: The correlation between men's intellectual flexibility at the time of the original study and their intellectual flexibility ten years later, shorn of measurement error, is 0.93. It would be erroneous to assume, though, that the high over-time stability of intellectual flexibility means that it is unaffected by adult experience; it might even be that this stability reflects unchanging life circumstances. In fact, we find that the effect of the substantive complexity of work on intellectual flexibility is striking — on the order of one-fourth as great as that of the men's ten-year-earlier levels of intellectual flexibility. This effect is essentially contemporaneous: The path from the substantive complexity of the job held at the time of the initial survey to intellectual flexibility at the time of the follow-up survey ten years later is small and statistically nonsignificant, while the path from the substantive complexity of the current job to current intellectual flexibility is much more substantial and is statistically significant.[7]

The reciprocal effect of intellectual flexibility on substantive complexity is still more impressive than the effect of substantive complexity on intellectual flexibility. This effect is entirely lagged, that is, it is the men's intellectual flexibility at the time of the initial survey that significantly affects the substantive complexity of their current jobs, and not their current intellectual flexibility. The longitudinal analysis thus demonstrates something that no cross-sectional analysis could show—that, over time, the relationship between substantive complexity and intellectual flexibility is truly reciprocal. The effect of substantive complexity on intellectual flexibility is more immediate: current job demands affect current thinking processes. Intellectual flexibility, by contrast, has a time-lagged effect on substantive complexity: current intellectual flexibility has scant effect on current job demands, but considerable effect on the future course of one's career. Cross-sectional analyses portray only part of this process, making it seem that the relationship between the substantive complexity of work and intellectual functioning were mainly unidirectional, with work affecting intellectual functioning but not the reverse. Longitudinal analysis portrays a more intricate and more interesting, truly reciprocal process.

The data thus demonstrate, beyond reasonable doubt, what heretofore could be stated only as a plausible thesis buttressed by presumptive evidence—that the substantive complexity of work both considerably affects, and is considerably affected by, intellectual flexibility.

My colleagues and I have recently completed two further analyses that extend these conclusions. A much more extensive longitudinal analysis of job conditions and intellectual flexibility (Kohn and Schooler, in press) confirms that the substantive complexity of work affects intellectual flexibility not only when prior levels of intellectual flexibility and pertinent aspects of social background are taken into account but also when all other structural imperatives of the job are taken into account as well. We further find that substantive complexity is not the only job condition that affects intellectual flexibility; several other job conditions that stimulate and challenge the individual are conducive to intellectual flexibility. But, clearly, substantive complexity plays a key role, not only because it has such a great effect on intellectual flexibility, but also because it provides the principal mechanism through which other job conditions affect intellectual functioning.

In another analysis (Miller et al., 1979), we found that the substantive complexity of work is as important for women's psychological functioning as it is for men's. In particular, a causal analysis using measurement models similar to those described above, but limited to cross-sectional data, shows the contemporaneous effect of substantive complexity on intellectual flexibility to be at least as great for employed women as for employed men.

These findings come down solidly in support of those who hold that occupational conditions affect personality and in opposition to those who believe that the relationship between occupational conditions and personality results solely from selective recruitment and job molding. Admittedly, personality has great importance in determining who go into what types of jobs and how they perform those jobs; in fact, our analyses underline the importance of these processes. But that has never been seriously at issue. What has been disputed is whether the reverse phenomenon — of job conditions molding personality — also occurs. The evidence of our longitudinal analysis supports the position that it does occur.

In particular, this analysis adds to and helps specify the growing evidence that the structure of the environment has an important effect on cognitive development (Rosenbaum, 1976) and that cognitive processes do not become impervious to environmental influence after adolescence or early adulthood but continue to show "plasticity" throughout the life span (Baltes, 1968; Horn and Donaldson, 1976; Baltes and Schaie, 1976). Our findings reinforce this conclusion by showing that intellectual flexibility continues to be responsive to experience well into midcareer. In fact, it appears that the remarkable stability of intellectual flexibility reflects, at least in part, stability in people's life circumstances. Intellectual flexibility is ever responsive to changes in the substantive complexity of people's work; for most people, though, the substantive complexity of work does not fluctuate markedly.

This analysis demonstrates as well the importance of intellectual flexibility for substantive complexity. I think it noteworthy that this effect appears to be lagged rather than contemporaneous. The implication is that the structure of most jobs does not permit any considerable variation in the substantive complexity of the work: job conditions are not readily modified to suit the needs or capacities of the individual worker. But over a long enough time — certainly over a period as long as ten years — many men either modify their jobs or move on to other jobs more consonant with their intellectual functioning. Thus, the long-term effects of intellectual flexibility on substantive complexity are considerable, even though the contemporaneous effects appear to be negligible.

Our models, of course, deal mainly with the events of midcareer or later. I think it reasonable to assume that men's intellectual flexibility in childhood, adolescence, and early adulthood have had a considerable effect on their educational attainments, and our data show that educational attainment is very important for the substantive complexity of the early jobs in men's careers. Since the substantive complexity of early jobs is a primary determinant of the substantive complexity of later jobs, it seems safe to infer that intellectual flexibility's long-term, indirect effects on the substantive complexity of later jobs has been even greater than our analysis depicts.

The reciprocal relationship between substantive complexity and intellectual flexibility implies an internal dynamic by which relatively small differences in substantive complexity at early stages of a career may become magnified into larger differences in both substantive complexity and intellectual flexibility later in the career. If two men of equivalent intellectual flexibility were to start their careers in jobs differing in substantive complexity, the man in the more complex job would be likely to outstrip the other in further intellectual growth. This, in time, might lead to his attaining jobs of greater complexity, further affecting his intellectual growth. Meantime, the man in the less complex job would develop intellectually at a slower pace, perhaps not at all, and in the extreme case might even decline in his intellectual functioning. As a result, small differences in the substantive complexity of early jobs might lead to increasing differences in intellectual development.

SUBSTANTIVE COMPLEXITY AND VALUES

We have not yet done longitudinal analyses to test the hypothesis that substantive complexity directly affects values or self-conception or social orientation—in fact, anything other than intellectual flexibility. Still, intellectual flexibility is the crucial test. Because of its remarkable stability, intellectual flexibility offers the most difficult challenge to the hypothesis that substantive complexity actually affects psychological functioning. Moreover, intellectual flexibility is intimately related to values, self-conception, and social orientation. It is an important link between social class and self-directed values and orientation (Kohn, 1969, pp. 186-187; Kohn and Schooler, 1969). Thus, demonstrating the causal impact of substantive complexity on intellectual flexibility gives us every reason to expect that substantive complexity affects values and orientation, too. In future analyses of the longitudinal data, we shall assess the hypothesized causal effect of substantive complexity on values, self-conception, and social orientation. For now, the two-stage least-squares analysis of the cross-sectional data provides a strong prima facie case that substantive complexity affects not only intellectual flexibility but also values and orientation. Extrapolating from intellectual flexibility to psychological functioning more generally, I would argue that there probably are continuing reciprocal relationships between the substantive complexity of work and psychological functioning throughout men's entire careers.

I would argue further that, at least within this economy and culture, the psychological effects of the substantive complexity of work are essentially the same for all segments of the work force. It might be thought, for example, that the substantive complexity of work would affect the psychological functioning of middle-class men more than that of working-class men. Not so. Substantive complexity has similar effects of comparable magnitude in all social classes. Moreover, these effects are much the same regardless of the sector of the economy in which the job is located, the type of industry, or the degree of bureaucratization (Kohn and Schooler, 1973). But there is insufficient evidence from other countries, cultures, and political and economic systems to judge whether the psychological effects of the substantive complexity of work transcend Western culture, industrial society, and a capitalist economic system.[8]

PROCESSES OF LEARNING AND GENERALIZATION

Why does substantive complexity have such widespread ramifications for personality? This question is still largely unanswered. Our findings suggest that the simplest type of learning-generalization process is operating here: that there is a direct translation of the lessons of the job to outside-the-job realities, rather than some indirect process, such as reaction formation or compensation (Breer and Locke, 1965). Thus, men who do complex work come to exercise their intellectual prowess not only on the job but also in their non-occupational lives. They become more open to new experience. They come to value self-direction more highly. They even come to engage in more intellectually demanding leisure-time activities. In short, the lessons of work are directly carried over to nonoccupational realms.

Several alternative interpretations have been advanced, but none has been adequately tested. One such interpretation is that doing more (or less) substantively complex work leads to a stronger (or weaker) sense of control over the forces that affect one's life, and that this sense of controlling or not controlling those forces influences one's self-concept, in particular, one's self-esteem. But why is it necessary to accord so strategic a role in the causal chain to "locus of control"? Why not say, more directly, that people who do substantively complex work come to think of themselves as capable of doing difficult and challenging tasks—and thus deserve respect in everyone's eyes, including their own? Similarly, people who do substantively simple work come to think of themselves as capable of nothing more than this simple-minded stuff.

I think the most reasonable hypothesis is the most straightforward: that in an industrial society, where work is central to people's lives, what people do in their work directly affects their values, their conceptions of self, and their orientation to the world around them — "I do, therefore I am." Hence, doing substantively complex work tends to increase one's respect for one's own capacities, one's valuation of self-direction, one's intellectuality (even in leisure-time pursuits), and one's sense that the problems one encounters in the world are manageable. There is no need to posit that locus of control or any other aspect of values and orientation plays a necessary intermediary role in this process; the substantive complexity of work can directly affect all aspects of people's conceptions of reality.

It is, however, entirely possible that the process by which substantive complexity affects values and orientation may be mediated, at least in part, through intellectual flexibility. Increased intellectual flexibility may, for example, increase one's valuation of self-direction and one's tolerance of different beliefs; decreased intellectual flexibility may result in greater valuation of conformity to external authority and increased authoritarian conservatism. What makes this causal chain more plausible than interpretations positing an intermediary role for locus of control or any other aspect of values and orientation is that intellectual flexibility is qualitatively different from these other psychological phenomena: it represents not content of thought, but process of thought. Many of the psychological processes affected by substantive complexity involve thinking: valuing thinking for oneself, being tolerant of other people's thinking for themselves, and thinking through one's own moral standards. The hypothesis that intellectual flexibility plays a strategic intermediary role in explaining the effects of substantive complexity on values and orientation is in principle testable, and we shall try to test it with our longitudinal data.

Still another possible interpretation is that occupational conditions do not affect all people similarly, but differently, depending on the individual's own needs, values, and abilities — the so-called "fit" hypothesis. Our analyses do not support this interpretation. We repeatedly find, for example, that the substantive complexity of work has much the same effects regardless of whether men value intrinsic or extrinsic aspects of their work more highly (Kohn and Schooler, 1973; Kohn, 1976). But these analyses have been broad-gauge, and more detailed analyses of pertinent subpopulations might require us to modify our views. Moreover, our analyses of this issue have thus far not been longitudinal. But since our data demonstrate that people's values and even their abilities are affected by their job conditions, it is clear that only longitudinal assessments can be conclusive.

Our studies have led me to conclude that the intrinsic meaning and psychological impact of a job result not just from the status or income or interpersonal relationships that the job provides but also — and especially — from the meaningful challenges the work itself poses (or fails to pose). The most important challenge is that of mastering complex tasks, that is, the substantive complexity of the work. Our data indicate that substantive complexity affects people's psychological functioning regardless of their needs, values, and personal capacities and regardless of their social class (but, of course, the type of work one does is intimately related to one's social class; so, too, are one's values). What matters most about work, in short, is not any of its attendant rewards or social experiences, but the work itself.

Moreover, the relationship between work and psychological functioning is quintessentially reciprocal. There is an ongoing process, throughout all of adult life, whereby the occupational conditions encountered by the individual both mold his psychological processes and in turn are molded by his personality and behavior. No theory of adult personality development that fails to take account of the ongoing effects of occupational (and, presumably, other social) conditions can be regarded as realistic. By the same token, no social psychology of occupations that fails to take account of the ongoing effects of individual psychological functioning can be regarded as realistic.

Notes

1. Our primary source of data is a sample survey of 3,101 men, representative of all men employed in civilian occupations in the United States. These men were interviewed for us by the National Opinion Research Center (NORC) in the spring and summer of 1964. For more detailed information on sample and research design, see Kohn, 1969, pp. 235-264. In 1974 NORC reinterviewed a representative subsample of these men for us; this time, the wives (and, where applicable, one of the children) were interviewed, too. For detailed information on the follow-up study, see Kohn and Schooler (1978) and Kohn (1977).

2. Our principal indices of psychological functioning measure subjective reactions to the job itself (that is, job satisfaction and occupational com-

mitment), valuation of self-direction or of conformity to external authority (both for oneself and for one's children), self-conception (self-confidence, self-deprecation, fatalism, anxiety, and idea conformity), social orientation (authoritarian conservatism, criteria of morality, trustfulness, and receptiveness or resistance to change), alienation (powerlessness, self-estrangement, and normlessness), and intellectual functioning (intellectual flexibility, intellectuality of leisure-time activities). For detailed information about our definitions of these concepts and our methods of indexing them, see Kohn, 1969, pp. 47-58, 73-84, 265-269; Kohn and Schooler, 1973, pp. 99-101; Kohn, 1976, pp. 114-118.

3. Specifically, these twelve crucial occupational conditions are: (1) ownership/nonownership; (2) bureaucratization; (3) position in the supervisory hierarchy; (4) closeness of supervision; (5) routinization of the work; (6) substantive complexity of the work; (7) frequency of time-pressure; (8) heaviness of work; (9) dirtiness of work; (10) the likelihood, in this field, of there occurring a sudden and dramatic change in a person's income, reputation, or position; (11) the probability, in this line of work, of being held responsible for things outside one's control; and (12) the risk of loss of one's job or business.

4. The concept "substantive complexity" has been the subject of much research that goes considerably beyond the issues addressed in this essay. Many writers have adopted the concept and used it for such diverse purposes as reinterpreting the status-attainment model (Spaeth, 1976), proposing a new method of classifying the occupational structure of the U.S. economy (Temme, 1975), reassessing the psychological effects of complex role sets (Coser, 1975), interpreting the effects of fathers' occupational experiences on their sons' occupational choices (Mortimer, 1974; 1976), and searching out the sources of powerlessness (Tudor, 1972).

5. To validate this index, which is specifically tailored to each respondent's description of his own job, we have compared it to assessments of the average level of complexity of work with things, with data, and with people for the entire occupation, made by trained occupational analysts for the *Dictionary of Occupational Titles* (United States Department of Labor, 1965). The multiple correlation between our index of substantive complexity and the independently coded *Dictionary* ratings is 0.78—sufficiently high to assure us that our appraisals of substantive complexity accurately reflect the reality of people's work.

6. The two-stage least squares technique is described in detail by Kohn and Schooler (1973) and the references cited therein. This method attempts to "purge" each variable of the effects of all others with which it is reciprocally related by estimating from other pertinent data what each individual's score on that variable would have been if the other variables had not had an opportunity to affect it. These estimated scores are then used as independent variables in the (second stage) multiple-regression equations.

7. Concretely, the time-lagged path (that is, from substantive complexity in 1964 to intellectual flexibility in 1974) is 0.05 and the contemporane-

ous path is 0.18. A path of 0.18 might not under ordinary circumstances be considered striking; but a continuing effect of this magnitude on so stable a phenomenon as intellectual flexibility is impressive, because the cumulative impact will be much greater than the immediate effect at any one time. Continuing effects, even small-to-moderate continuing effects, on highly stable phenomena become magnified in importance. The effect of the substantive complexity of work on intellectual flexibility is especially noteworthy when we take into account that we are dealing with men who are at least ten years into their occupational careers.

8. Such evidence as we have from other countries is based on only approximate indices of substantive complexity. This evidence suggests that substantive complexity has psychological effects similar to those we have found in the United States, in West Germany (Hoff and Grueneisen, 1977a), in Italy (Pearlin, 1971; Kohn, 1969), in Ireland (Hynes, 1977), and in Peru (Scurrah and Montalvo, 1975), but probably not in Taiwan (Olsen, 1971). For a detailed discussion of these findings, see Kohn (1977). More definitive information may come from studies now being undertaken in Poland by Kazimierz Slomczynski, Jadwiga Koralewicz-Zebik, and Krystyna Janicka, and in West Berlin by Wolfgang Lempert, which use more precise indices of substantive complexity.

References

BALTES, PAUL B. 1968. Longitudinal and cross-sectional sequences in the study of age and generation effects. *Human Development*, 11:145-171.

BALTES, PAUL B., AND K. WARNER SCHAIE. 1976. On the plasticity of intelligence in adulthood and old age. *American Psychologist*, 31:720-725.

BLAU, PETER M., AND OTIS DUNCAN. 1967. *The American occupational structure*. New York: Wiley.

BLAU, PETER M., AND RICHARD A SCHOENHERR. 1971. *The structure of organizations*. New York: Basic Books.

BLAUNER, ROBERT. 1964. *Alienation and freedom: the factory worker and his industry*. Chicago: University of Chicago Press.

BREER, PAUL E., AND EDWIN A. LOCKE. 1965. *Task experience as a source of attitudes*. Homewood, Ill.: Dorsey.

COSER, ROSE LAUB. 1975. The complexity of roles as a seedbed of individual autonomy. In *The idea of social structure: papers in honor of Robert K. Merton,* ed. L. A. Coser. New York: Harcourt Brace Jovanovich.

COTTRELL, W. FRED. 1940. *The railroader*. Stanford: Stanford University Press.

DUNCAN, OTIS D., DAVID L. FEATHERMAN, AND BEVERLY DUNCAN. 1972. *Socioeconomic background and achievement*. New York: Seminar Press.

HOFF, ERNST-HARTMUT, AND VERONIKA GRUENEISEN. 1977a. Arbeitserfahrungen, Erziehungseinstellungen and Erziehungsverhalten von Eltern. In *Familiare Sozialisation: Probleme, Ergebnisse, Perspektiven,* ed. H. Lukesch and K. Schneewind. Stuttgart: Klett.

———. 1977b. Personal communication (unpublished data).

HORN, JOHN L., AND GARY DONALDSON. 1976. On the myth of intellectual decline in adulthood. *American Psychologist*, 31:701-719.

HYNES, EUGENE. 1977. Personal communication (unpublished data).

JÖRESKOG, KARL G. 1969. A general approach to confirmatory maximum likelihood factor analysis. *Psychometrika*, 34:183-202.

KOHN, MELVIN L. 1977. Reassessment, 1977. In *Class and conformity: a study in values*. 2nd ed. Chicago: University of Chicago Press.

———. 1976. Occupational structure and alienation. *American Journal of Sociology* 82:111-130.

———. 1969. *Class and conformity: a study in values*. Homewood, Ill.: Dorsey. (2nd ed., Chicago: University of Chicago Press, 1977.)

KOHN, MELVIN L., AND CARMI SCHOOLER. In press. Job conditions and intellectual flexibility: a longitudinal assessment of their reciprocal effects. In *Factor analysis and measurement in sociological research: a multidimensional perspective*, ed. E. F. Borgatta and D. J. Jackson. Beverly Hills: Sage Publications.

———. 1978. The reciprocal effects of the substantive complexity of work and intellectual flexibility: a longitudinal assessment. *American Journal of Sociology*, 84:24-52.

———. 1973. Occupational experience and psychological functioning: an assessment of reciprocal effects. *American Sociological Review*, 38:97-118.

———. 1969. Class, occupation, and orientation. *American Sociological Review*, 34:659-678.

MILLER., JOANNE, CARMI SCHOOLER, MELVIN L. KOHN, AND KAREN A. MILLER. Women and work: the psychological effects of occupational conditions. *American Journal of Sociology*, 85:66-94.

MORTIMER, JEYLAN T. 1976. Social class, work, and the family: some implications of the father's occupation for familial relationships and sons' career decisions. *Journal of Marriage and the Family*, 38:241-256.

———. 1974. Patterns of intergenerational occupational movements: a smallest-space analysis. *American Journal of Sociology*, 79:1278-1299.

OLSEN, STEPHEN. 1971. Family, occupation, and values in a Chinese urban community. Ph.D. diss., Cornell University.

PEARLIN, LEONARD I. 1971. *Class context and family relations: a cross-national study*. Boston: Little, Brown.

ROSENBAUM, JAMES E. 1976. *Making inequality: the hidden curriculum of high school tracking*. New York: Wiley.

SCURRAH, MARTIN J., AND ABNER MONTALVO. 1975. *Clase social y valores en Peru*. Lima, Peru: Escuela de Administracion de Negocios Para Graduados.

SEWELL, WILLIAM H., ROBERT M. HAUSER, AND DAVID L. FEATHERMAN, eds. 1976. *Schooling and achievement in American society*. New York: Academic Press.

SPAETH, JOE L. 1976. Cognitive complexity: a dimension underlying the socioeconomic achievement process. In *Schooling and achievement in*

American Society, ed. William H. Sewell, Robert M. Hauser, and David L. Featherman. New York: Academic Press.

TEMME, LLOYD V.1975. *Occupation: meanings and measures.* Washington, D.C.: Bureau of Social Science Research.

TUDOR, BILL. 1972. A specification of relationships between job complexity and powerlessness. *American Sociological Review,* 37:596-604.

UNITED STATES DEPARTMENT OF LABOR. 1965. *Dictionary of occupational titles.* Washington, D. C.: United States Government Printing Office. 3rd ed.

WHYTE, WILLIAM F. 1969. *Organizational behavior: theory and application.* Homewood, Ill.: Richard D. Irwin.

——. 1961. *Men at work.* Homewood, Ill.: Dorsey.

——. 1955. *Money and motivation: an analysis of incentives in industry.* New York: Harper.

PART FOUR

Individual Adaptation and Development in Adulthood

TEN

Transformations during Early and Middle Adult Years

SINCE ERIK ERIKSON opened the door to adult development back in the 1950s, we psychoanalysts have been trying to make sense of what we see. Since what we see is so much more than we can talk about because of the constraints of our theoretical language, it is time to try to create a language that corresponds to the subject. What I am proposing in this essay is not a new language to replace existing psychoanalytic language, as has been proposed by Roy Schafer, but an additional set of terms designed to capture the sense of movement, direction, and struggle that all of us experience during adulthood, especially when we confront the problems of work and love.-

The basic concept is *transformation*. Growth is defined as a transformation. A transformation is an expansion of self-definition. The self-definition is essentially a license to be, and while operating within that license, a person feels minimal conflict or anxiety and a maximum sense of security. While functioning outside that license, there is anxiety, conflict, and a minimum sense of security until the license is redefined. The boundaries of the self-definition are usually blended into everyday behavior, but become almost palpable when an expansion or growth is taking place via risk-taking behavior in a novel situation. Risk-taking behavior creates anxiety and a sense of internal prohibition against proceeding. The direction of growth and process of transformation are expressed by the tension of vital signals — away from stagnation and claustrophobic suffocation toward vitality and an expanded sense of inner freedom. The process of transformation may be illustrated by a case history.

THE CASE OF NICOLE

What follows is a two-year period in the life of Nicole, during her thirty-sixth and thirty-seventh years.

At thirty-seven she has been married for fifteen years and has four boys ranging from age five to thirteen. She is a vivacious, bright, charming woman who exudes warmth and vitality within an overall sense of solid settledness. Her love of life includes the embroidered stories of her children's mishaps and discoveries and an unusually strong pleasure in her husband's company. Not only are they the best of friends who talk about everything and share their inner lives, but they are great lovers on their frequent trips when spontaneity and zaniness rule the day. He is a successful, hard-working professional and they have abundant material goods which they see as toys to play with. Up until Nicole was thirty-six, she was very happy to be a full-time mother and wife. That way of life afforded her enough time for her own activities, which included photography, reading several books a week, and being on the board of an experimental school. She is literate and appreciates the good phrases of others as well as her own, such as, when referring to her life with four small boys, "my life is one long, interrupted conversation."

Around thirty-six, Nicole found herself wanting more out of life, partly in response to her youngest child's going to school and partly out of a desire to use and develop certain talents outside of the home that represented vital parts of herself. She wanted to add something to her established life. She did not want to leave home or give up what she enjoyed and was not offended by the work of motherhood and wifehood. But like many educated women, she felt uncomfortable when asked at cocktail parties what she "did" in life — and when she found herself initially labeled "just a housewife." On a conscious level, there was a rather simple and easy solution in sight, for since she enjoyed photography and had been doing quite a bit for the school, she thought she might establish a part-time photography business. In order to do it on her own time and still be around home during crucial hours, she had a darkroom constructed in the guest room. One thing led to another and soon an acting agency wanted to give her steady work as a portrait photographer.

At this point, on the verge of commercial success, she put aside her photography. She bumped into her first internal obstacle! Working and selling herself commercially contradicted her unrecognized dream of continuing to be the special loved child who was stroked for being talented but who never really had to discipline herself or compromise her talents in the service of making an income. Her mother's labeling her photographic interest as "only a phase" strengthened, but did not cause, the internal obstacle—the unconscious self-definition. While she was in the midst of working through this internal struggle, her parents moved in. They took over the room that had been her studio and darkroom and just as the sink and plumbing were being ripped out she developed a pain in her stomach. Within a day she was in bed with a full-blown peptic ulcer which required medication and care for over two weeks. During the next year she did not touch her photographic equipment (which had been moved to an outside darkroom) nor unsheathe her camera. Several months later her father developed symptoms of brain cancer and died within six months. His illness occupied all of her life and his loss was mourned painfully. He was not only a father but also a very special intellectual companion who had the same love of life that she herself had, and that her mother had never been able to share. She was left with her own grief, the absence of a buffer between herself and her mother, and the grief of her four children, who dearly loved their grandfather.

Her mother's grief seemed to overpower Nicole. She was unable to express her own feelings when her mother was around. Her mother intimated that only she who lost her husband had the right to express her loss, while Nicole, who had a loving husband and a young family, had no such right. It was partly because of the burden of her mother's presence six months after the death of her father that she came to see me, and partly because she felt stuck in life. She was constantly on the edge of ulcer symptoms that were unresponsive to special diet and medication.

At this point being stuck meant that the self-initiated expansion of her self-definition—allowing her to exercise her talent in photography in a way recognized by the world—had been impacted by a conjuction of inner and outer forces: her wish to remain the pure, admired, talented, untested little girl, and the lack of support from her mother, who perceived her only as a dilettante. The symbolic ripping out of her right to be a photographer with the ripping out of the plumbing translated into a visceral ripping peptic ulcer.

Why did this competent, capable woman of thirty-seven continue to respond so absolutely to her mother's rather minor disapproval of her urgent growth need, especially since she had full support of her husband and a proud response to her photography from her boys? A bit of history is needed to understand the power of her mother.

Nicole was the bright, adored first child in a family of three. Her mother worked downstairs in a dry goods store and was available only during lunchtime until Nicole was four. Aunts and cousins did the adoring and caretaking. When her brother was born she was mightily offended, as are most children by the birth of a sibling, but continued and exaggerated her pleasing ways to get the adoration, admiration, and attention of those around her. When she was six years old the family moved across the country, and although she received more absolute time from her now nonworking mother, her mother's new importance and centrality left Nicole with a sensitive stomach in response to her mother's fluctuations of affection and withdrawal. She remained a "good girl" throughout her adolescence, became the girlfriend to her mother, and, after a brief period of work following college, married her husband in a great romantic flourish which continues to this day.

Though she was an exemplary wife and mother to her own family, she had not been an exemplary daughter in her mother's eyes because she, unlike her five-year younger sister, refused to play child to her mother and to imitate and agree with all of her mother's ways. In the role of wife and mother, she had been her own person and quite autonomous. Only when she began to go beyond the confines of that self-definition into the work world did her mother's power over the course of her life reassert itself. It is because of that move that she lost much of her relative autonomy.

What are the dynamics of this shift of autonomy in this healthy adult person? Nicole, by virtue of being a full-time mother, was doing more than reflecting her commitment to her children and exercising the assets of her personality that allowed her to be such a good mother. It is true that she was warm, open, loving, psychologically minded, empathic, and interested in the complexity of the growth of her children, that she was able to be involved with them and have perspective on them at the same time, and that she enjoyed her life as a mother. But it is also true that in so doing she was being the opposite of, and better than, the part-time mother of her early childhood. In crossing the line of self-definition and becoming a worker-mother she would be unconsciously committing the same crime her mother perpetrated on her as she judged it while a child. In that sense, becoming a worker-mother was not just a conscious choice to expand her horizons in her thirty-seventh year of life but was an act that destabilized a major defensive tactic imbricated into the life structure, opening the door to the buried, angry conflict between herself and her mother and to the angry, mother-deprived child that had been covered over by the adored child and loving adult. Also aroused were memories of being the rejected child who was angry at her brother's birth, hence might be angry at all men, and might even be angry at her own boys. Not only was the door opened to unresolved hurt and anger by becoming a worker-mother, but another, and maybe more primitive, dilemma was joined that heretofore had been avoided. As she became more like her mother of early childhood, might she not become exactly like her, and lose herself in the bargain — the ubiquitous primitive fear of becoming encased within our earliest blurred image of the first love object?

The problem with this condensed explanation is that it smacks of speculation and historical reductionism and cannot be proved or directly observed. But one can observe directly the myths and fantasies and false ideas that are part of Nicole's consciousness during the thirty-seventh year of her life. And it is to this that I turn — her current mythic misinterpretations of reality that stand on their own as valid dynamics but are also the data for the above condensed formulation. It is important to keep in mind in what follows that each of the ideas and fears are "believed" to be part of reality until they are clear enough to be challenged as possible misinterpretations. They exist just beyond focus in the dark interior or are embedded in unformulated assumptions about the external world. These false ideas are the operative barrier to growth and the functional boundary of the self-definition.

Underlying the first articulated, rather benign version of the internal obstacle — not being willing to relinquish the ideal of the special child — were a series of more basic fears. The first mythic fear Nicole encountered was that her desire to have things for herself would erupt uncontrollably as she took the first step into the life of worker-mother. Since she had been "too good" as a girl and gave "too much" to her children and husband in return for their praise, she feared that she would totally and suddenly abandon the role of mother-wife that was beginning to feel obligatory. On the other hand, she recognized that she enjoyed her home and family. Only after articulating her fear of having a greedy, impulsive child inside of her that would act contrary to her conscious wishes to integrate a work life with a mother life was she able to realize operationally that she had options along the way and that she was not really in an either/or position. With that she began to process the greedy child images as archaic parts of herself that, once acknowledged as such, were controllable. The internal dialogue helped her understand how much she had performed for her mother's love. Following that insight, she had a burst of fury at her mother for continuing to subvert her efforts at individuation by rewarding her only when she was a sweet little girl-woman.

Following this episode she found she could no longer read two or three books a week. Out of the fuzzy-headed inability to concentrate she began to see images of Lady Macbeth and a knife plunging into a body. She became in touch with her second mythic fear—that in order to grow, she would have to fight her mother to the death. Access to the demonic fury within her led to the realization that the killer imagery belonged to an archaic battle displaced onto a rather vacuous current battle with her mother who indeed stood against her change but was in no position to stop her. The greedy child image was transmogrified into the killer-child or killer-mother image; but once held up to the light of day, that imagery could no longer endure or control so absolutely.

Next Nicole discovered that she believed that she could change only if she could get her mother to change. Though she resented performing for affection and praise, she also felt she was hooked on it. When she went against her mother, and her mother was cold in response, she first felt a pain in her stomach, then felt very angry, and then felt a tremendous urge to retreat and do what her mother wanted. Since her mother's withdrawal of love was translated viscerally to Nicole's belly, she believed she could go forward only if she could get her mother to admire, understand, and endorse her strivings. If she could convince her mother to praise her for becoming a worker-mother, then she could avoid the primitive, unconscious kill-or-be-killed battles, and silence the pain in her stomach that made her feel her mother must ultimately win in any standoff.

When Nicole asked herself why she did not probe and proceed along various career lines experimentally, she discovered the next myth blocking her path. The first reason that came to her was the familiar and popular fear of rejection, that is, she might ask for the job and not get it. Imagining how that might feel, she saw how much she wanted to preserve her self-image of the special child who is loved and adored and gets whatever she wants because she is so vivacious and bright. A deeper understanding followed—fear of being accepted, not rejected, was what kept her from experimenting. Going to work in *any* real job was a step down from the position of the special child. Being accepted on the job was a loss both of the special-child image of the past and of the future ideal career. Since she was so good with words, she had reason to believe that she could write better than many contemporary authors. Someday she hoped to use that talent. Any beginning job in photography would be interpreted as a relinquishment of that talent, as if, once entering the work world, she was not free to move from her initial entry position.

She next challenged the myth that her children and husband could not survive without her and that she could not survive without them. She went on a trip to New York with a friend. On the way to the airport she had a strange worry that a killer earthquake might occur in Los Angeles while she was away.

Having worked her way through these first five mythic obstacles, she encountered the most powerful one to date. It left her in bed for two days with stomach pain. The strength of her marriage rested in part on total openness with her husband. She had been discussing with him her conflicts and desire about work, and as she became more firm in her resolve she felt him to be irritated with her and to reject her sexually. She was no longer able to arouse him in the way she had before. At first she thought that she was doing something terribly wrong, then she thought there was something terribly wrong with him. He must hate women since he had such a hateful mother! Her ulcer began to act up as she came to the conclusion that her husband's reaction faced her with a choice. He was saying, indirectly, that she must be a caretaker and mother to him or he would be angry and punish her. She was not allowed to be a competent working woman in this marriage. To have her new self was to lose her man. To be sick in bed with stomach pain was the result of the conflict that seemed unresolvable and was at the same time an attempt to resolve the conflict by instituting the dialogue with her husband in which she was the taken-care-of-child and no longer the threatening competent woman. Furthermore, it got her out of the resentful role of having to be the mother to him while not being allowed to be a self to herself. She responded to his transitory shift as if it were an absolute statement that he did not give her permission to change. He temporarily became the absolute authority replacing the original absolute authority over her growth, her mother. At the moment that she went to bed she thoroughly believed the myth that some other person could continue to have veto power over her path of growth and development and that she had encountered that person in the husband she totally trusted. Her closest friend had become her worst enemy.

The corollary appeared to be that men, generically, will not allow women to leave home. She unraveled that overgeneralization. In response to her stress and ambivalence about being on the school's executive board, her husband suggested she resign. Her first interpretation was that her enemy wanted to return her to the confines of the home — a variation of barefoot and pregnant. As she probed the matter more deeply, she discovered that she wanted to resign from the board because belonging was tied to the identity of being the mother-volunteer rather than the mother-worker she was aiming toward. After that insight she remembered the conversation with her husband differently, and saw how she selectively fed him information and almost demanded that he suggest she resign from the school board in order to displace the responsibility for the decision onto him and to battle with him rather than with her own separation-depression fears about leaving the major role of her adult life. She was pleasantly surprised to find that when she admitted to herself that she wanted money and power in her own right, she was able to resign from the school board in a diplomatic and timely way; and as a bonus surprise, the surging sense of power made her feel more sexual and lustful rather than less so. She engaged in some pattern-breaking sexual activities with her husband that had previously been fantasies, and after an initial period of wish-fulfilling fear that she might become hypersexual and go crazy with lust, she settled into a new, more open, uninhibited sexual life with her husband — the kind that she had been able to have on trips with him but had never been able to carry off at home while surrounded by children's bedrooms.

Soon she began to believe that she was too strong for her husband, and that in fact she must sacrifice her capacities to his ego — the opposite of her earlier belief that he was such a strong, potentially destructive enemy that he could refuse her permission to grow. In the current belief, he became a little boy, and the sacrifice she resented most was the joyous, fun-loving part of herself that was the frivolous and zany counterpart at times to his solid, sometimes too serious view of life and pleasure. It was too much like the play that went on in reverse between her joyous father and drab mother. Her belief that *her* strength was overpowering alternated with the opposite belief that she was really a little girl. If she showed her strength clearly, she would lose her husband, and then if her strength waned, she would have no protector. After dealing with this last complicated set of barrier images, she once again took up photography.

This brought to the surface the next false belief: now that she had everything — a direction, internal permission to work, and a family that loved her — it was too much! She was too lucky; some evil must befall her. The evil eye must be there, watching and waiting for the time to strike.

After challenging that superstition by taking a pleasure trip with her husband, a rather intellectualized barrier surfaced. Was she becoming her mother? Was she voluntarily leaving her children the same way her mother had voluntarily worked? Did she really want a career outside of the home or was she doing unto her children what was done unto her in some kind of primitive retaliation?

Several weeks later her career interest took a twist and she found herself with a whole series of creative ideas about how travel agencies might better customize service. Ideas were coming to her fast and furious out of the blue. She might become a travel agent, work part-time, still be around for the children, and at the same time participate in a great love of hers, traveling. A very exciting integration was taking place. She knew she was ready to act and called several travel agencies to find out how to get trained. While talking to one agency owner, who was about to get rid of her, she said, "You really ought to interview me; I'm quite special." This took him by surprise and he listened to her account of why she would be a good travel agent and agreed to interview her; within two weeks she was working happily and with a great deal of energy and vitality. Then she encountered the last false belief standing in her way. She believed that her mode of selling and servicing clients would have to be like that of her saleswoman mother, who survived the great Depression by exploiting every opportunity to earn a little more. She came to recognize how different she was from her mother. Her own style and ethics and circumstance in life were so different. She would service all of her clients the way she would service her friends and family.

After beginning to work, she still had to deal with members of her family. Her mother's belittling, nonsupportive attempt to return her to the little girl role failed. She dealt with it firmly and understandingly, though she resented her mother's envy. Her husband had some minor troubles adjusting, complained of her being unavailable around dinnertime, and had a mild hypochondriacal attack. These responses by the important people in her life were seen clearly because she was not hampered by the false belief that she was not entitled to do what she found herself doing. She had gone through an odyssey of mythic barriers and arrived at a new self-definition which included her right to work, and from that perspective the reverberations in her family were seen for what they were: as temporary responses to change, and not as evidence that what she was doing was wrong, dangerous, and destructive. She had truly undergone a transformation of self.

Nicole is a real person whose case personalizes and concretizes principles of human behavior here subsumed under the concept of transformation. Nicole illustrates the following ten properties of the transformational processes.

(1) A transformation implies a *shift in the defensive system* imbricated into the current life structure that is being disturbed. Initially Nicole had to deal with the fear she was "really" an out-of-control greedy child who would destroy the valued parts of her life if she changed the controlling boundaries of that life. The "bad" child was banished by the life structure of the "good" mother. At the moment she starts her transformational odyssey she's faced with the fear that she will either expose an untameable, shameful child or stay stuck in an encrusted defensive identification.

(2) *False ideas* make up the operative barrier to growth and the functional boundary of self-definition. These ideas are "believed" until they surface. They form a second underground vision of reality which we will call childhood consciousness.

(3) The processing of these false ideas is *not intellectual*—it is a particular form of internal dialogue. Only after the diffuse anxiety is funneled into the charged belief that "I really am an uncontrollable greedy child" could that "reality" image be questioned and contradicted by the adult reality view that "I have options, choices and time." Until then, the rational reality state was powerless to contradict the childhood reality state because there was no point of contact. In order for this internal dialogue to take place, Nicole had to trust herself enough to suspend the protective device holding that dangerous self-image in check. She had to "allow" the surfacing of the greedy child to take place.

(4) The self-definition boundary is composed of a *series of linked false ideas,* the surfacing and disposition of one leading to the advent of the next. Since there is a confusion-anxiety-clarity sequence surrounding each false idea, it is easy to mistakenly interpret the presence of familiar anxiety as evidence of no progress, as regression — when in fact it may be a sign of progression.

(5) At some points in the transformational process there is the experience of *warfare.* As the drive to expand and become whole meets the provisional boundary of the self-definition in the form of these false ideas, there is an impact and a sense of being arbitrarily held back, analogous to the sensation a child must feel when stopped from climbing out of a playpen. There is an unseen enemy to our imperative movement — a primitive superego image internally laden and elaborated by the memories of real experiences with imperfectly empathic parents and arbitrary authorities. I suspect the force and fierceness of this enemy within partly reflects the narcissistic dimension of our particular parents' need for us to be "their way."

(6) The *location of the enemy* is always in doubt. It is hard enough to consider that we are often the enemies to our own growth imperative and to accept as fact our ambivalent attitude toward change and internal freedom; but it is doubly hard to keep that focus when at times there are real foes to our progress in the persons of our spouses and bosses. It is easy to transpose the internal conflict to a battle with another person; it is temporarily relieving, serves to objectify, and gives hope since the other person, no matter how powerful or important, is much less powerful than the primitive superego imagos within. Sometimes we make a friend into an enemy unnecessarily with some help from a slippage of logical thinking, "If I hurt, someone responsible for me must be hurting me," or "If he or she isn't completely helpful, he or she must be intentionally hurtful."

(7) There are also *friends to our growth,* those who respond openly to what we are becoming, those who endorse and confirm our expanded selves. These too may be spouses and bosses; and when they are, they get an added measure of our love, loyalty, and creativity. Often we have to seek confirmation outside of our established intimacies and workplace, because our former self is too densely interwoven into the surrounding social system by labeling, or mutual conspiracies with our spouse or employer. New friends, new work, and new loves attach themselves to our need to confirm and vitalize fragile parts of ourselves through other peoples' eyes and love. All parts human are originally born in mutuality.

(8) *The fluidity of destructive imagery interferes with intimacy.* In Nicole we saw this through her visceral response and through a series of contradictory false ideas. Originally her stomach lining was being ripped by her mother, when she caused the darkroom plumbing to be removed; then it was her husband who sent her to bed with stomach pain. The barriers to intimacy were erected in situ when the trusted parents and husband were experienced as destructive enemies. But the same barriers were also constructed when the destructive imagery resided within — when Nicole imaged herself destroying her mother or believed herself to be too strong and overwhelming for her husband.

(9) The *outcome* of a successful transformation is a new level of passion for life, accompanied by a greater sense of internal freedom and power. Conversely, an impacted transformation is accompanied by an enfeeblement of passion, and very often symptoms of stress disease. It is like driving a car with the brake on.

(10) A significant transformation always affects *those close to us,* bringing out the best and the worst in them, just as it brings out the best and the worst in ourselves as we temporarily lose our autonomy

and struggle with the false ideas and destructive imagery of our archaic selves.

In the case of Nicole, we see that work and love were subtly and powerfully affected by the processes of transformation. I see transformation as the central concept of adult development. If we are to understand the subtle day-to-day changes as well as the large crises in work and love, we must appeal to these central, ongoing processes whereby each of us is driven by maturational necessity to be more whole, to include within us disenfranchised parts, and to be as internally free as we are capable of being. We do this in steps throughout our life and rarely reach a steady state with either our work or our love life, although any particular career or any particular love may last us a lifetime. But within that career and within that love relationship there is constant renegotiation in an attempt to keep the career and love relationship as confirming and allowing of our emerging parts and as free from the position of "enemy" as possible. The physiology of work and love is as complicated, or more complicated, than organ physiology.

The transformation of Nicole was large and dramatic. We encounter those transformations when we make career changes or major substitutions in our love life. But we are also undergoing transformations on an everyday basis that are not as dramatic but are just as compelling as we strive for higher levels of intimacy, greater freedom of sensuality, increased license to use talents heretofore underutilized, in order to reach a greater confidence in our own authority and to overcome internal prohibitions which unnecessarily restrict our fullest humanity. All of this is done in equilibrium with our family and others close to us at home and work. All this is done within a certain historical period, within a culture and a subculture. Also there are some systematic changes with age that affect the surfacing of various issues of work and love. The workplace subculture is one aspect of this complicated mosaic that can substantially affect the transformational process.

OBSTACLES TO TRANSFORMATION PROCESSES IN THE WORKPLACE

Ideally, the process of transformation in the workplace proceeds as it did with Nicole. Her initial work was being a mother and wife. She responded to the vital signs of stagnation, discovered her own inner direction, and then pursued the path it indicated. Although her original choice of paid work was photography, she changed along the way in response to another set of urges that surfaced. Now she's happy as a travel agent. That work confirms many parts of her and has an idiosyncratic meaning which makes it relevant to her life. The success of the process is measured by her sense of vitality, the feeling that she is moving on and creating.

Most of Nicole's transformation work was recognition and identification of internal obstacles. That is not the case for a person in a large corporation or professional organization where external obstacles blend with internal obstacles. Each workplace subculture has its own dynamics and pressures and shapes us by offering rewards when we fit ourselves into the role dictated by the relevant stereotype or the organizational chart rather than following the charting process taking place within us. The workplace is not organized for human development and hence inevitably conflicts with the transformational process.

OBSTACLE 1: STEREOTYPING

In some careers, the structural characteristics allow the transformational process to proceed relatively freely. For example, doctors and lawyers can shift interests within their broad, open professions without sacrificing money or status and without having anybody looking over their shoulders marking their report cards. But even in these professions where one can change the pace and direction of work rather easily, doctors sometimes leave medicine and lawyers sometimes leave law; they leave their only adult "work family." Although medicine offers many opportunities and may indeed fit individual talents and temperament, it also imposes a certain concomitant definition of adultness, including the heavy responsibilities of incessant duty and obligation to others, and of being serious and following safe routines most of the time. At times doctors and lawyers find themselves too constrained by these obligations (not the work itself) and leave the profession in order to regain their playfulness or express other vital parts of themselves submerged under the stereotype, just as Nicole had to escape from the stereotype of "housewife."

OBSTACLE 2: DEFINING SUCCESS AS POWER

The temptation to go up the vertical ladder in large, pyramidal organizations is so great that employees hardly recognize new, internally generated interests or else consider them to present a security-threatening conflict. In organizations that are exciting and on the move, the temptation to move up becomes a demand imposed by management policy. For example, one aggressive, leading organization rotates its managers every eighteen to twenty-four months, rewarding those who become most visible in their new assignment, shape up their suborganization, and show a profit. This is without regard for inner processes or long-term effects of "fit." There is a powerful inducement and opportunity to go up the vertical ladder as quickly as possible and become a "real man." Those who stay in the system characteristically work twelve- to fourteen-hour days year after year and end up married to their jobs and in trouble with their families. It is known as a young man's organization in which nobody seems happy but all are making a lot of money. Once caught in the whirlpool effect of that social system it is hard to retrieve one's autonomy and to find one's own inner direction and transformational track. The excitement is all "out there" in the unending challenges and the opportunities to become a powerful man. The organization seems to be a complete definition of life.

OBSTACLE 3: ALLOWING WORK TO SANITIZE LIFE

Work plays into our defensive system by making us feel big and important and ridding us of feelings of inadequacy or human frailty or inner complicatedness. The workplace sanitizes us as we become part of it, but a vicious spiral is born because it is a compensatory system. The only effective way to quiet our fears about the human condition is to first acknowledge them; instead, when we bury the disavowed yet omnipresent reality messages about the human condition we experience by getting "bigger," we do not quiet our fears at all — we keep them at the same constant, unresolved level. This keeps us on a treadmill. Often, the only way a transformational process can take place within this work setting is through failure or stress disease, both of which require a questioning of the workplace ideology and the meaning of work in life. Another unfortunate way a transformation sometimes starts is through the trauma of separation and divorce when the spouse can no longer bear the incompleteness of the "too successful" worker.

OBSTACLE 4: CHANGING FOR ECONOMIC REASONS ONLY

In the last several decades there has been an effort to humanize the workplace, and recently there has been a demand on the part of the workers, when job competition is not too stiff, to have work that is challenging and meaningful and offers opportunities to learn and grow. This demand competes with demands for rank and money and in many instances is a more powerful factor than either of those customary rewards or the threat of loss of job. If an organization is responsive to the demand for more meaningful work and helps people accordingly, the transformational process is abetted. This requires an open dialogue between employer and employee in which everyone's goals or requirements are clearly stated.

In one large electronic manufacturing company, Joe, a thirty-six-year-old man who had been an accountant for a manufacturing division, insisted that he needed to become a line manager in that division and was accorded the opportunity. Two years later he is still very excited about his job and explained to me that accountants sit on the sidelines and watch and are not "real" men because they are in such a safe position, whereas he needed at that time of his life to prove to himself that he was capable of dealing with responsibility, pressure, excitement, and the risk of making decisions that could be wrong. He had to explore his doubts that he was still his mother's protected child while in the unassailable position of accountant. The job change was really part of a transformational process. This man would have left that company in order to seek the new opportunity because he felt the urge so strongly and because he was the kind of person who honored those urges even though he did not understand their origin and full meaning until after the had accomplished his purpose. He received no increase in rank or salary from his change of job and in fact forfeited a faster track in order to change his self-definition.

OBSTACLE 5: CONFLICTING INTERESTS BETWEEN COMPANY AND EMPLOYEE

All organizations are not equally responsive and all people are not as clear or insistent as Joe about what they want. Growth can be impacted by organizational or economic reality. In some organizations employees are afraid of asking for a change because organizations view such requests as acts of disloyalty or as disruptions. They want their employees to stay in their current positions because this is most efficient or fits their organizational concept. Joe's request for a change might have caused a conflict with his superior, who may have needed him to carry out a function and found it difficult or time consuming to replace him. It might not have been realistically possible for him to change within that organization, and if the job market was tight he may not have had an opportunity in another organization. Under those circumstances his growth would have been hindered and he would have been a good candidate for a stress disease. Undoubtedly Joe's interest in the work of accounting would have diminished and been filled with conflict. His work would not be a vital, creative part of his life as it is today.

Trying to accommodate where we no longer fit is a more difficult process today than it was forty years ago when adapting to a situation was of higher and more pervasive value. Now we expect our growth to be facilitated, and blockage is doubly frustrating. Few of us can do exactly what we want in life and compromises are always being made, but to the extent that we do what we have to do to survive and prosper and at the same time do work that is confirming of our transformational process, we can enjoy rather than endure the work part of our life.

WORK AND AGE

When we begin our worklife in the twenties or earlier, we start with assumptions about work that originate in childhood and reflect our parents' values as well as our own reparative fantasies. These ideas have not been tested and are contaminated by an idealizing process in which we hope that the work not only will be pleasurable but also will aid us in overcoming feelings of inadequacy, smallness, and uncertainty. When we attach ourselves to particular work, we are likely to stay with it because, if we are successful, it confirms our status as adults. In return for this gift of adultness, we tend to accept the explicit and implicit value system of the particular organization or career, becoming narrower in relation to our full potential while becoming deeper in relation to a specific real-life competency. The work becomes us, not just our activity of choice. We tend to bluff and pretend to more competencies than we actually have in the early twenties and then fill in our arrogated confidences with the experience of competency by the end of the twenties.

Work during the twenties serves so many developmental functions that it makes most of us willing to work long and hard without questioning seriously the fundamental value of what we are doing and why we are doing it as long as we are constantly feeling better about ourselves. To the degree that a job becomes a career and becomes an open pathway to escalation in the future, the sense of optimism increases with the sense of competency. When the job is not linked to escalating roles, that optimism is blunted. Much of this is class-linked; middle-class managers have much more optimistic viewpoints in the twenties than hourly workers, whereas, for example, unemployed members of minorities have no reason for optimism since their growth is often stopped at a crucial stage as a result of prejudice.

These generalities of the twenties are true for both men and women, but for women they are complicated by the issue of maternity. Since early childhood a man has been socialized to believe that he must find meaning in his work and that he is a captive of the workplace. Most women expect to have an option: to work outside the home or to work inside the home. For those women who choose to work outside the home during their twenties, it is a period of increasing competence and confidence as long as the issue of having a child is in abeyance. The fear of becoming too caught up in the work world is always present for those who intend to have children, whereas their male counterparts do not have that concern. Work, then, is confirming of one part of the woman and in competition with the other part — the mothering part of the woman. For those women who become mothers and give up outside work during the twenties, there is a tendency for confidence to be eroded because status support for motherhood as a career is lacking in this society and because the task of motherhood is almost impossible. There is no opportunity to improve one's rank in motherhood as there is in an organized career where projects are completed and promotions granted. Although the women may be exercising sets of skills that will be useful to her personal development later in life — empathy, intuition, and emotional range — these are not premium skills in the work world which dominates our value systems and grants official adultness to those in their twenties eager for an anchor outside the parental home. There is a tendency in the twenties still to believe that there is one right way to do things and that there are real adults in this world. During our twenties we tend to do what we think we should be doing and therefore judge ourselves by arbitrary internal standards. Awareness of the transformational process is constrained by these arbitrary standards which seem to inhere in the world "out there" and must be accepted, we think, as "reality." Therefore, most of our growth work is done "out there" as we respond to social and economic necessity.

By the end of the twenties, this frame of reference seems to come to a natural end as we achieve sufficient competence to ensure that we are truly adults who can handle the adult enterprise of work and will not return whimpering to our parents' home for board and care. There is also a dawning recognition that we have paid a high price for this achievement. We begin to question self-imposed limitations upon our future career course. The arbitrary standards are found to be "in here." In work situations we feel quite competent and consequently frustrated by less competent managers. We are still willing to work hard but are becoming more interested in working hard to maximize our own growth, personally defined, as compared to the twenties when we honored the competing motive of doing what we should do to prove that we were adult enough to master the tasks as defined by others. During the early thirties, we begin to be a more divided self and a more interesting self. Although we want to push forward into our career, we are also questioning the ways we want our career to go to complement our expanding self. As long as it rids us of our childhood mythic smallness, we are not capable of totally surrendering work as a defense, but the grip of work as a defense is lessening in favor of work as a self-defined and slowly discovered meaningful activity. We accept new assignments with more question and more frequently ask whether we really want to do them.

This process of questioning and seeking occupies a relatively small part of our time and energy in the early thirties but grows to larger proportions during the midlife decade, thirty-five to forty-five. If in response to the questioning and accelerated transformational process we engineer better and better fits between our inner needs and current job activity, the questioning process is satisfied and work continues as a labor of love. If, on the other hand, the questioning process does not lead to shifts and changes that are small but cumulative during the course of the thirties, our suppressed growth develops into a major break that demands psychological work. This break may take several forms: renewed repressions, often fortified by alcohol or acting out; prematurely becoming old, dull, and dutiful; psychological or physiological symptoms; deterioration of interest level and concentration; or other mental disturbances requiring the reconsideration of the meaning of work. These are the potential midlife crises which may or may not end in midcareer shifts.

In the midlife period, while striving for authenticity and generativity as the organizing themes of the transformation processes, serious and urgent questioning takes place about the meaning of work. During this time of profound changes and major revitalization opportunities it is most important to identify idiosyncratic meanings of work. Underutilized talents and capacities are still locked away, defensively isolated in response to one's childhood thinking about the core of the self. For example, one medical doctor discovered that he had worked unsuccessfully as an academic researcher until he was forty years old because he was afraid that he would look "greedy" if he were a private practitioner. He had been warned during most of his young life not to be "greedy" like his bad uncles. He should help people, as did his devoted civil-servant father. As an adult he came to see his father not so much devoted as scared, too security conscious, and dull. He found himself very much the same at age forty, when symptoms mimicking a muscle-wasting disease forced him to reflect on his life's choices. Then he recognized that he wanted to make money to support his four children (even if that represented greed) and that he loved to teach students and treat people rather than do research upon them. His decision was confirmed as "right" several years later when he was given an outstanding teacher award; at that time he talked with deep commitment about his concern for students, a concern that he was able to exercise only after he left the unsatisfactory and low-paying researcher role and became a visiting professor from the domain of "rich" private practitioners. He no longer labeled as "greedy" making a decent living and doing the work for which he felt he had talent. This outcome occurred only after psychological work that followed the same lines portrayed in the case of Nicole. With a revitalized interest in work, the muscle-wasting symptoms disappeared and a new relationship with his own family began. He became generative and authentic in one swoop.

Midlife is a dramatic period for those women who began a dialogue with themselves in their early thirties about returning to the workplace after a career as wife and mother. This is illustrated in the life of Nicole, who succeeded in her transformational effort relatively easily because the optimal set of circumstances in her life joined with her talent for processing the inner dialogue. She could reflect on archaic ideas without being dominated by them or scared off by the anxiety generated as they approached consciousness. The transformations related to work during this age period are usually much more difficult for most women I have known and treated. Often there is a turbulence that lasts for years, disrupting the marriage and occasionally destroying it.

THE CONFLICT BETWEEN INTIMACY AND GROWTH

We return to the case of Nicole once more. While contented in the self-definition of mother-wife and feeling good about herself, she formed an equilibrium and silent conspiracy with her husband that fortified and enhanced her sense of being a lovable and loving woman. Her husband's love for her confirmed that part of herself. In return, she did the same for him. As long as she looked at herself as primarily a mother-wife, she confirmed, within that arrangement, his sense of being a caring, loving man-husband-father. When she began to change, she upset that balance. When she perceived her husband as disapproving of that change and withdrawing his love or being irritated with her, she was tempted to sacrifice her growth. At those times he became confining to her new growth, while confirming of her old and still valued self. If she had stopped at any of those points, he would have been the one who kept her in the old position and maintained her "label" as *only* wife-mother. He would have become the enemy to her forward movement and self-expansion. Their love would be scarred because her transformational process did not go to completion.

INTERFERENCE 1: THE INTERNAL OBSTACLE EXTERNALIZED

Nicole's husband would have become the enemy because of her misperception of the quantity and quality of his disturbance that her changing the contractual conspiracy of mutual confirmation had caused. She would have created the enemy and reacted to her creation as if it were real and their intimacy would have been disturbed by the anger directed at the superego-like figure of her husband. The internal obstacle projected onto the spouse, supported by qualitative evidence, but not quantifiably accurate, would have disturbed the intimacy.

INTERFERENCE 2: THE EXTERNAL OBSTACLE

On the other hand, if Nicole's huband had been a different kind of man, he might have responded belligerently to his experience — Nicole's withdrawing from him the conspiratorial confirmation of his lovable maleness. That withdrawal may be aggravated by another phenomenon. In the midst of a powerful transformational process we tend to be more closely guarded and less demonstrably loving because we temporarily slip into the dangerous world of primitive power imagery which may at any moment turn out to be external reality. So Nicole's husband was also losing Nicole's usual day-to-day demonstrations of love.

Thus Nicole's husband was affected by two losses — the automatic change of the mutual confirmation compact and her subtle withdrawal that accompanied a dangerous transformational process. His pain was felt on a visceral level. Anger was the response to the "unfair" disruption of his life.

Such an initial response can be the beginning of a new reality to the intimate couple in which he truly becomes the enemy to her new growth. It is not a matter of misperception or projecting the internal obstacle but a matter of a new reality being created and being sustained by the inner dynamics of the husband. His response disturbs the intimacy.

The principle at work is what I call developmental envy.[1] The partner who is growing fastest is temporarily leaving the other partner behind and in pain and induces developmental envy which can be either the source of new growth for the partner or the source of anger targeted at the fast-growing partner. In the case of Nicole, this was a major transformation and a potential major interference with the relationship.

Her growth therefore upsets his defensive equilibrium and he can either restore the defensive equilibrium by blocking her changes or he can make use of the gap in his defensive armament to accelerate his own transformational processes. Ideally, the hurt in response to her growth can be the beginning of his growth if properly understood and accepted as part of the inevitable flux of change and of the push-pull rhythm that occurs between two people who are close over time. Without that understanding, most of us react automatically to the loss caused by change with initial anger.

In the case of Nicole, there was a salutory ending and both partners profited by her growth work. It could easily have been otherwise and another divorce might have been recorded in the national statistics or another unhappy love life endured for the benefit of the children or the illusion of security.

THE DIALECTIC OF GROWTH AND INTIMACY

Our love relationships are always in one or another position in a cycle that is organized and driven by the inexorable need to grow. The best times are when neither partner is confusing the other with an internal obstacle nor suffering in response to the other's withdrawal. That is the steady state of two autonomous self-sufficient people interdependent but not dependent upon each other in the old childhood way. (The childhood way is when there must always be one big one and one small one, one all powerful and one relatively helpless.) Between the steady states, one partner is growing more rapidly than the other. It is the transformational and developmental envy dynamics that make up the rhythm of joys and disturbances within an intimate relationship. It is these dynamics gone awry that account for separations and divorces, some of which turn out to be beneficial for both partners, some of which turn out to be disastrous for both partners, and some of which benefit one partner but not the other. In some cases divorce and separation are a failure of love because neither party is capable of doing what is necessary to both grow and help the slower-growing partner respond affirmatively to that growth. At other times the divorce and separation are triumphs of love because one partner loves himself enough to risk growth and accept the consequences.

LOVE AND AGE

Many of the age considerations that apply to work obtain also for the issues of love. During our twenties, when we are establishing ourselves as adults, and facing outward more than inward, we automatically establish bonds in our love life. They consist of contracts and conspiracies that temporarily support our sense of adultness, maleness, femaleness, and competence by using the other person's confirming presence and attitudinal relationship to us. In that sense there is a deep dependence on the other as part of our defensive system, hence a vulnerability when the other person changes and a powerful need to keep him to the terms of the initial contractual love relationship. To the degree that the confinement inherent in this arrangement is tolerable and to the degree that the arrangement supports the primary developmental task of achieving competency and parental independence, conspiracies go largely unquestioned during the twenties. Breaches are patched by a rational solution and promises to try harder next time.

When, in the late twenties and thirties, as a result of an internal dialogue concerning the arbitrariness of the taken-for-granted assumptions about life, the conspiracies begin to unravel, the interior of the marital relationship becomes more ragged, confused, uncertain; yet at the same time it becomes richer and more complex. As the partners grow in response to their own inner voices, they develop more complicated maps of themselves and each other. They become more tolerant of each other's complexity and hold each other less rigidly to the simple criteria of the twenties. As they grow there is a new engagement with a subtle interaction between the two of them. The simplified images of self and the other give way to the experience of interaction and introspection, and the optimism that accompanies idealization diminishes. At the same time this is often a period when there are young children in the family, which makes the staying together more important and more difficult. Young children in the family tend to inhibit large transformational changes that disrupt the fabric of the family. On the other hand, the presence of our growing children rekindles unsolved developmental dilemmas of our own childhood. This pushes the transformational processes forward while burdening us with the confusion between self and other, present and past. All in all a complex set of forces impinges upon the conspiracies of bonding during the thirties, making them come to the surface and be challenged, but also rendering the challenging difficult. We are brought closer to the true complexity of the human mind and emotions that are ignored in romantic myths or idealized notions of how life could be.

As we enter the midlife period there is an increasing need for a clear and fuller self-definition, in response to the sense of urgency about time left to live. We strive for a deeper authenticity which requires the further challenging and unraveling of those conspiracies in which the attitude and behavior of the other still dominate our self perception and defensive armor. We need to suspend and disrupt defenses as much as possible in order to have a deep internal dialogue with the remaining negative self-images that control access to cut-off parts of ourselves. To the degree that a partner requires us to maintain a specific defensive stance or live up to an old label, he or she inhibits that process and we withdraw. If the doctor who was afraid of the label "greedy" had had a wife who tried to hold him to the defensive identity of being a devoted researcher, his transformational work would have been that much harder than it was, just as Nicole's work would have been harder if her husband had tried to hold her to a defensive identity that did not include the use of her powers—power in women being confused with the deep negative self-image of nasty-unlovable. Midlife men and women trying to recapture functions sacrificed to early adulthood choices frequently are traveling in different directions, coming out of two different sets of experience if they have had a traditional marriage. This has been loosely described by others (including Jung) as men taking in their feminine parts and women taking in their masculine parts; men become more affective and women become more instrumental.

I understand this as a transformational process about sensations in men and powerfulness in women. One man described the successful outcome of this process: "I now feel the knowledge of my head in my body—there's a sensation in my left arm talking to me; when I'm right about something I know it through and through." For men this is a very exciting reunion taking place. Hence we hear of men becoming more in touch with beauty (the "visceral" experience of a breeze or a sunset is novel), requiring more affection, no longer being able to shut out home problems and go off to work because the pain sticks, wanting more intense relationships, being ready to cry, loving and tending their children with greater depth, seeking more sensuality in life, being more ready to make love than war, and intensely reacting to the unavailability of any of these sensations with another sensation—a frustration persistent enough to command effort and sacrifice in the search for relief.

Along with the awareness of body sensations as an end in themselves and as sources of information comes intolerance of the previously accepted reality at home and at work. At work the hypocrisies and narrowness become apparent and at home the interferences with intimacy and intensity become intolerable. In many instances the midlife man is becoming just what his wife wanted all along—someone more like her, someone more aware of life outside the sterilized work world.

But often the timing is terrible! The woman's relationship with sensations is also changing as part of her psychological work on her transformation. Intense sensations are associated with vulnerability, surrender, and frustrated dependence. To viscerally experience the other person's needs, wants, demands, and anxieties requires a mandatory servicing of those demands. It takes it out of the realm of choice: Do I want to? Is it necessary? Is it fair? Is it good for me? Just as men have to steel themselves on Monday morning to face the brutal facts of work, so women have to steel themselves in order to go out into the world in a new and different way. They develop a new attitude toward the modality of sensations—at least a temporary blocking off.

When this occurs in women, their husbands' demands for sensations and intimacy are felt as demands for regression and surrender. Hence there is a painful love gap created that is both real and not real, necessary and unnecessary.

I cannot end this essay without at least mentioning what I believe to be a major motif coursing below the surface of all of these specifics. During the adult years we strive to become more liberated from ideas that were generated in childhood and persevere in adulthood even though they constrain us. These ideas still deliver a piece of the prized illusion of absolute safety. As in the case of Nicole, we encounter these false ideas during the process of transformation as we strive for expanded licenses of the self. But we also encounter these false ideas in the course of our daily life, in ways unrelated to a specific transformational effort, just because we arrive at a new age and hence a novel position in the life cycle. Then heretofore silent assumptions surface as they are contradicted by experience.

As we modify the ideas of our childhood we gain a fuller ranging freer mind. We give up a piece of the illusion of absolute safety. Judgments based on a more solid view of life as it is give us as much real safety as we can have in a complex changing world without reliable fortune-tellers.[2] As I see it, there is a constant maturational push throughout adulthood to free the mind and achieve the sense of inner freedom and spaciousness that accompanies that quest.

The transformational processes described in this essay are at the center of this maturational push, just as they are central to the issues of the work and love forums that connect our inner and outer life. The transformational processes are more complicated than I have been able to present and are well known to all of us under other labels. I have created this language in order to collect these processes under one roof in honor of the adult experience. We are continuously transforming ourselves — within a community, out of the past into the future, with and within a complex mind, trying always to gain a little more liberty to be what we are becoming.

Notes

1. This concept was first elaborated in a jointly authored paper with Renée Gould.

2. In another work, *Transformations: Growth and Change in Adult Life* (New York: Simon and Schuster, 1978), I have analyzed more completely the illusion of absolute safety as it organizes the phases of adult life between sixteen and fifty.

ELEVEN

Changing Hierarchies
of Commitment in Adulthood

MARJORIE FISKE

UNLIKE MANY OTHER students of adult life, I have found the models of continuing growth through adult life to be of limited use in important segments of our society. Extensive research on a sample of middle-and lower-middle-class adults suggests instead a paradigm that emphasizes the importance to individuals of commitments during the adult years — especially commitments to work and to love. At a time of rapid social change that has brought greater longevity, earlier retirement, and earlier freedom from child-bearing and child-rearing obligations, coping patterns in terms of changing commitments in the decades of middle and later life take on new significance. My research suggests that among mainstream Americans, at least, the potential for growth during these years may become stunted. Why this is so and how it relates to the ability to sustain commitments invites conjecture and analysis.

This chapter will focus on how people in various walks of life, at this time and in this culture, perceive the changes around them, as well as those within themselves, and the way in which these perceptions influence their values, commitments, and behaviors. Digressions are tempting, and bear on such elusive questions as whether social changes are destroying any tendency that the individual may have to develop and sustain deep commitments to love, work, integrity, or even the preservation of the self and the race. Longitudinal studies stretching over a quarter century or so present evidence of characterological change. There seem to be fewer autonomous, self-generating people in the more recent studies (holding status and occupational level roughly constant). Superficially, this might be interpreted as an increase in "other-directedness" as observed by David Riesman (1950) over a quarter century ago. The nature of this other-directedness is, however, very different, and might be interpreted as a substitute for *inner*-directedness. There is an increasing need to be told how to think, feel, and behave. This need becomes particularly visible in the rapidly increasing numbers of people of all ages who crowd into the proliferating encounter and consciousness-raising groups and seek to suffer the ordeals demanded by charismatic "religious" leaders, including, as we have recently learned, voluntary mass suicides.

Most people in Western societies would probably agree that the senses and sensibilities of the individual are under greater bombardment than ever before, the shattering result being what Leo Bersani (with the plays of Genet as a prime example) calls "persons in pieces" (1976). Seeking survival in comparative comfort, many people appear to utilize whatever fragment of the self best fits the demands of the immediate situation. The sociologist Irving Rosow has called this "chameleon" behavior (1965); the psychoanalyst Robert Lifton used the term "Protean man" (1971). Interestingly, in a more recent work (1976), Lifton seems to be trying to put Humpty Dumpty back together again. He believes that something close to a "mass experience" is occurring, and that its aim is to re-symbolize work. "Perhaps for the first time in history, very large numbers of men and women are beginning to demand harmony . . . a reasonable equation between work and 'works' " (p. 142). The "masses" he cites, however, are work communes and radical caucuses in professional societies — in other words, elites, founders of a new way of life whose efforts are probably doomed to the fate of similar efforts in earlier periods of American history.

A quarter century of studying the life histories of young and older people prompts in me the undemocratic suspicion that there is a widening gap between the commitments and life-styles of academics and artists and the rest of the population, and that it is far wider than it was before World War II. A critical difference seems to be in the capacity to be alone, which the nature of their work forces on academics and artists, at least from time to time. Among others, Frank Barron (1963) in his studies of creativity and creative people, and Abraham Maslow (1954) in his early work on self-actualizing people (whom he had a great deal of difficulty in tracking down), have both pointed out that these sorts of people have stronger needs for periodic solitude than others. The shift from a mainly rural to an urban society, and the rapid growth of the mass media that accompanied it, may well have reduced both the need and the capacity for being alone, and perhaps along with it the capacity for some kind of self-realization, however humble.

To take one example of a solitary activity, twenty years ago there were still readers of books among sixty to ninety-year-olds in all walks of life. There also were many inner-directed people who did not need to be told what to do, people who found meaning in their lives, and who had a strong sense of their own dignity and worth. They liked, or needed, to be alone periodically, with or without the ideas of other people as found in books of their own choosing. Solitude helps a person to keep the inner and outer boundaries of the self — to borrow Bernard Landis' (1970) concept — in a bearable equilibrium between permeability and impermeability, and to find his own center. As Montaigne long ago noted, you cannot realize yourself if you do not know who you are, and you can only find that out by occasionally — or frequently — seeking solitude. Although I know of no research on the subject, I suspect that a day spent in solitude may well produce more restorative and self-centering dreams than one in which the senses have been bombarded by the sight and sound of many people, including those projected by television.

There are few, if any, solitude seekers in our present longitudinal study of normative transitions in adulthood, in which we have been intensively studying middle-class and lower-middle-class people for the past ten years. Our people range now from about twenty-seven to the midseventies, and the often dramatic shifts in their hierarchies of commitment over relatively short periods of time suggest the possibility of recurring periods of identity diffusion (Erikson, 1968) over far shorter intervals than I had reason to expect. My assumption, partly research-based, was that continuity in commitments to others (including love), to mastery (including work), and to moral, religious, generative, and altruistic values is essential to the sense of continuity of self. As they grew older, it was the "deviants" — those who had strong commitments to begin with and sustained them (and who in many other respects are more complex than their stage/age peers) — who became more despairing, anxious, and sometimes ill. Those who reordered their commitments, or who all along had few, or whose main concerns were self-protective, self-indulgent, or both, were far more likely to be satisfied with their ways of life. It is probable that more complex and autonomous people can grow old gracefully and comfortably in our time only if they belong to a more privileged class, where life-style options remain more open. It is regrettable indeed that the more self-generating people among the great middle-class majority of our population become, as they reach late middle and old age, deprived of the arenas in which they could serve as role models for the generations behind them, and for whom later life becomes the period of greatest frustration.

THEORIES OF CHANGE

In the past two decades four major frameworks have evolved within which questions bearing on psychosocial change in adulthood are being studied. One, strongly influenced by theorists of childhood such as Freud and Piaget, is *stage theory*. As in studies of the earlier periods of life, when stage theory is applied to adulthood, the implicit assumption is one of unfolding, of progression toward a more complex and wiser self. Most notable and influential of this school is, of course, Erik Erikson. He is also, interestingly enough, more flexible in his use of this framework than some younger scholars who, influenced by his work, have adopted stage theory as the paradigm for their own work. Recent scholarly works in the field include those of Roger Gould (1978), David Gutmann (1977), Lawrence Kohlberg (1973), Daniel Levinson et al. (1978), and Jane Loevinger (1976). More popular approaches include those of Nancy Mayer (1978) and Gail Sheehy (1976).

Closely related are the theories of *self-actualization* or self-realization, such as those of Kurt Goldstein (1940), Gordon Allport (1955; 1937), Abraham Maslow (1954), and Charlotte Bühler and Fred Massarik (1968). An assumption of growth in adulthood underlies these works, too, but it is not demarcated by stages and stage-linked crises, chronological or otherwise. Rather, growth is an on-going process. There may be temporary stressful periods, even periods of regression, but they are, so to speak, in service of the ego, and a part of slowly unfolding growth. Such crises as do develop are far more likely to be idiosyncratic than they are to be linked with normative, expectable changes in adulthood (see also Neugarten, 1977; Neugarten and Hagestad, 1976). The third and fourth paradigms may best be described, respectively, as *dialectic* and *eclectic*. Working toward a dialectic theory of psychosocial change in adulthood occupied the last several years of Klaus Riegel's life, and although it is far from finished, his theory has much appeal for scholars seeking ways of integrating personal and sociohistorical change (Riegel, 1977). In this developing theory, there is no underlying premise of progressive growth in the individual or in society, though it is by no means precluded.

Newcomers to an adult life course perspective are increasing.

They include scholars such as the philosopher David Norton (1976), who has developed a flexible stage theory which is not inherently developmental, and the psychologist David McClelland (1975); both of these men have adapted their stages from those of Erikson. Several others recently attracted to issues relating to psychosocial change in adulthood have brought their own paradigms with them, and have fewer *a priori* assumptions about the nature and direction of psychosocial change in adulthood, except for the conviction that it exists. As a group, they might best be called *eclectic*. My own work also fits into the eclectic category, but with a very strong inclination toward the dialectic. Studies of the perceptions and behaviors of a wide variety of people moving across their allotted time span seem to make a certain degree of eclecticism necessary, at least for now.

Also included among relative newcomers to the study of middle and late middle age are George Vaillant (1977), Robert Sears (1977), and Pauline Sears (Sears and Barbee, 1977). All three inherited longitudinal studies; participants in Vaillant's research are now in their early fifties and those in the Sears' research a decade or so older. Vaillant's framework is essentially that of coping and adaptation, and he has adopted an innovative model of adaptive (and maladaptive) defenses. The model used by Pauline and Robert Sears, who inherited Lewis Terman's large sample of "gifted children," is centered in achievement and satisfaction in the work and family spheres of life. The samples represent the higher echelons of American society. The Vaillant study consisted of male graduates of an elitist university, whereas the Terman study, fortunately, included both sexes — fortunate because gender differences in most dimensions of life far exceed age or stage differences found within either sex group alone.

Other fairly recent work includes an innovative ongoing study of chronic stress and coping among men and women in their early fifties and sixties (Lazarus, 1978), and a related study of treated and untreated persons undergoing acute and severe stress (Horowitz, 1977). Both of these studies developed in part from the Longitudinal Study of Transitions reported in this chapter, and are conceptually and methodologically integrated with it within the Human Development and Aging Program, University of California, San Francisco (Fiske, 1979b). Finally, the now classical longitudinal studies of the Institute for Human Development, University of California, Berkeley, initiated by Harold Jones in the early thirties, are becoming more eclectic as the associated scholars have become increasingly impressed with the strong message of the accumulating data: much more goes on in adulthood than can be predicted by lingering effects of childhood circumstances or by personality traits developed through adolescence (Brooks, in press; Clausen, 1972; Haan, 1970).

Perhaps a better way to describe the above studies than "dialectic" or "eclectic" would be to say that the investigators believe that, in a field half a century younger than child development, it is advisable to keep all options open and to involve the approaches of as many disciplines as possible. The adoption of self-actualizing, developmental, personality, or normative crisis theories may be premature. To take stage theory as one example, there is evidence that such a framework yields very sizeable "deviant" cells even among more privileged segments of our society (Vaillant, 1977). Similarly, Gutmann's theory of change in mastery styles from active to passive to magical is not clearly supported in our data. Young men declined in active mastery, for example, between ages eighteen and twenty-three; women in our preretirement group, on the other hand, preferred the active mastery style and showed no decrease in this preference five years later (Hodges, pending). The cross-cultural generalizability of this theory has also been questioned (Simpson, 1974). Since the higher levels, and especially the highest, of most stage theories (including that of Loevinger, perhaps the most rigorous of them all) come close, and inevitably so, to expressing the scholar's philosophy of man, cross-class and cross-cultural inconsistencies would seem to be inevitable. Even studies of privileged members of the culture in which the stage theories were developed require a shift in conceptual gears as we move from the early to the later stages. Jean Piaget, for example, in writing about adulthood, ventures bravely but perhaps uneasily into a looser definition of formal operations "in different areas according to their aptitudes and their professional specializations" (1972, p. 10). Jane Loevinger's highest stage is integration, a rather imprecise term with many possibilities for interpretation (1976). In Robert Lifton's highest stage, one must come to terms with death, play, and transcendence (1976). Lawrence Kohlberg's last stage is summed up as the autonomous functioning of conscience, and his own studies clearly indicate that his is not "pure" stage theory; even Harvard students regress (1973). Erik Erikson's stages, on the other hand, have come increasingly to suggest an ongoing dialectic between the self and society.

We all need a vision of the human potential. That this is true of scholars is self-evident, judging from the burgeoning interest in adult life-stage theory. That it is also true of an impressively large segment of others in this country is reflected by the enormous popularity of Gail Sheehy's recent book (1976) and by the increasing use of her term "passages" in magazines (including advertisements for self-help groups). The most satisfactory way to gain insight into the human potential is through knowledge of social history, of individuals — first hand, biographical, or autobiographical — and of a variety of carefully selected and described cohorts followed over long periods of time. We must not abandon these rich sources (Goertzel et al., 1978; Spicker et al., 1978; White, 1975). They explicate the variety of the ways in which people may mature (or not) and grow old, and include backward and forward movements which may occur in rapid succession. Most important, they examine, as did Erikson's biographical studies (1969; 1958), the interrelationship between society and individual. It is this which needs close attention before we can build sound theories of change in the adult life course, and methods of testing them.

TOWARD A FLEXIBLE PARADIGM

Our evolving theoretical framework came about after it became clear that little of what we were learning in our longitudinal studies of adult transitions fit comfortably into existing frameworks. In many ways the successive protocols of the 216 men and women participating in our study made their own demands for a very flexible paradigm. Schooled as we were in various developmental approaches to the study of children and adults, the initial framework for the study was couched in terms of continuities and growth in goals and values and their congruence with behavior. A principal hypothesis was that the maintenance of such congruity would prove to be a critical component of the adaptive process as the individual moves across his or her life course (Lowenthal, 1971). A major expectation was that persons who were growth-oriented, and those with value continuity in spheres such as work and love, would be most fulfilled, in their own terms, and best adapted by whatever measures were used. This expectation was not realized.

In terms of both retrospectively perceived and prospectively anticipated values, the sense of well-being was far more likely to be associated with the sense of past and future change in goals and behavior patterns than with continuity (Thurnher, 1975). The question that most troubled me was whether direct queries about values and goals were tapping the hierarchy of realistic priorities and decisions that pattern the individual's behavior throughout the days, weeks, and years. After close reading of very detailed life histories, the insightful reader can usually sense a commitment hierarchy at the time the life stories were told or written. The person speaking or writing may or may not be aware of the revelation. I am not referring to the neurotic repetition of what Erich Fromm (1966) has called the "life plot," though some dynamics of this sort may be involved for some people. That their major commitments were not always obvious to the people we are studying became apparent several years ago when we first began to study them.

One of our major areas of inquiry was consistency and inconsistency in value hierarchies and the relevance thereof to adaptation at successive life stages; consequently we often spent two or more hours on direct, though open-ended, questioning in this sphere. What the reviewer of these life histories sensed as a person's basic value structure often differed strikingly from that person's own very conventional responses to interviewer queries ranging from the most global (such as what is life all about) to a rank ordering of specific past, present, and future goals. As one strategy for getting closer to the truth, we conducted a cluster analysis of selected adjectives from a lengthy checklist, derived from the Block Q-Sort (Block, 1961), designed to probe into the concept of the self. The rationale for this procedure was that such a semiprojective approach would bring us closer to the wellsprings of choice and behavior. In examining the terms in which individuals describe themselves and how those terms change through time, we circumvent the tendency of most people to rise to a potentially ennobling occasion such as being directly queried about their values and aspirations. Furthermore, the adjective checklist was filled out by the participants themselves, in privacy, and therefore with considerably more anonymity than in a face to face interview.

The resulting clusters of self-selected characteristics we have named interpersonal, altruistic, competence/mastery, and self-protective. (There is at least one other, reminiscent of Allport's old schema, which one might call aesthetic, but the self-concept checklist does not provide a basis for "operationalizing" it.) Such commitments may be brought into play in any or all of the changing arenas of the adult life course. A work setting, for example, may provide the arena for interpersonal, altruistic, or self-protective intentions as well as those relating to mastery or competence.

Interpersonal commitment is deeply imbedded in psychoanalytic theory, more recently "socialized" and "culturalized" by, notably, Harry Stack Sullivan and Erik Erikson. For many interviewees, interpersonal relationships at their place of work are at least as important as they are in the nonwork contexts of their lives, and, among persons holding routine jobs, often more highly valued than the nature of the work itself. Among circumstances conducive to the development and strengthening of interpersonal relationships on the job is *esprit de corps*. This sense of unity may emanate from the top down, or "horizontally" among people working for a common objective so appealing that they feel united regardless of the hierarchical structure of the organization. (Such work situations, however, are rare among the people we studied.) By contrast, a sense of unity or fellowship with one's peers at work may be rooted in shared and mutually reinforcing resentments against superiors; in large organizations, the more common and less challenging target is the ubiquitous, anonymous "they." In many blue-collar occupations, playful competitiveness among men may develop spontaneously, with or without encouragement from above. The more hazardous the work, the stronger seems to be the sense of camaraderie engendered by such competition. Women working in contexts where they are excluded from, or ignored by, such cohesive groups of males may themselves unite in scorn or self-defense. Or they, too, may become playfully competitive with each other in aggressive or flirtatious attempts to penetrate the barriers more or less explicitly erected and defended by men.

In addition to such group affiliations, the work arena may provide a universe from which deep and lasting dyadic relationships develop. Whether such friendships are more common in one occupation than another has not been studied, but appears probable. In our middle-to-lower-middle-class group they were infrequent, but many participants in the more "elitist" samples report that some of their deepest and most lasting relationships developed through their work. Among the less privileged, it appears to be the family network which is most likely to include close personal relationships, satisfying and otherwise. As Ann Swidler demonstrates in Chapter 6, there are dramatic changes in norms in regard to marriage, the nuclear family, and the extended family. If they reach all strata of our society, these changes may well weaken the strongest interpersonal bonds of all, those of love, mutuality, and intimacy.

The second cluster of commitments, which we are calling *altruistic* in a rather broad sense (integrated/generative would be more apt but is awkward), includes ethical, philosophical, and religious allegiances, and also encompasses Erikson's concepts of generativity and integrity. Obviously, the organizational structure and goals of the workplace and the behavior of others in the workplace may strengthen or weaken commitments of this type. Some of the so-called midlife crises one finds in life histories, in clinical studies, biographies, and, increasingly, in fiction and the mass media may be attributed to conflict between individual commitments and organizational methods and goals. The timing of such conflicts varies in accordance with career trajectories common to particular occupations. When a man confronts the realization that his occupational career has peaked, not only is he likely to feel anxious and insecure, but he may be prompted to reflect on his work life in terms of such questions as: "What was or is it all for?" Some men attribute their plans for early retirement to a disparity between their own values and ethics and those of the organization. A few seem to mention such conflict as a highly respectable rationalization, for in fact they wish to retire early for quite hedonistic reasons.

The women in our study of transitions, for their part, pay little attention to the methods and goals of their occupational settings. As is true for their interpersonal commitments, their more altruistic values are directed to the child-rearing arena. For such women, a midlife conflict may be triggered by a sense of failure of mission as mother or by the realization that their child-rearing days are over. The subsequent struggle, for many, is between what they may view as a moral imperative to settle for being a "good" wife, and their growing awareness of a need for new arenas outside the confining sphere of the family where their commitments—interpersonal, instrumental, altruistic, or self-indulgent—may find expression.

Our third commitment category, one which Robert White (1963) suggests is an instinct, is competence, with its concomitant sense of effectance. It includes some degree of autonomy, and, for some, creativity; for the time being, we are calling this category *mastery,* used in a broader sense than the term "instrumental" suggests. In adulthood, one's work is the most common arena for its fulfillment, especially for men. In the still prevailing male-dominated occupational and familial structures of our society, men tend to have few conflicts in this domain before they reach their occupational peak — providing that their fellow workers and superiors, and ideally their wives as well, applaud or at least acknowledge their effectiveness. Somewhere between the beginning of the postparental stage and the beginnings of preoccupation with the retirement stage (which we suspect is triggered not so much by entering the postparental phase as by occupational peaking), many men seem to become weary of all this self-assertion and regret that they have, to varying degrees, sacrificed interpersonal or other commitments in its behalf. Their assessments of the bind they feel themselves to be in are most likely to be reflected in projective materials, where strong dependency needs emerge. This shift from work to interpersonal commitments, theoretically developed by Carl Jung, later documented by David Gutmann (1977), may not be class or status linked. The studies by George Vaillant (1977) and Robert Sears (1977) both lend support to such a thesis among far more privileged late middle-aged men than those we studied, who express their sentiments more directly. Among women, however, there well may be class differences. As they seek more mastery in work or elsewhere, women in our study become less concerned with the interpersonal sphere, whereas women in Terman's gifted sample, half of whom have professional careers, show no such shifts (Sears and Barbee, 1977).

Conflict between interpersonal and mastery commitments at middle age may or may not result in, or exacerbate, marital discord, depending in part on its timing. If wife and husband experience conflicts at the same time, the former seeking more mastery (in work or otherwise), the latter more love or support, the problems of each become confounded by awareness that any resolution which would free one of them might well threaten the marriage. In our groups, some women find a compromise solution: they stay home and become increasingly assertive there, responding to their husbands' needs for nurturance by becoming "bossy," as many of their spouses put it. Thus, while for these middle-aged and older men the natural arena for interpersonal commitment is or becomes the family network, for some women it may become the context for the expression of the emerging commitment to self-assertion and mastery, not only in their relationships with their husbands but, unfortunately, with their adult children as well.

A *sine qua non* for all forms of commitment is a fourth, which might be called self-preservation or *self-protectiveness*. This rubric, in a commitment framework, is one which needs considerable refinement for both theoretical and empirical reasons. For the moment, we are using it to blanket such diverse concerns as physical, economic, and psychosocial survival and well-being. The self-protective way of living includes at least two very different trajectories, one reflecting a lifelong need for continual reinforcement so deep-seated and pressing that it precludes the development of serious commitments of other kinds, and the other a commitment to comfortable survival which originates later in life and increases with age. Late middle-aged men in our study of transitions reflect a growing commitment of this kind and its accompanying change in life-style, and it tends to replace commitment to mastery.

One advantage of a commitment framework is that it transcends dichotomies which, while convenient for the researcher, result in oversimplification of the issues. Work/leisure is one such that has been perpetuated far too long. Some sociologists (and a few psychologists) study work, others leisure. As a result, reports of individuals' activities become so rigidly compartmentalized that it is impossible to analyze the functional interrelationship of the two arenas and the changes in that relationship which occur at various stages of life. By contrast, when we study activities within a substantive framework of the meanings and satisfactions that the people studied attach to them, we find that "careers" in the two spheres often bear a dialectic relationship to each other (Pierce, in press).

Of course there are some people who do allocate their activities (and their meanings) in a strictly dichotomous fashion. For them, the bifurcated checklists are no doubt appropriate. On the other hand, as our life histories show, most people, when asked to think about it, assess the activity and time allocations of their lives in a much more complex fashion. Confronted with a checklist, they have difficulty in deciding whether a particular undertaking is work or nonwork. On a strictly behavioral level, they can tell us how much time they spend "on the job," but this is a geographic rather than a functional allocation ("I was working" equals "I was *in* the office" or "I was *on* the job").

The subjective significance of the distribution of time is hinted at in reports such as "Whatever I'm doing, I'm preoccupied with my job," or "My job is so routine that I think about lots of other things while I do it," or "I am one of those people who watches T.V., does needlepoint, talks, and thinks about how to redecorate the living room all at the same time." Like most human subtleties, however, this one is difficult to translate into researchable terms. For a start, if we ask people an open-ended question about what they like or dislike, or are committed or antipathetic to, in their rounds of living, and, only after such activities have been identified, ask them about the contexts in which they occur, we are very likely to find themes common to work and nonwork spheres alike, themes denoting meaning, which is the essence of commitment. To give some examples, a man or woman might cite as either challenging or frustrating such situations as winning battles through several layers of bureaucracy; dealing with real or alleged experts outside their own fields of expertise; making their own decisions; attending large ritualistic gatherings; coping with disorderly or recalcitrant material objects, be they piles of documents, ice cube trays, or computers; dealing with situations which, on one side or the other, involve manipulation or trickery; making friends; or even selecting appropriate clothing. Such circumstances arise both in work and nonwork settings, and the stance adopted toward them in occupational and nonoccupational contexts not only tells us something about the salience of various areas of commitment but also suggests the extent to which the work and nonwork arenas are functional equivalents. Similar crossovers could be readily traced in arenas other than the work place. For example, the ostensibly interpersonal sphere of family living may not only provide a setting for the budding expression of mastery and decision making, as it does among some middle-aged women, but for the fulfillment of aesthetic commitments (rearranging objects, redoing the house, inside or out), or escape from direct interaction ("shared" television, or the head behind the newspaper).

The four commitments that emerged from the analysis of attributes of the self-concept are quite different from the values reported when interviewees were asked to arrange cards in rank order. For example, what we are calling a mastery commitment did not correlate with instrumental values, nor altruistic commitment with religious/philosophical values, nor even interpersonal with interpersonal, though the adjectives clustering from the self-concept checklist and those defining goals were quite similar. Obviously we were tapping, as we had hoped, a different level of the self than that reached through a direct approach. In support of this thesis is the fact that some of these deep-seated commitments are very significantly correlated with a set of ratings designed to get at resources (as well as deficits) in a kind of dual, nonmedical model of adaptation.[1] Among people facing the postparental stage there was (at the time of the first interview) a strong correlation between a high ranking on satisfaction and a strong commitment to mastery among men. Among middle-aged women, many of whom were thinking about going back to work (or finding a more interesting job), there was an even more significant relationship between a strong commitment to mastery and a high rating on growth.

There were marked differences between the sexes and within each sex group in both the hierarchical arrangement and the strength of commitments at the time of our first contact with participants. Among the most clear-cut patterns are what we might call the "diversified," that is, people equally committed in three or more areas, a pattern which in turn can be subdivided in terms of its comparative strength (that is, degree of commitment). At the other extreme are those who put nearly all of their eggs into one commitment basket. The surprise came, however, when we compared the baseline hierarchies with those that emerged five years later when most had passed through the normative transitional periods they were sampled to represent. (At the first contact our subjects were high school seniors, newlyweds, people whose youngest child was a high school senior, and a group planning to retire within two years; see Lowenthal et al., [1975].)

Despite the fact that most of the people in each of the four groups had experienced the same anticipated transition in the intervening five years, there was, to me at least, an astonishing amount of variability in the patterns of change in their commitment hierarchies. First, one might reasonably expect to find considerable consistency in these hierarchies over time. Second, since each group was undergoing the same kind of "typical" transition for their life stage — to the empty nest, for example, or into retirement — it would seem reasonable to suppose that, in this socioeconomically homogeneous group, those who change would do so in similar directions. The great diversity of these changes over a five-year span is illustrated by the personal graphs of two of our subjects (figs. 11.1, 11.2). It is not irrelevant to add, in light of the influence of situational change on personal change, that both the woman and the man had changed jobs.

Another way to examine these changes is to place each individual within his or her transitional group. Figure 11.3 shows the change in commitment to mastery among late middle-aged women, and Figure 11.4 shows change in moral and altruistic commitments among men in the somewhat younger "empty nest" stage. Figures 11.5 and 11.6 show changes in self-protectiveness among those originally selected as preretirees. Most of the men had retired from their main lifetime jobs; a few had (new) part-time jobs and two had new jobs. Among those women who worked, most had retired; two were still working. The average age of this group was by this time sixty-three. More men and women increased in self-protectiveness than decreased, though fewer women than men did so, and those women who decreased the most in self-protectiveness were those whose commitment to mastery increased.

COMMITMENT, SOCIAL CHANGE, AND GENERATIVITY

These are "average" people. For them, as perhaps for all people, agreement with Erikson's conviction that generativity — responsibility for the next and succeeding generations — should be the aim of those in midlife takes not only faith but fortitude, especially in our era of change, not least because we are at a loss as to the content of such re-

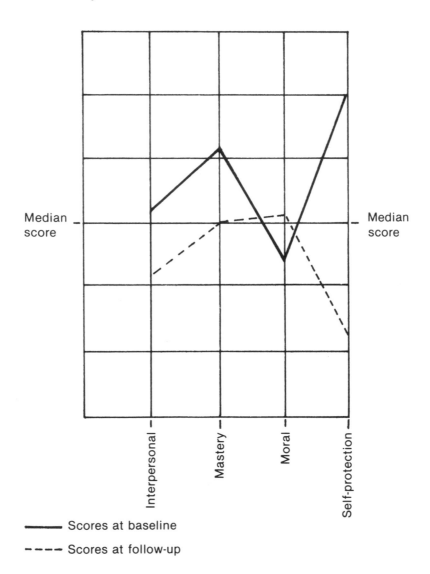

Median
score

Median
score

Interpersonal

Mastery

Moral

Self-protection

———— Scores at baseline

– – – – Scores at follow-up

Figure 11.1 • Mrs. M. R.: change in commitment scores.

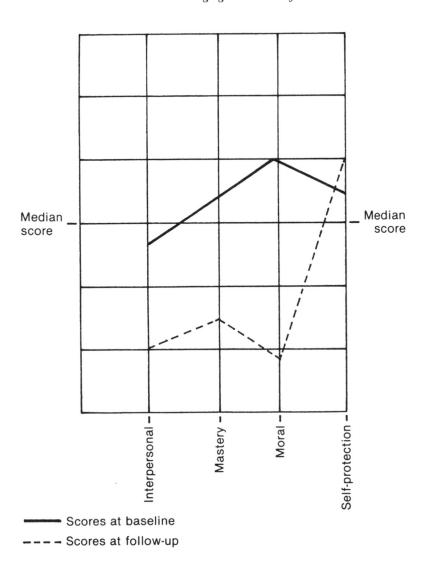

Figure 11.2 • Mr. F. C.: change in commitment scores.

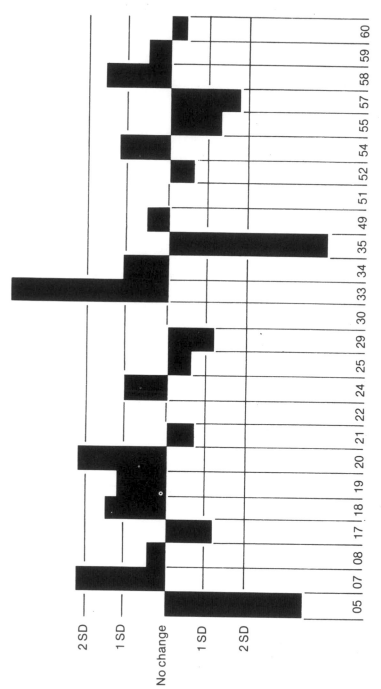

Fig. 11.3 Preretired females (by subject number): change in commitment to mastery.

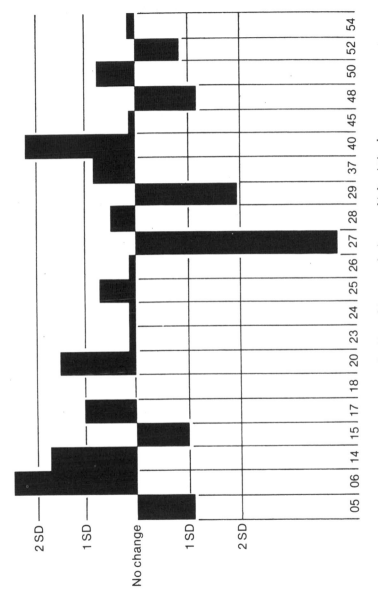

Fig. 11.4 Empty-nest males (by subject number): moral/altruistic change.

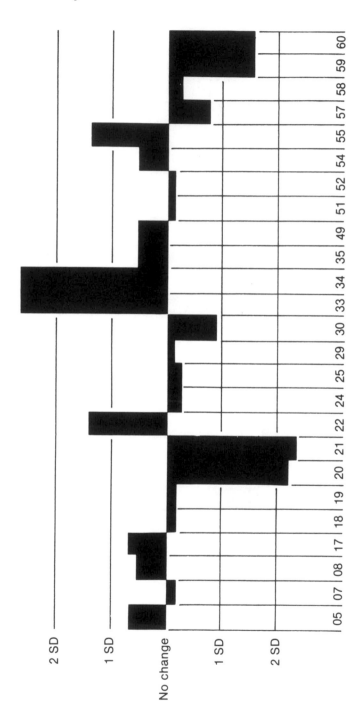

Fig. 11.5 Preretired females (by subject number): self-protection change.

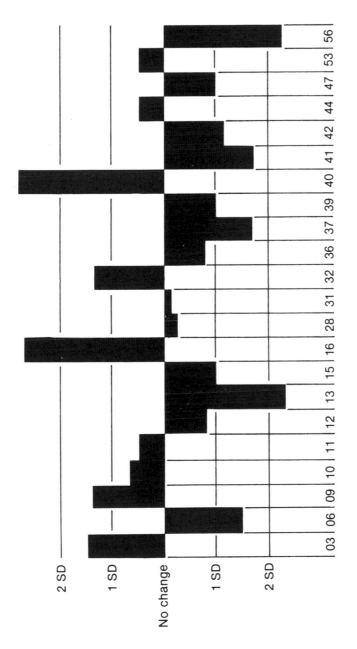

Fig. 11.6 Preretired males (by subject number): self-protection change.

sponsibility. Since the Middle Ages, at least in Western societies, the self-conscious task of many young people, especially but not only university students, has been not only to learn but to question the heritage of wisdom bequeathed by their elders. Middle-aged and older leaders of those societies rarely felt threatened in their own beliefs and values; their certitudes were strong. In recent times, there has not only been resurgence of questioning (and among some of the elders as well), but its content changes more rapidly than among former generations. There were generational clashes about values of the Protestant Ethic and imperialism after World War I and the later Great Depression in many Western societies. After World War II, however, family and tradition-centered norms came to be accepted, with evidence of relief, by the majority of the then young. Child-centeredness and family togetherness features flooded the women's journals of that time. The world was shrinking, impinging, and the war had made people realize, as perhaps never before, that the world could be unbelievably brutal and cruel as well. Home became the refuge, and the more nineteenth- and early-twentieth-century values people could restore, the safer and more sheltered they felt, especially since political, religious, and scientific certitudes were becoming increasingly difficult for a moderately intelligent and well-read person to accept.

The other side of the coin, of course, was the sense that the individual can do little or nothing in the face of such overwhelming forces of evil and terror as those unleashed in Germany, Italy, Japan, and, as it turned out, the Soviet Union—or, for that matter, in the face of the overwhelming power of the military and industrial complexes which in many countries were rapidly acquiring control, at home and abroad as well.

Then came Korea and Vietnam, and the student rebellions of the sixties. After the anomie and retreatism of those who were young in the fifties, the renewed activism among youth was heady, for themselves and for many of their elders as well, including teachers and parents. Whether or not they agreed with the philosophies and actions of their offspring, at least the young were doing something, and that was far better, for most liberals at least, than their own passivity in the previous decade. Now, in the late seventies, there are no hippies in the Haight, there are ambitious and studious young people in the universities, and there is unemployment among recent graduates in the humanities and the social and behavioral sciences. While the shrinking of "generations" may be occurring even more rapidly in Israel, in much of the West it nevertheless proceeds at least twice the pace of what today's late middle-aged people experienced when they were in school.

The hopes and anxieties of parents for their children are not rejected today in the way "over-thirty" people were rejected in the sixties, but with this rate of social change, what salience can our "generativity" legacy and the transmission of our values have? Some say the best one can do is teach the young to be flexible and to bow with whatever winds of change may blow. Others believe that the pendulum is again changing direction. *Roots* (Haley, 1976), which portrays the quest of a black man for identity, is symbolic of a swing toward renewal of a sense of past periods in history in which we hope to find anchorage. The millions of readers and television viewers of Haley's story and of "Holocaust" may or may not be prophetic of a widespread reawakening of the belief that, by tracing relationships between past and present, we strengthen the power of each individual to help mold the future.

Peter Marris (1975) reports intriguing similarities in effective ways of coping with a variety of personal and social changes in several cultures, and illustrates the idea of a dual approach to adaptation with a somewhat different set of concepts than those of our "balance" concept. The balance, in his terms, is between the conservative impulse and the innovative, and the objective is the achievement of a sense of continuity in the meaning of one's life. He is very convincing in his development of the thesis "that the impulse to defend the predictability of life is a fundamental and universal principle of human psychology" (p. 3). This impulse, rooted in the need to maintain continuity of the self, is seriously threatened by changing events and processes as wide-ranging as bereavement, slum clearance, colonization, revolution, and the accelerating advances of science. When meaning is threatened by unpredicted events, even a move to another house, it is important to realize that many changes are losses of the familiar and predictable, even though intrinsically they may at the same time represent gains or improvements (as in slum clearance).

Interpreting Marris' work from a somewhat different perspective, we might conclude that if we recognize and anticipate that a change will be disruptive and allow a moratorium for self-repair, we are likely to emerge the stronger for it. Such moratoria provide the opportunity to rearrange and to recenter our commitments. In this way, we find within ourselves the sense of continuation which is our chief bulwark against the onslaught of changes in ourselves, in our personal milieux, and in the supports and impingements of the wider world which interlace with our more private ones. The process takes patience and faith in one's inner power for recovery. While this may sound a bit mystical, strong support warranting such faith is found not only in religious and philosophical thought (Norton, 1976), but in the insights of Harry Stack Sullivan (1953), who was convinced that belief and hope constitute very strong drives toward health in most people. In a large-scale, short-term, longitudinal study of six hundred people ranging in age from sixty to the early nineties, we found Sullivan's concept to be remarkably well-supported (Lowenthal and Berkman, 1967). If this is true of the old and very old, the middle-aged certainly have no reason, despite the many changes they confront, not to trust themselves to recover from whatever trauma they may inflict. Patience is required because, Emile Coué (1922) to the contrary, it is not a matter of saying over and over to one's self, "every day and in every way I am getting better and better." Self-recovery from trauma and change is by no means entirely conscious, but it does require a measure of relaxation in self-renewing solitude. Some people appear to be incapable or afraid of being alone; somewhat paradoxically, these are frequently persons who most likely acquire, early or late in life, a self-protective life-style, including the kind of distraction and sensory bombardment offered by the media, travel, and large gatherings. It is as though they must avoid both listening to themselves think and experiencing peace and quiet that for others offer the natural maturational processes time to yield their restorative results.

The committed, as they undergo inner and outer change, find new meanings in their lives when they allow themselves the moratoria required for coping with successive life stages within a rapidly changing sociohistorical context. They do not forget, in Norton's words, that "the object of whole-hearted commitment is not the world but oneself, as the moral task of self-actualization. This must be stressed because of the frequency with which persons in the situations of choice objectify the determinants of choice and neglect themselves. In effect such persons look to the world to make the choice for them . . . They forget that what is to be decided is not what is, but what is to be done by themselves . . . The possibilities of choice are not first in the world but initially in persons . . . What one chooses wholeheartedly is the self one shall strive to become, a becoming that contributes to the world" (1976, p. 195).

The first commitment then, is to self-discovery—and rediscovery. The others follow. True enough, and the philosopher cannot be faulted for not going on to remind the reader that for some the pace of change in the outer world could be incapacitating, completely overwhelming their own processes of self-rediscovery and renewal of commitment. Thus, a social behavioral scientist cannot with clear conscience conclude only on a philosophical note, appealing though it is. Commitments to work and to love must be renewed at middle age and other stages of life not only within oneself but within an outside world to which we ourselves, when younger as well as older, are contributing a conflicting mixture of the old and the new.

From an individual perspective, the more we know about the ambiguities within ourselves and the worlds in which we live, the more probable it becomes that we can learn to tolerate them. The more gifted among us even learn to synthesize some of the ambiguities; out of such syntheses comes growth.

Caring endows the intimate dialogue with truth. The truth in our close relationships is a source of strength which can enable those of us in middle and later life not only to nurture and treasure autonomy in ourselves and our children, but by our words and actions to contribute to the dialogue between the private and public spheres of our ever more complicated worlds. Only by our individual contributions toward a synthesis of public and private values and behaviors can we endow our young with the courage not to retreat when they become old. And only if we — and they — do not retreat will the generations that come after us be able to mold themselves instead of becoming puppets. The velocity of some changes in the outer world are generating winds to which we dare not bow. We middle-aged may have few eternal truths or treasure troves of values to bequeath, but we are old enough to know that there comes a time when one must stand up and be counted.

Notes

Research supported by the National Institute on Aging, Grant No. AG-00002 (and formerly by National Institute of Child Health and Human Development Grants No. HD-03051 and HD-05941).

1. These ratings, which we spent a year or so in developing, were undertaken by an interdisciplinary team, including two distinguished psychoanalysts. They were based on reviews of the entire protocols (except for the structured research instruments), which sometimes covered fifty to a hundred typed pages. For additional details, see Lowenthal, Thurnher, Chiriboga and Associates (1975), Chapters 5 and 6.

References

ALLPORT, GORDON. 1955. *Becoming*. New Haven: Yale University Press.

———. 1937. *Pattern and growth in personality*. New York: Holt, Rinehart, and Winston.

BARRON, FRANK. 1963. *Creativity and psychological health: origins of personal vitality and creative freedom*. New York: Van Nostrand Reinhold.

BERSANI, LEO. 1976. *A future for asyntax: character and desire in literature*. Boston: Little, Brown.

BINSTOCK, ROBERT H., AND ETHEL SHANAS, EDS. 1976. *Handbook of aging and the social sciences*. New York: Van Nostrand Reinhold.

BLOCK, JACK. 1961. *The Q-sort method in personality assessment and psychiatric research*. Springfield, Ill.: Charles C. Thomas.

BROOKS, JANE. In press. Social maturity in middle age and its development antecedents. In *Present and past in midlife,* ed. D. Eichorn. New York: Academic Press.

BÜHLER, CHARLOTTE, AND FRED MASSARIK, EDS. 1968. *The course of human life*. New York: Springer.

CLAUSEN, JOHN A. 1972. The life course of individuals. In *Aging and society*. Vol. 3, *A sociology of age stratification*, ed. M. W. Riley, M. Johnson, and A. Foner. New York: Russell Sage.

COUÉ, EMILE. 1922. *Self-mastery through conscious autosuggestion*. London: Allen and Unwin.

DiRENZO, GORDON J., ED. 1977. *We, the people: American character and social change*. Westport, Conn.: Greenwood Press.

ERIKSON, ERIK H. 1969. *Gandhi's truth*. New York: Norton.

———. 1968. *Identity: Youth and crisis*. New York: Norton.

———. 1958. *Young man Luther: a study in psychoanalysis and history*. New York: Norton.

FISKE, MARJORIE. 1979a. *Middle age: the prime of life?* New York: Harper and Row.

———. 1979b. Tasks and crises of the second half of life: resources and stumbling blocks. In *Handbook of mental health and aging,* ed. J. E. Birren and R. B. Sloane. Englewood Cliffs, N.J.: Prentice-Hall.

FROMM, ERICH. 1966. The problem of the Oedipus complex. Paper presented at Langley Porter Neuropsychiatric Institute Staff Meeting, University of California, San Francisco, April 20, 1966.

GOERTZEL, MILDRED GEORGE, VICTOR GOERTZEL, AND TED GEORGE GOERTZEL. 1978. *Three hundred eminent personalities*. San Francisco: Jossey-Bass.

GOLDSTEIN, KURT. 1940. *Human nature in the light of psychopathology*. Cambridge: Harvard University Press. (Rpt. New York: Schocken Books, 1963.)

GOULD, ROGER. 1978. *Transformations: growth and change in adult life*. New York: Simon and Schuster.

GREGORY, MICHAEL S., ANITA SILVERS, AND DIANE SUTCH, EDS. 1978. *Sociobiology and human nature*. San Francisco: Jossey-Bass.

GUTMANN, DAVID C. 1977. The cross-cultural perspective: notes toward a comparative psychology of aging. In *Handbook of the psychology of aging,* ed. J. E. Birren and K. W. Schaie. New York: Van Nostrand Reinhold.

HAAN, NORMA. 1970. Personality and intellectual changes in adulthood. In *Developmental psychology today,* ed. J. Aronfreed et al., Del Mar, Cal: CRM Books.

HALEY, ARTHUR. 1976. *Roots.* New York: Doubleday.

HODGES, RUTH. Pending. Ego mastery styles and the adult life course. Ph.D. diss. University of California, San Francisco.

HOROWITZ, MARDI J. 1977. Adjunct study of stress response among non-treated patients. Privileged communication, Human Development and Aging Program, University of California, San Francisco.

KOHLBERG, LAWRENCE. 1973. Continuities in childhood and adult moral development revisited. In *Life span developmental psychology,* ed. P. Baltes and K. W. Schaie. New York: Academic Press.

LANDIS, BERNARD. 1970. *Ego boundaries. Psychological Issues,* 4, no. 4, monograph 24. New York: International Universities Press.

LASCH, CHRISTOPHER. 1978. *The culture of narcissism: American life in an age of diminishing expectations.* New York: Norton.

———. 1977. *Haven in a heartless world: the family besieged.* New York: Basic Books.

LAZARUS, RICHARD. 1978. The stress and coping paradigm. Paper presented at conference on The Critical Evaluation of Behavioral Paradigms for Psychiatric Science, Gleneden Beach, Oregon, November.

LEVINSON, DANIEL J., CHARLOTTE DARROW, EDWARD KLEIN, MARIA LEVINSON, AND BRAXTON MCKEE. 1978. *The seasons of a man's life.* New York: Knopf.

LIFTON, ROBERT JAY. 1976. *The life of the self.* New York: Simon and Schuster.

———. 1971. "Protean man." *Archives of General Psychiatry,* 24:298-304.

LOEVINGER, JANE. 1976. *Ego development: conceptions and theories.* San Francisco: Jossey-Bass.

LOWENTHAL, MARJORIE FISKE. 1971. Intentionality: toward a framework for the study of adaptation in adulthood. *Aging and human development,* 2:79-95.

LOWENTHAL, MARJORIE FISKE, PAUL L. BERKMAN, AND ASSOCIATES. 1967. *Aging and mental disorder in San Francisco: a social psychiatric study.* San Francisco: Jossey-Bass.

LOWENTHAL, MARJORIE FISKE, MAJDA THURNHER, DAVID CHIRIBOGA, AND ASSOCIATES. 1975. *Four stages of life: a comparative study of women and men facing transitions.* San Francisco: Jossey-Bass.

MARRIS, PETER. 1975. *Loss and change.* New York: Doubleday/Anchor Books.

MASLOW, ABRAHAM H. 1954. *Motivation and personality.* New York: Harper and Bros.

MAYER, NANCY. 1978. *The male midlife crisis: fresh starts after 40.* New

York: Doubleday.

McClelland, David. 1975. *Power: the inner experience.* New York: Irvington.

Neugarten, Bernice L. 1977. Personality and aging. In *Handbook on the psychology of aging,* ed. J. E. Birren and K. W. Schaie. New York: Van Nostrand Reinhold.

Neugarten, Bernice L., and Gunhild O. Hagestad. 1976. Age and the *psychology of aging,* ed. J. E. Birren and K. W. Schaie. New York: Van stock and E. Shanas. New York: Van Nostrand Reinhold.

Norton, David L. 1976. *Personal destinies: a philosophy of ethical individualism.* Princeton: Princeton University Press.

Piaget, Jean. 1972. Intellectual evolution from adolescence to adulthood. *Human Development,* 15:1-12.

Pierce, Robert C. In press. Dimensions of leisure. I: Satisfaction. *Journal of Leisure Research.*

Riegel, Klaus F. 1977. History of psychological gerontology. In *Handbook of the psychology of aging,* ed. J. E. Birren and K. W. Schaie. New York: Van Nostrand Reinhold.

Riesman, David. 1950. *The lonely crowd: a study of the changing American character.* New Haven: Yale University Press.

Rosow, Irving. 1965. Forms and functions of adult socialization. *Social Forces,* 44:35-45.

Sears, Pauline S., and Ann H. Barbee. 1977. Career and life satisfaction among Terman's gifted women. In *The gifted and the creative: a fifty year perspective,* ed. J. Stanley, W. George, and C. Solano. Baltimore: Johns Hopkins University Press.

Sears, Robert R. 1977. Sources of life satisfactions of the Terman gifted men. *American Psychologist,* 32:119-128.

Sheehy, Gail. 1976. *Passages: predictable crises of adult life.* New York: Dutton.

Simpson, E. L. 1974. Moral development research: a case study of scientific cultural bias. *Human Development,* 17:81-106.

Spicker, Stuart F., Kathleen M. Woodward, and David D. Van Tassel, eds. 1978. *Aging and the elderly: humanistic perspectives in gerontology.* Atlantic Highlands, N.J.: Humanities Press.

Sullivan, Harry Stack. 1953. *Interpersonal theory of psychiatry.* New York: Norton.

Thurnher, Majda T. 1975. Continuities and discontinuities in value orientation. In Marjorie Fiske Lowenthal, Majda Thurnher, David Chiriboga, and associates, *Four stages of life: a comparative study of women and men facing transitions.* San Francisco: Jossey-Bass.

Vaillant, George. 1977. *Adaptation to life.* Boston: Little, Brown.

White, Robert W. 1963. *Ego and reality in psychoanalytic theory. Psychological Issues,* 3 no. 3, monograph 11. New York: International Universities Press.

———————— TWELVE ————————

Toward a Conception
of the Adult Life Course
———— DANIEL J. LEVINSON ————

THE PRECEDING CHAPTERS give evidence that we know much more about work and love than we do about the meaning of being an adult or about the place of adulthood in the human life cycle. In the initial chapter, Neil Smelser urged that the study of work and love be placed in the broader context of the study of adulthood, and he noted that our research about adult life is severely limited by a scarcity, ambiguity, and fragmentation of theory. In this concluding chapter I want to reconsider some of the issues he raised, to identify several theoretical perspectives on adulthood currently accepted by investigators in this field, and then to present my own theoretical framework for the adult life course.

There are good reasons to identify childhood and adolescence as phases of life that have a certain unifying character within which to study particular events and processes of change. Clearly, adulthood is not a single phase of life in the same sense. For one thing, it lasts too long: it covers the fifty or more years that people ordinarily live after adolescence. For another, tremendous changes occur over the course of the adult years. Therefore, rather than identifying adulthood as a single, unitary stage, we need to consider whether a sequence of phases or age levels may exist within adulthood, as it does in the preadult years.

Little research has been done to determine whether there exists any underlying order in the progression of adult life—whether, for example, it makes sense to speak of a sequence of stages or periods in adulthood. The most generally held assumption is that it does not.

We now have no widely accepted conception—or even several competing conceptions—of a sequence of age levels in adulthood. Investigators often use terms such as youth, maturity, the middle years, and old age to signify such divisions. However, these terms are given diverse meanings, often by a single writer, and the prevailing attitude is one of mistrust toward any general schema of age levels.

If we are to advance our knowledge of adulthood, we must take more seriously the idea of *sequence*. We must study the evolving character of the individual's life—what Smelser has called the "contour"—during the adult years. The most apt name for this research domain is "the study of the adult life course." This name is purely descriptive. It does not imply any single theoretical approach; yet it does suggest the major issues with which all theories must deal. The term "adult" requires us to consider more carefully what we mean by adulthood and its relation to other segments of the life cycle. The term "life course" highlights the idea of sequence and temporality, of stability and of change over time. It embraces all the components of living that have thus far been studied mainly in isolation: occupational history; marriage and family roles; changes in personality, bodily functioning, and other characteristics of the organism over time; and participation in various groups, institutions, classes, and cultures. The life course is the raw material that every theory must attempt to explain. It is also the stuff of which biographies are made.

How can we think about the adult life course? Numerous concepts have been used to examine features of adult life. However, most of the work to date is based on three theoretical perspectives. These are: personality development in adulthood; adult socialization (the shaping influence of social systems on individual roles and careers); and adaptation (coping with major life events). I shall discuss these in turn, as well as a fourth perspective stemming from my own research: the evolution of the individual life structure.

The personality development, socialization, and adaptation perspectives have been widely used in psychology, psychiatry, and the social sciences. Some research has utilized two or more of these perspectives, often without distinguishing between them clearly. Other studies have gathered data on a set of measurable variables, with no systematic theoretical aim. If we are to discover the significant variables and construct appropriate measuring instruments, further clarification of these theoretical perspectives is necessary. Each deals with a crucially important aspect of adult life. By itself, however, each is too narrow to provide a comprehensive understanding of the course of adult life. Together, they may enable us to use and then go beyond the intuitive insights that until now have been available only in great literature. An important task for the future is to combine the first three perspectives within a single framework that provides a more comprehensive view of adulthood. The fourth perspective, based on the concept of the evolution of the individual life structure, is an effort in this direction.

PERSONALITY DEVELOPMENT IN ADULTHOOD

The concept of development is of central importance in psychology and biology. To the extent that development occurs, it is a primary source of order in the life course. A developmental perspective is fundamental to our understanding of the sequence of stages or phases in the preadult years: infancy, early childhood, middle childhood, puberty, and adolescence. It is generally assumed that this sequence has its origins in a genetic program. The sequence is thus based on a maturationally given process, an unfolding from within. External conditions can affect the process; they may speed up or retard the timetable, and in the extreme case may prevent further development altogether. Thus, from this perspective, external conditions are seen as operating on a developmental program that originates within the organism.

The idea of personality development in childhood and adolescence is now well established, and we have learned a great deal about the developmental principles and timetables that shape the life course during these years. Much less is known about personality development in adulthood. The most common assumption is that adolescence is the last developmentally determined period in the evolution of personality; individual personalities may change during the adult years, but these changes are produced by external influences rather than by a developmental sequence. The field known as "developmental psychology" has been largely confined to the study of childhood and adolescence. Recently the term "life-span developmental psychology" has become fashionable, but it still represents a hope more than a well-defined field of study.

Sigmund Freud has probably exerted the greatest influence on our understanding of child psychology and its implications for adult life. Through his insights we know how clearly the early emotional experience of the child is reflected in the personality of the adult. Unfortunately, since Freudian theory assumes that personality development does not extend beyond adolescence, it provides a limited understanding of the nature of adulthood as a time of life.

The theorist who can most appropriately be regarded as the

founder of the study of adult development is Carl G. Jung. During his thirties Jung was Freud's disciple; subsequently he developed his own school of depth psychology. Of the many issues on which they differed, none was more important than that of personality development in adulthood. Jung accepted the main outlines of Freud's conception of personality development in the preadult years, and he believed as well that the individual's life in early adulthood is largely dominated by the instinctual impulses that were so central in Freud's view. Jung maintained, however, that development need not end here. He observed a process of "midlife individuation," which begins at about age forty and may continue throughout the remaining years. He referred to forty as "the noon of life" (1971). His own creative work after forty was devoted chiefly to understanding the individuation process in the afternoon and evening of life. Until recently, Jung's ideas have been largely ignored by the established academic disciplines. This situation is beginning to change, as important new theoretical steps are being taken to integrate the various approaches to depth psychology with the social sciences.

The next major figure, and the contemporary theorist who most represents the study of adult development, is Erik Erikson, whose theory of the human life cycle was first published in detail in *Childhood and Society* (1950). It is a charming irony that a book with this title should provide a basis for the next generation's work on the study of adulthood and society. Erikson posited eight age levels or segments of the life cycle from birth through old age, and for each segment he proposed a distinctive stage in ego development. The first five ego stages cover the years from infancy (the stage of trust versus mistrust) to adolescence (identity versus confusion). These stages have captured the greatest interest and are the ones that Erikson has described most fully. Less interest has been shown in the last three ego stages, intimacy versus isolation, generativity versus stagnation, integrity versus despair. Moreover, Erikson himself has written less about these stages. His biography, *Gandhi's Truth,* provides a rich account of the problem of generativity in the years from forty to sixty, but it does not offer a more detailed conceptualization of this stage. At present there is no theoretical consensus, and little systematic evidence, regarding the status of the adult stages in Erikson's theory. I believe that the value and validity of this important concept of the adult ego stages will become more evident when it is placed within the context of the evolution of the life structure (Levinson et al., 1978).

Despite Erikson's considerable influence, very few others have taken up his challenge to study the life course as a whole and to examine it from the multiple vantage points of society, history, and personality. Many have admired Erikson but few have truly followed his example. In academic psychology, the study of adult personality development has never truly caught on. The idea of development continues to be associated primarily with childhood, and researchers generally assume that the personality remains relatively stable during adulthood. Their main interest is in showing how the adult personality operates as a determinant of individual choice and adaptation. If a personality does change in adulthood, this is usually seen as a result of therapy or of a massively important event (such as loss, illness, or uprooting) rather than as part of an intrinsic developmental process. A major exception is Roger Gould (1978), whose view of adult personality development is summarized in chapter 10 of this volume.

Indeed, the very question of adult personality development has remained ambiguous and "touchy" in academic psychology. The difficulties are reflected in an important paper by Bernice Neugarten (1968), one of the leading figures in this field. Although strongly committed to the idea of adult development, she tells us that she has chosen not to use this term. She begins with the observation that "a psychology of the human life cycle has been slow in making its appearance." In seeking to explain this, she notes that "biological and sociological perspectives have not yet been integrated into an overarching theory of human behavior, nor have they been combined even in describing a meaningful context against which to view psychological change over the life cycle." She continues:

> The primary problem is that we lack a developmental psychology of adulthood in the sense that we have a developmental psychology of childhood. Because the term "development" has been used with such a wide variety of philosophical as well as scientific meanings, it will be strategic for purposes of the present discussion to avoid the awkward juxtaposition of the terms, "adult" and "development", and to speak of the need for a psychology of adulthood in which investigators are concerned with the orderly and sequential changes that occur with the passage of time as individuals move from adolescence through adulthood and old age.

In the climate of academic psychology, the terms "adult" and "development" have indeed formed an "awkward juxtaposition." Nonetheless, it is clear that the "psychology of adulthood" Neugarten advocates is truly a developmental one. Moreover, the two problems she mentions are intimately related: in order to create a developmental psychology of adulthood, we must join the biological, psychological, and sociological perspectives into a more integrated conception of the life cycle. Neugarten makes this point more directly at the conclusion of her article: "If psychologists are to discover order in the events of adulthood, and if they are to discover order in the personality changes that occur in all individuals as they age, we should look to the social as well as to the biological clock, and certainly to social definitions of age and age-appropriate behavior" (p. 146).

My views are in essential agreement with Neugarten's, but I want to state the matter more bluntly: We cannot learn much about personality development in adulthood as long as we operate within a purely psychological framework. Our thinking must become more sociological if we are to study adult personality development more effectively. We must take account not only of the person but also of the person's engagement in society. The sharp splitting that now separates psychology from its sibling disciplines, especially sociology, has kept all these disciplines from forming a comprehensive conception of of the life cycle. Psychologists must do more than include "social factors" such as class and race as variables in statistical analyses of adult personality changes. We must have a sociological perspective. If we persist in the provincial effort to establish a pure psychology of the life cycle, we will continue the difficulties Neugarten has described. Only when we have a comprehensive theoretical framework can we understand specific issues such as personality change or adaptation to major life events.

ADULT SOCIALIZATION

We turn now to the perspective of socialization, which points to the importance of external social and cultural influences on the temporal phasing of the life course. Whereas development represents an unfolding from within, socialization reflects a molding from without. Just as there seem to be timetables based on laws of inner growth, so, too, is the life course shaped by timetables governing our roles and careers in various social groups and institutions. The developmental perspective has great significance in disciplines that deal primarily with the individual, such as psychology, psychiatry, and biology; the socialization perspective has similar significance in disciplines that deal primarily with society and the patterning of our collective lives, such as sociology, anthropology, and history. Although they are not in principle antithetical, the two perspectives are often seen as antithetical and have become the focal points for continuing controversy among the "individual" and "social" sciences. Little has yet been done to bring them together into a more unified framework.

The socialization perspective deals with the ways in which every social system (class, culture, organization) shapes the roles and outlook of its members. In every society numerous roles are open to the individual, relating to membership in occupation, family, gender, class, religion, and other groups. For example, every society shapes its members' lives by its system of age stratification that defines a series of age grades or levels (Van Gennep, 1960; Eisenstadt, 1956; Riley, Johnson, and Foner, 1972; Riley et al., 1969; Riley and Foner, 1968; also see LeVine's chapter in this volume). Each age grade has its distinctive rights and obligations. There are often rites of passage that legitimize and celebrate movement from one grade to another. Educational, religious, and other institutions transmit the cultural meanings of age and prepare their members for age-linked changes in social status and role.

A person's role in any social system evolves over time. The term "career" refers to the relatively patterned sequence of role change. Thus, an occupational career involves a series of positions and roles within one or more occupational worlds. We speak also of the career of parent, spouse, student, athlete, patient. Each person has multiple careers which, singly and in their interweaving, form basic elements of the life course.

The study of careers begins with the institutional nexus in which they occur. For example, the occupational structure defines particular occupations, each containing a set of roles and careers. A career timetable identifies a series of levels of advancement as well as the approximate age at which a person should normally reach a given level. Similarly, the marriage-family career involves a series of socially patterned stages, such as courtship, marriage without children, family with children at home, empty nest, grandparenthood, and beyond.

Most sociological studies have focused on a single career sequence within a delimited social context, typically occupation or family. Studies of the occupational career often note in passing that a person's work may be influenced by events outside the work context, but sociologists have generally not investigated the individual life course in its complex patterning. They may identify stages within a single career, but they are reluctant to identify stages in the individual life course. This narrowness is due partly to the specialization of fields within sociology. The expert in occupational careers usually has little interest in the family, religion, or other systems.

Another source of difficulty for the analyst is the phenomenon of career dissynchronization: individuals progress at different speeds within their multiple careers. One person at forty may be very advanced occupationally yet in an early stage of family life, while another at the same age has near-adult offspring and more limited occupational status. Stages in the family cycle, and in the individual career as spouse and parent, are not closely synchronized with stages in the occupational career. The biographer must consider the patterning of a person's multiple careers over time. Socialization theory and research have not yet seriously confronted this problem.

In an excellent essay highlighting the merits and limitations of a socialization perspective, John Clausen (1972) points out that the concept of developmental stages is useful in the "formative" preadult years, and perhaps in old age, but is of little value during the main adult years. The adult's life is divided into a number of discrete roles, each with its own temporal phasing. He endorses the study of aging, in the sense that age is an important variable for the individual and for society. However, since the significance of age differs from one group, institution, and role to another, and since a person's various careers proceed at different rates, Clausen does not expect to find a more generalized sequence of individual development. This means, in effect, that sociology can appropriately study single careers, but it cannot develop a general theory of the individual life course. Clausen is explicitly stating a position that is held implicitly by most sociologists in the field of adult socialization.

This position produces a basic dilemma. If we focus only on single, disparate roles, without considering the ways in which they are joined or integrated in a broader pattern, how can sociology contribute to a general theory of the individual life course? Clausen addresses this dilemma in his concluding paragraph:

> In this essay we have been concerned with the ways in which age gives patterning to the life space and to the sequence of roles, relationships, and activities that make up the life course. Within all segments of society the years provide a structure of expectations, opportunities and challenges. If these are to a considerable degree integrated by the individuals who experience them, they remain largely unintegrated insofar as a general theory of the life course is concerned. Perhaps it is unrealistic to think of a theory of the life course. Perhaps we can only look forward to more limited theories relevant to aspects of the life course—for example, more adequate theories bearing on types of role transition in different kinds of social settings. It is hoped that the present essay has at least indicated some of the elements that will be incorporated in more adequate formulations in the future.

While recognizing the problem, Clausen doubts that it can be solved; perhaps sociology is overreaching itself in seeking a general theory of the life course — we may be doing all we can when we study specific roles in specific settings. In this, too, Clausen is giving voice to an assumption widely held by sociologists.

· A comprehensive theoretical framework for studying the individual life course will certainly not obviate the need for study of particular roles, career sequences, and age stratification systems, just as it will not obviate the need for study of adult personality development. However, we must learn how to think systematically about the individual life as an imperfectly integrated whole, and about the evolution of this life over time. Our understanding of the life course must give a major place to careers, which are among its basic elements, and to the ways in which institutions socialize their members throughout their careers. The theoretical problem is to develop a way to regard a person's careers in various systems as components of the overall pattern of living.

THE ADAPTATION PERSPECTIVE

The adaptation perspective is fundamental to psychology and the social sciences. It has often been used in the study of major life events such as moving out of the parental home, entering a new job, getting promoted or fired, as well as illness, loss, and change of various kinds. These events play an important part in the individual life course. How a person adapts to them is important not only to the individual but also to the groups, institutions, and social settings in which they occur.

The basic paradigm here is that adaptation (response, coping, adjustment) to a given event is conjointly determined by the specific stimulus, by the broader social context in which the event is situated, and by characteristics of the individual (such as values, skills, motives). By and large, personality-oriented psychologists tend to regard personality as the most important determinant of adaptation to major life events, whereas other psychologists and social scientists emphasize the influence of the external situation. It is generally acknowledged that both sets of determinants are important, but few studies give equal weight to both and few theories have equal room for both.

The adaptation perspective deals with single events in their own right. It does not require us to place the single events within the framework of the adult life course as a whole, and it does not deal with the problem of order and sequence in adult life. This is a crucial difference between the adaptation perspective and the two discussed previously. The personality development and socialization perspectives are concerned with the problem of temporal order in the life course and therefore provide some basis for the discovery of order.

An example of the adaptation perspective is given by Vaillant (1977). He studied the interrelationships of life adjustment (adaptation) and personality in a single sample of Harvard men at three successive ages, roughly twenty, thirty, and forty-five, with main emphasis on the last age. His measure of quality of life adjustment in the midforties correlated significantly though modestly with a personality measure of psychological health or ego strength. The data suggest that the individual's level of adjustment at a given time is influenced by his personality. Vaillant's study has less to say about the nature of the adult life course and adult personality development. It provides a fairly elaborate picture of the subjects at three different age levels, but it does not yield a clear view of the life course as it evolves from one age to another. Although the data on personality stability and change are not conclusive, since the measures change somewhat over the years—a hazard of longitudinal research—Vaillant finds some evidence for stability on the personality measures. This fits his psychoanalytic theory in which adolescence is the last developmental period. On the other hand, his interviews with the men in their forties indicate that some of them have changed in important respects. It is not clear whether these changes reflect an underlying pattern of personality development. This is not a major issue for Vaillant, since he regards adulthood primarily from an adaptation perspective.

Marjorie Fiske and her associates provide another way of using the adaptation perspective (Lowenthal et al., 1975; Chapter 11). They identify four "stages of life," each stage being defined in terms of a particular role transition, such as leaving the parental home or dealing with the empty nest. Using lengthy, semistructured interviews, they obtained data regarding the person's anticipation of a transition and subsequent adjustment to it. They relate variations in adjustment to factors such as gender, age, and personal values. However, they treat transitions as specific events. They do not study the process of role transition itself; that is, they do not delineate a sequence of living over a span of months or years.

Fiske's research offers rich data regarding adaptation to four life events, but its relevance for a conception of the adult life course and for a theory of adult development is unclear. The events are not actually stages of life but are, rather, turning points in the occupational or familial career. Thus, retirement is a key transition in the occupational career—but it is not a stage in the overall pattern of living. We can determine whether retirement is part of a more general change in the character of a person's life only by studying the entire life pattern (including family, leisure, political, religious, and civic involvements, and self, in their complex interweaving), and how this pattern changes over the years. This was not done in the Fiske study; and to do it would carry the authors well beyond their model of adaptation to single events.

The study of major life events has much to contribute to our understanding of specific adaptations in adult life, but a wider perspective is required if we are to gain a fuller understanding of the adult life course. We must define "event" more broadly and place it within a long-term process of change.

When our concern is with the life course, I suggest that we identify major life events as "marker events." This term accentuates the importance of regarding a single happening as one step within an extended sequence. For example, marriage, retirement, and the death of a loved one are, in some respects, concrete events. They ordinarily occur on a particular day or, at most, over a span of a few days or weeks. They are often symbolized by a specific ceremony or dramatic occasion (such as a wedding, funeral, or graduation). However, the meaning and impact of the event can be understood only if we place it within a longer sequence that begins much earlier and continues well beyond. For example, retirement as an event may be identified by a ceremony or by the date engraved on a gold watch, but the process of retiring starts months or years before the ceremony and continues for months or years afterward. A marker event thus serves to punctuate and dramatize a relatively extended, complex sequence of change. If we focus too narrowly on the event itself, we lose sight of the deeper process. Other aspects of this sequence, though less dramatic or less accessible to investigation than the marker event, may yet be of fateful importance in the life course.

Divorce, for example, is a significant life event from almost any perspective. That it is usually regarded as an event in its own right is indicated by the amount of research on the incidence of divorce in different populations and age levels and on various ways of coping with the immediate aftermath. From a life-course perspective, however, we note that divorce may occur at very different points in different sequences. It may happen precipitously, after the first signs of conflict in a previously tranquil marriage. Or a poor but seemingly stable marriage of fifteen or twenty years' duration may suddenly be shattered after an incident of a kind that had been endured many times before. A couple may separate after a period of severe conflict and then spend months or years exploring the possibilities of reconciliation before finally settling on divorce.

Just as divorce is usually the culmination of a difficult period lasting from a few months to many years, the aftermath is equally variable in character and duration. In the simplest case, the wounds heal quickly and the person goes on to a new life with few traces of the previous marriage. The simplest case is also the rarest. Especially when there are children, termination of the marriage leaves a great deal to be dealt with in subsequent years: the relationships continue in new forms and exert their influence on the lives of all the family members. Divorce in a technical sense is an event, but from the perspective of the life course, it is a moment in a much longer sequence of individual and family conflict, separation, transition, and restructuring.

Moreover, the sequence of family breakup is greatly influenced by roles and relationships outside the family. Occupation, in particular, is heavily interpenetrated with marriage and family life. One's occupational endeavors strongly influence, and are influenced by, relationships with spouse and children. This obvious point has been virtually ignored in theory and research, which generally focus on one domain to the exclusion of the others. Marriage, divorce, and the empty nest are regarded primarily as events within the context of family life. Job promotion, change, and retirement are studied within the context of occupation. In research, rarely do the twain meet.

I am saying, then, that major life events can be examined from at least two perspectives. From an adaptation perspective, we treat the event as a single, distinct occurrence, identify various modes of adaptation to it, and investigate its determinants (in the external environment and within the person) and its consequences. From a life-course perspective, on the other hand, we treat the specific event as a marker of a broader and more extended sequence. Our focus is not on the event as such but on the segment of the life course of which it is a part. To adopt this perspective, however, we must have at least a preliminary theory of the adult life course. Theory that deals mainly with adaptation to specific events is necessary but not sufficient for the study of the life course.

THE EVOLUTION OF THE INDIVIDUAL LIFE STRUCTURE

The fourth perspective begins with the concept of the individual life structure and provides a way of thinking about the evolution of this structure. This perspective creates a space in which personality, career socialization, and marker events can be examined conjointly within a more encompassing view of the life course. It is offered not as a replacement for the other perspectives but as an additional approach that permits us to study individual lives over time in greater psychological and social complexity.

The concept of the individual life structure is the product of a study that my colleagues and I began in 1967 (Levinson et al., 1978). We studied forty men drawn from four diverse occupations: hourly workers in industry, executives, biology professors, and novelists. All were between thirty-five and forty-five years old. Each man was interviewed five to ten times for a total of ten to twenty hours. His task: to tell the story of his life. Given several hundred pages of transcript for each man, it was then our task to reconstruct the individual life course and to look for commonalities as well as differences among the forty lives.

At the start, we used all three of the perspectives noted above in trying to make sense of our subjects' lives. We would focus at one moment on the significance of a dramatic marker event and then shift to the socializing influence of a work organization or the reenactment of a childhood personality theme in the adult marital relationship. Our previous training in clinical psychology, social psychology, sociology, psychiatry — and various mixtures thereof — had given us some skill in dissecting particular components of living, but it also hampered our attempt to form a more integrated view of the individual life course. During the first few years of the study we made progress in specific areas, but I often despaired of reaching my primary goal.

The idea of the individual life structure emerged in fits and starts. The key problem, we discovered, was to free ourselves from the initial focus on personality, or on career, or on some other aspect of living, and to focus instead on the overall pattern of living and its evolution over time. Once the new idea had taken shape, it seemed an "obvious" solution to the problem. Even after we had developed an intuitive notion of the life structure and could begin to use it in our biographical analyses, a long and painful process was required to conceptualize it more explicitly and place it within a broader theoretical framework. Investigators constrained by more rigid timetables do not have the luxury — or the struggle — of this kind of intellectual evolution.

My main emphasis here is on the life course of men. Our initial studies of women suggest that women go through the same periods as men in early adulthood, but there are important differences in the issues they face and the ways they traverse the periods. Despite the growing concern with gender in recent years, very little research has yet been done on the adult development of women. We need to learn more about both genders in order to understand either.

The life structure is the pattern or design of a person's life, a meshing of self-in-world. Its primary components are one's relationships: with self, other persons, groups, and institutions, with all aspects of the external world that have significance in one's life. A person has relationships to work and to various elements of the occupational world; friendships and social networks; love relationships, including marriage and family; experiences of the body (health, illness, growth, decline); leisure, recreation, and use of solitude; memberships and roles in many social settings. Each relationship is like a thread in a tapestry; the meaning of a thread depends on its place in the total design.

The life structure as a whole, and every component in it, has both external and internal aspects. The external aspects have to do with the persons, social systems, and other outside realities with which the person is involved. The internal aspects are values, desires, conflicts, skills—multiple parts of the self that are lived out in one's relationships. Our analysis must begin with the overall life structure. Once that has been characterized, we can examine in more detail the ways in which its components operate.

The life structure stems from the engagement of self with the world. To be truly engaged with the world, one must invest important parts of the self in it and, equally, must take the world into the self and be enriched, depleted, and corrupted by it. In countless ways we put ourselves into the world and take the world into ourselves. Adult development is the story of the evolving process of mutual interpenetration of self and world.

One or two components (rarely as many as three) have a central place in the life structure. Others are more peripheral, and still others are completely detached from the center. The central components, which have the greatest significance for the self and for the evolving life course, receive the largest share of one's time and energy and strongly influence the choices made in other aspects of life. The peripheral components are easier to detach and change; they involve less investment of the self and are less crucial to the fabric of one's life. We found that occupation and marriage-family are usually the central components, though there are significant variations in their relative weight and in the importance of other components. This finding is consistent with Freud's comment that the capability for working and for loving are the hallmarks of mature adulthood.

The life structure may change in various ways. A component may shift from center to periphery or vice versa, as when a man who has been totally committed to work starts detaching himself from it and involves himself more in family life. A formerly important component may be eliminated altogether. Or the character of a man's relationships within a given component may change moderately or drastically. For example, a man may enrich and deepen his existing marital relationship; he may modify the nature and meaning of his work, without changing occupations; or he may leave his present marriage or occupation in search of a basic change.

When we used the concept of life structure in analyzing the biographies of our men, we found that the life structure evolves through a relatively orderly sequence of periods during the adult years. The essential character of the sequence was the same for all the men in our study and for the other men whose biographies we examined. These periods shape the adult life course.

The sequence consists of an alternating series of structure-building and structure-changing (transitional) periods. The primary task of a structure-building period is to form a life structure and enhance life within it: a person must make certain key choices, form a structure around them, and pursue his values and goals within this structure. Even when a person succeeds in creating a stable structure, life is not necessarily tranquil. The task of making major life choices and building a structure is often stressful indeed and may involve many kinds of change. A structure-building period ordinarily lasts six or seven years, ten at the most. Then the life structure that has formed the basis for stability comes into question and must be modified.

A transitional period terminates the existing life structure and creates the possibility for a new one. The primary tasks of every transitional period are to reappraise the existing structure, to explore the various possibilities for change in self and world, and to move toward commitment to the crucial choices that form the basis for a new life structure in the ensuing period. Transitional periods ordinarily last about five years. Much of our lives is taken up with separations and new beginnings, exits and entries, departures and arrivals. Transitions are an intrinsic part of development, but they are often painful.

As a transition comes to an end, one starts making crucial choices, giving them meaning and commitment, and building a life structure around them. The choices are, in a sense, the major product of the transition. When all the efforts of the transition are done — the struggles to improve work or marriage, to explore alternative possibilities of living, to come more to terms with the self — choices must be made and bets must be placed. One must decide "This I will settle for," and start creating a life structure that will serve as a vehicle for the next step in the journey.

It is worth emphasizing that the transitions are major periods in their own right. They have the same weight in the sequence as the structure-building periods, and they occupy almost as many years of our lives. The transitional periods are essential in the shift from one life structure to another, and the process of structural change is in urgent need of study.

It is important to distinguish between transitional periods in the evolution of the life structure and transitions of other kinds. A transition is a process of change from one structure or state to another. A career transition, for example, occurs when a person shifts from one occupational role to another. Following the death of a loved one, a person goes through a transition in which he or she grieves the loss and transforms the relationship to the other, who now exists primarily as an internal figure. Various transitions may occur within a life-structure transition (as well as in other periods); it is important both to keep them analytically distinct and to study their interrelations.

My view of a sequence of alternating structure-building and structure-changing periods has much in common with various developmental stage theories such as those of Jean Piaget (1970), Lawrence Kohlberg (1969), and Jane Loevinger (1976), but there are important differences as well. All of us regard development as the evolution of a structure — be it a cognitive structure, a moral structure, an ego structure, or a life structure. The others identify a series of stable stages (structures), separated and linked by intervening transitions. For them, too, the concept of transition is important, but their emphasis has been more on the structure than the transitions. Their stages, unlike mine, form a hierarchical progression from "lower" to "higher" levels on a developmental ladder. The periods in my theory form an invariant sequence over time, but one period is not seen as higher or more advanced than another. The imagery is more that of the seasons in the year: each is necessary, each has its proper place in the total cycle, and.each has its value within a single, organically evolving process. In this respect, the life structure periods are similar to Freud's psychosexual stages and Erikson's ego stages; each of them is characterized by certain developmental tasks and dilemmas rather than by specific developmental achievements. Finally, all of the other theories posit stages in the development of psychic (cognitive, psychodynamic) structures, whereas my periods refer to structures of living that have both inner and outer aspects.

In his recent book *Structuralism* (1970), Piaget makes a statement that vividly highlights our similarities and differences. He writes: "Structure and genesis are necessarily interdependent. Genesis is simply transition from one structure to another, nothing more; but this transition always leads from a 'weaker' to a 'stronger' structure; it is a 'formative' transition" (p. 141). Like Piaget, I regard development as the evolution of structure. Transitions are always formative and, indeed, transformative. In preadult development a transition may always lead, as Piaget says, from a weaker to a stronger structure. In the evolution of the adult life structure, however, things are more complicated and our knowledge and theory are more primitive. A given life structure is not necessarily stronger (more differentiated, more functional, or developmentally more advanced) than the preceding one. Moreover, the criteria for evaluating the relative "strength" of a structure are probably more complex or ambiguous in adulthood than in preadulthood. For the present, at least, I prefer not to build in evaluative assumptions; it seems more fruitful for the immediate future to focus chiefly on the nature of the successive life structures and the processes of change. In time, as we gain more wisdom about the myriad forms of individual lives, we can cautiously begin to evaluate the many forms of developmental advance and decline. The present ambiguities about developmental levels in adulthood tend to put off many psychologists who conceive of development solely in terms of an advance from lower to higher levels. In the study of adult development, however, we cannot limit ourselves to childhood-centered models.

ERAS AND PERIODS IN ADULTHOOD

Before describing the series of developmental periods in early and middle adulthood, I need to introduce briefly the concept of eras. Eras form the macrostructure of the life cycle; they provide a rough map of the underlying order in the life course as a whole, from birth through old age. The developmental periods provide a more detailed map of the life course; they form transitions between the eras and generate change within each era. Although the main emphasis here is on the periods, I want to emphasize that the conception of the life cycle and its component eras is an essential framework for the study of particular age levels.

The first era, *preadulthood,* extends from birth to about age twenty-two. This is the time of most rapid bio-psycho-social growth, during which the organism moves from helpless infancy through childhood, puberty, and adolescence to the beginnings of the capability for living as a relatively independent, responsible adult. It is the era that has been most fully studied, especially from a developmental perspective.

The second era, *early adulthood,* lasts from roughly age seventeen to forty-five (fig. 12.1). The Early Adult Transition period, from seventeen to twenty-two, is devoted both to the termination of preadulthood and to the initiation of early adulthood, and is thus part of both eras. Early adulthood is the adult era of greatest energy and abundance, and of greatest contradiction and stress. Biologically, the twenties and thirties are the peak years of the life cycle. In social and psychological terms, early adulthood is the season for forming and pursuing youthful aspirations, establishing a niche in society, raising a family, and, as the era ends, reaching a more "senior" position in the adult world. This can be a time of rich satisfactions in terms of love, sexuality, family life, occupational advancement, creativity, and realization of major life goals. But there can be crushing stresses, too: undertaking the burdens of parenthood and, at the same time, of forming an occupation; incurring heavy financial obligations when one's earning power is still relatively low; having to make crucially important choices regarding marriage, family, work, and life-style before one has the maturity or life experience to choose wisely. Early adulthood is the era in which we are most buffeted by our own passions and ambitions from within, and by the demands of family, community, and society from without. Under reasonably favorable conditions, the rewards as well as the costs of living are enormous.

Before early adulthood ends, a new era, *middle adulthood,* gets underway. Middle adulthood starts at about forty. The Mid-life Transition, from forty to forty-five, is a developmental period that links the two eras and is part of both. Middle adulthood lasts from about forty to sixty-five. During this era our biological capacities are below those of early adulthood, but normally still sufficient for an energetic, personally satisfying and socially valuable life. The great philosopher-historian Ortega Y Gasset (1958) has suggested that people aged forty-five to sixty form the "dominant generation" in every society. In politics, industry, science, and the arts — in all social institutions — the main leadership comes from this generation. Unless our lives are hampered in some special way, most of us during our forties and fifties become "senior members" in our own particular worlds, however grand or modest they may be. We are responsible not only for our own work, and perhaps the work of others, but also for the development of the current generation of young adults who will soon enter the dominant generation.

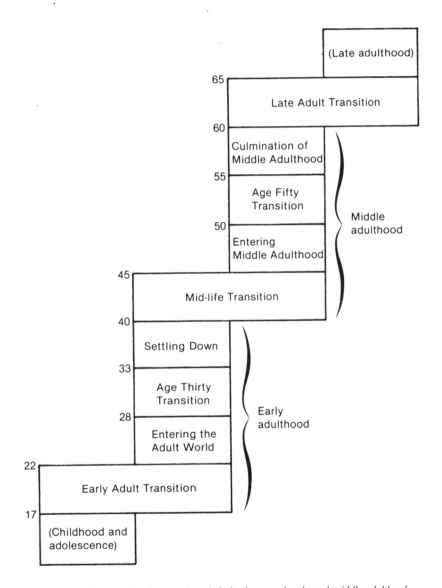

Figure 12.1 • *Developmental periods in the eras of early and middle adulthood.*

In middle adulthood, we can become more compassionate, more reflective and judicious, less tyrannized by inner conflicts and external demands, more genuinely loving of self and others. Without development of this kind, we face a middle adulthood of triviality, stagnation, and decline. The move into middle adulthood is thus a crucial phase of adult development.

Finally, the period of the Late Adult Transition, from about sixty to sixty-five, brings about both the completion of middle adulthood and the start of the next era, *late adulthood.*

We have found that each period begins and ends at a well-defined modal age, with a range of about two years above and below this average. The idea of age-linked periods in adult life goes against conventional wisdom. Nevertheless, these age findings have been so consistent in our initial research and in subsequent studies that I offer the concept of age-linked periods as a hypothesis that deserves extensive testing in various cultures.

Within early and middle adulthood, the life structure evolves through the following periods:

The Early Adult Transition (age seventeen to twenty-two) is a developmental bridge between adolescence and early adulthood. The boy-man is on the boundary between the childhood world, centered in the family, and the early-adult world with its new responsibilities, roles, and life choices. One task of the Early Adult Transition is to terminate the adolescent life structure. A young man has to modify existing relationships with important persons and institutions, and modify the self that formed during preadulthood. A second task is to make a preliminary step into the adult world: to explore its possibilities, to imagine oneself as a participant in it, to make and test some tentative choices before fully entering it.

The second period we call *Entering the Adult World* (age twenty-two to twenty-eight). Now a young man has to fashion a first life structure that provides a link between the valued self and the adult society. He must shift the center of gravity of his life from the family of origin to a new home base that is more truly his own. He has to explore the available possibilities, arrive at a crystallized (though by no means final) definition of himself as a novice adult, and live with his initial choices regarding occupation, love relationships, life-style, and values. He tries, often with limited success, to build a life structure in which he can pursue his youthful dreams and aspirations.

The Age Thirty Transition (twenty-eight to thirty-three) provides an opportunity to work on the flaws in the first adult life structure and to create a basis for the second structure that will be built in the following period. The exploratory quality of the twenties is ending and a man has a sense of greater urgency. He asks: What have I done with my life? What new directions shall I choose?

When a man of twenty-eight or twenty-nine examines his life, he usually finds a lot to be concerned about. Some men have a relatively stable, organized life, but one that excludes crucially important parts of the self. If a man recognizes this, he is likely to feel that his life is a sham, an unwanted compliance with the dictates of parents or society, and a betrayal of what he holds most dear. Or, a man with several strong interests pointing in different occupational directions may be plagued by dilemmas of choice. Or he may be married to a woman he cares for and yet have doubts about his love for her, about her feelings for him, about the durability of the relationship.

For other men, the life structure of the late twenties is relatively unstable, incomplete, and fragmented. Although a transient existence without heavy responsibilities may have suited him well for a while, the insecurity and rootlessness of this life begin to weigh on him. It is more distressing now if he does not have a wife or an occupation or a home base of his own. For most men — and for most women — the Age Thirty Transition is a time of moderate or severe crisis.

As the Age Thirty Transition ends, a man moves toward major new choices or recommits himself to past choices. A great deal hinges on the choices made at this time. If he chooses poorly and the new structure is badly flawed, his life in the next period will become increasingly painful.

The next period, *Settling Down and Becoming One's Own Man*, lasts from about thirty-three to forty. The major tasks now are to build a second adult life structure and, within this framework, to work toward the realization of one's youthful dreams. At the start of the period a man is on the bottom rung of a self-defined ladder and is entering a world in which he is a junior member. He tries to anchor his life more firmly, develop competence in a chosen craft, become a valued member of a valued world, and be affirmed in that world. The thirties is usually a time in which work, family, and other demands are at a peak.

From about thirty-six to forty there is a distinctive phase that we call Becoming One's Own Man. During this time there is a peaking of ambition: a man is eager to accomplish his goals, to become a senior member in his world, to speak more strongly with his own voice and have a greater measure of authority. The effort to become more manly in these respects may bring great rewards, but it also carries the burden of great responsibilities and pressures.

The imagery of the ladder is vivid in the late thirties. A man feels that by about forty he can no longer be a "promising young man"; it is time to achieve the goals he had set earlier and move into a senior position in the world he is just entering. By about forty-five he is already in a new world, though not necessarily the one he had sought earlier.

The next period, the *Mid-life Transition*, starts at about forty and ends around forty-five. It forms a bridge between early and middle adulthood and is part of both. For most men this is a time of great struggle within the self and with the external world. We have identified three major tasks of this period.

Perhaps the first task is to reappraise one's life, to examine critically the life structure developed during the Settling Down period. This arises in part from the person's heightened awareness of his mortality; recognizing that his remaining time is limited, he wants to use it wisely. At times he feels that the past is without value, that it provides no basis for building a future. As the life structure comes into question, a man is compelled to ask: What have I done with my life? What do I really get from and give to my wife, children, friends, work, community—and self? What is it I truly want? What are my talents and how am I using (or wasting) them? How satisfactory is my present life and how shall I change it to provide a better basis for the future? These are often painful questions to consider—but avoiding them is in the long run even more painful.

The second major task during the Mid-life Transition is to integrate the great polarities: Young/Old; Destruction/Creation; Masculine/Feminine; and Attachment/Separateness. Each of these pairs forms a polarity in the sense that the two terms represent opposing tendencies or conditions. Superficially, it would appear that a person has to be one or the other and cannot be both. In actuality, however, both sides of each polarity coexist within every person. At midlife a man feels young in many respects, but he also has a sense of being old. He feels older than the youth, but not ready to join the generation defined as "middle-aged." He feels alternately young, old, and "in-between." If he clings too strongly to the youthfulness of his twenties, he will find no place for himself in middle adulthood. If he gives up on the young, he will become dry and rigid. His developmental task is to become young-old in a new way.

The Destruction/Creation polarity presents similar problems of conflict and reintegration. The Mid-life Transition activates a man's concerns with death and destruction. He experiences more fully his own mortality and the actual or impending death of others. He becomes more aware of the many ways in which other persons, even his loved ones, have acted destructively toward him (with malice or, often, with good intentions). What is perhaps worse, he realizes that he has done irrevocably hurtful things to his parents, lovers, wife, children, friends, rivals (again, with what may have been the worst or the best of intentions). At the same time, he has a strong desire to become more creative and loving: to create products that have value for himself and others, to participate in collective enterprises that advance human welfare, to contribute more fully to the coming generations in society. In middle adulthood a man can come to know, more than ever before, that powerful forces of destructiveness and of creativity coexist in the human soul and can be integrated in many ways — though never entirely.

Likewise, every man at mid-life must come more fully to terms with the coexistence of masculine and feminine parts of the self. And finally he must integrate his powerful need for attachment to others with the antithetical but equally important need for separateness. The integration of these and other polarities is a great vision which many have sought to realize but no one can fully attain.

The third major task of the Mid-life Transition is to modify the life structure. In the midforties, as the Mid-life Transition ends, the life structure that emerges will differ in essential respects from the structure of the late thirties. Some men make decisive alterations in their lives as a result of divorce, remarriage, marked shifts in occupation, status, and life-style. Other men tend to "stay put" during the Mid-life Transition, remaining in the same marriage, job, and community. Even for these men, however, a closer look shows that important changes have occurred in the character and meaning of their relationships, work, and life goals.

At about age forty-five the Mid-life Transition is concluded. The main task of the next period, which we call *Entering Middle Adulthood*, is to build a new life structure for the launching of middle age. This structure comes into question in the *Age Fifty Transition*, which lasts from about fifty to fifty-five. For many men this transition is relatively smooth and undramatic. They use it to make minor changes in life structure, but continue on the same general path. For other men the Age Fifty Transition is a time of moderate or severe crisis. It is likely to be an especially difficult time for men who went rather smoothly through the Mid-life Transition, without examining themselves or making necessary changes in their lives. At fifty, the chickens may come home to roost.

In the *Culmination of Middle Adulthood*, the period from roughly fifty-five to sixty, the task is to build a second life structure within which one can work toward the major goals of this era. The *Late Adult Transition*, from sixty to sixty-five, brings about the completion of middle adulthood and the initiation of late adulthood.

Theoretically, the life structure forms a bridge between personality structure and social structure. It contains elements of both, but combines them in a new way and represents a separate level of analysis. I conceive of adult development as a sequence of periods in the evolution of the life structure. The idea of an orderly sequence of age-linked periods violates our usual assumptions about the adult life course. The first question it raises is: Does this sequence really exist, or is it just an artifact of a particular method or sample? When the initial positive evidence seems substantial enough to be taken seriously, a second question is raised: On what theoretical basis can this sequence be understood—what are its underlying sources or determinants? The sequence of life-structure periods cannot be derived simply from a maturationally given process of personality development in adulthood. It cannot be based on the socializing influence of any single social system such as occupation or family, nor on the interweaving of multiple systems (since the synchronization among them varies so widely). Nor does it follow directly from any known sequence of biological growth and decline. No one of the various human sciences holds the master key to the secrets of the life cycle, yet all are of major importance. The basic form of the adult life course, at this stage of human evolution, is conjointly determined by the maturational unfolding of the human psyche and the human body, and by the basic features of human society (as it has existed for, say, the last five or ten thousand years). In short, the order in the evolution of the individual life structure stems from multiple bio-psycho-social sources and not from any single source (Levinson et al. 1978). It cannot be described or explained by a unidisciplinary approach.

I have described a series of periods in the *evolution* of the life structure. It might be argued that we should not speak of them as periods in the *development* of the life structure. The word "development" is often understood to mean personality development, and the notion of developmental stages has commonly been taken to mean the unfolding of a maturationally given sequence or the gradual realization of an inner, genetically determined potential. The life structure periods, on the other hand, represent the combined influence of development and of socialization, as these terms are generally used. Since the external world is an intrinsic component of the life structure and a major factor in its evolution, the conventional meaning of development is too narrow.

There are important reasons, nevertheless, for identifying these as developmental periods, for speaking of the development of the life structure, and for regarding this as a theory of *adult development*. The periods are developmental in the sense that they shape the fundamental sequence of the adult life course. Each period is characterized by tasks that are in principle developmental: they define essential work that people must engage in if they are to form a way of living that is appropriate to their current time of life and that provides a basis on which further development can occur in subsequent periods. Finally, the perspective of the evolution of the life structure enables us to conceive of adulthood not as a static state nor as a random flux of events but as a sequence that evolves in accord with its own developmental principles.

The periods constitute a source of order in the life cycle. This order exists at an underlying level. At the day-to-day level of concrete events and experiences, our lives are sometimes rapidly changing and fragmented, sometimes utterly stationary. At the level of personality, we change in different ways, according to different timetables. Yet, I believe that everyone lives through the same developmental periods in adulthood, just as in childhood, though people go through them in their own ways. Each individual life has its own unique character. Our theory of life structure does not specify a single, "normal" course that everyone must follow. Its function, instead, is to indicate the developmental tasks that everyone must work on in successive periods, and the infinitely varied forms that such work can take in different individuals living under different conditions. Rather than imposing a template for conformity, it increases our sense of human potentialities and of the variousness of individual lives.

The validity and usefulness of this particular theory remains to be determined. No doubt it will change considerably as a result of further research and experience. I present it as empirically grounded theory, not as demonstrated truth. The need for more and better theory is obvious. The sciences of human life are now suffering from a lack of a vital, species-encompassing conception of the adult life course that can help us understand and deal with problems that confront us today. The present volume has tried to make a contribution to the development of such a conception.

References

CLAUSEN, JOHN A. 1972. The life course of individuals. In *Aging and society*. Vol. 3, *A sociology of age stratification,* ed. M. W. Riley, M. Johnson, and Anne Foner. New York: Russell Sage.

EISENSTADT, SHMUEL NOAH. 1956. *From generation to generation.* Glencoe, Ill.: Free Press.

ERIKSON, ERIK H. 1969. *Gandhi's truth.* New York: Norton.

————. 1950. *Childhood and society.* New York: Norton.

GOULD, ROGER. 1978. *Transformations: growth and change in adult life.* New York: Simon and Schuster.

JUNG, CARL G. 1971. The stages of life. In *The portable Jung,* ed. J. Campbell. New York: Viking. [This paper was first published in 1930. This book contains other selections dealing with Jung's conception of archetypes and the individuation process.]

KOHLBERG, LAWRENCE. 1969. Stage and sequence: the cognitive-developmental approach to socialization. In *Handbook of socialization theory and research,* ed. D. A. Goslin. New York: Rand McNally.

LEVINSON, DANIEL J., WITH CHARLOTTE N. DARROW, EDWARD B. KLEIN, MARIA H. LEVINSON, AND BRAXTON MCKEE. 1978. *The seasons of a man's life.* New York: Knopf.

LOEVINGER, JANE. 1976. *Ego development: conceptions and theories.* San Francisco: Jossey-Bass.

LOWENTHAL, MARJORIE FISKE, MAJDA THURNHER, AND DAVID CHIRIBOGA. 1975. *Four stages of life: a comparative study of women and men facing transitions.* San Francisco: Jossey-Bass.

NEUGARTEN, BERNICE L. 1968. Adult personality: toward a psychology of the life cycle. In *Middle age and aging: a reader in social psychology,* ed. B. L. Neugarten. Chicago: University of Chicago Press.

ORTEGA Y GASSET, JOSÉ. 1958. *Man and crisis.* New York: Norton.

PIAGET, JEAN. 1970. *Structuralism.* New York: Basic Books.

RILEY, MATILDA W., AND ANNE FONER. 1968. *Aging and society.* Vol. 1, *An inventory of research findings.* New York: Russell Sage.

RILEY, MATILDA W., ET AL., EDS. 1969. *Aging and society.* Vol. 2, *Aging and the professions.* New York: Russell Sage.

RILEY, MATILDA W., MARILYN JOHNSON, AND ANNE FONER, EDS. 1972. *Aging and society.* Vol. 3, *A sociology of age stratification.* New York: Russell Sage.

STEWART, WENDY. 1976. A psychosocial study of the formation of the early adult life structure in women. Ph.D. diss., Columbia University.

VAILLANT, GEORGE. 1977. *Adaptation to life.* Boston: Little, Brown.

VAN GENNEP, ARNOLD. 1960. *The rites of passage.* Chicago: University of Chicago Press. [First published 1908.]

Index

Abraham, Karl, 50, 53, 59, 60, 72
Adaptation perspective, 266, 273-276
Adler, Alfred, 57, 58, 60, 65
Adult life course: sequence in, 266; marker events in, 275-276; periods of, 279, 284-288; eras of, 281-284. *See also* Life course
Adulthood: impetus toward study of, 1-3, 265; as special subject, 3-4; issues in study of, 4-5; patterning in, 6; in American culture, 120-121, 125-127, 134-136; and self-realization, 136-139; and sexuality, 141; assumptions of age and sex in, 151-157; new ideal of, 157-161; variation by class and culture, 161-165; transcendence with aging, 166-170; as time of change, 174-175; and job complexity, 193; transformation as central concept of, 224; stages in, 265-266, 281-288
Affective mode: defined, 105; at personality level, 105-106; at cultural level, 105, 106; split from instrumental, 106-109, 117-118, 134, 235; and marital relationships, 117-118
Age: and work, 228-231; and love, 234-236. *See also* Aging
Aging: among the Gusii, 99; new concepts of, 151; and crossovers, 158; transcendence with, 166-170
Allport, Gordon W., 241, 245

Altruism, 246-247
Arber, Sara, 168
Aries, Philippe, 153
Arnold, Matthew, 110-111
Austen, Jane, 124

Bakan, David, 36
Baltes, Paul B., 202
Banks, J. A., 113
Banks, Olive, 113
Barbee, Ann H., 242, 248
Barnett, Rosalind C., 168
Barron, Frank, 239
Baruch, Grace K., 168
Bellah, Robert N., 169
Bellow, Saul, 133
Bem, Sandra L., 168
Bengston, Vern L., 159, 164
Bergman, Ingmar, 129
Bergson, Henri, 160
Berkman, Paul L., 260
Bernays, Martha, 36
Bersani, Leo, 239
Binswanger, Ludwig, 60, 70
Birth order, among Gusii, 90-91
Blau, Peter, 158, 193, 194
Blauner, Robert, 195
Bleuler, Manfred, 51, 54, 58
Bloch, R. Howard, 121
Block, Jack, 245